The Smithsonian Guides to Natural America

THE GREAT LAKES

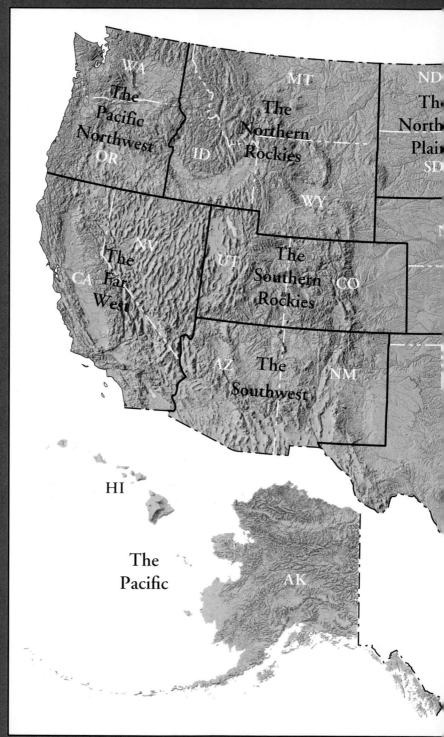

WA

The
Pacific
Northwest

OR

MT

The
Northern
Rockies

ND

The
North
Plai

SD

ID

WY

NV

The
Far
West

CA

UT

The
Southern
Rockies

CO

AZ

The
Southwest

NM

HI

The
Pacific

AK

The following labels appear on the map:

Northern New England

ME

VT

NH

Wisconsin

Michigan

The
Great
Lakes

NY

The Mid–Atlantic States

MA
CT RI

Southern New England

IA

The Heartland

IL

Indiana

Ohio

PA

MD DE

MO

WV

VA

KY

Central Appalachia

The Atlantic Coast

TN

NC

The South Central States

AR

SC

GA

The Southeast

AL

MS

LA

FL

THE GREAT LAKES
WISCONSIN – MICHIGAN – INDIANA
OHIO

THE SMITHSONIAN GUIDES TO NATURAL AMERICA

THE GREAT LAKES

OHIO, INDIANA, MICHIGAN, WISCONSIN

TEXT

Michele Strutin

PHOTOGRAPHY

Gary Irving

PREFACE

Thomas E. Lovejoy

SMITHSONIAN BOOKS • WASHINGTON, D.C.
RANDOM HOUSE • NEW YORK, N.Y.

Front cover: Pictured Rocks National Lakeshore, Lake Superior, Michigan
Half-title page: Painted trillium
Frontispiece: Rock Harbor, Isle Royale National Park, Michigan
Back cover: Black swallowtail butterfly; red trillium; mink

THE SMITHSONIAN INSTITUTION

SECRETARY I. Michael Heyman
COUNSELOR TO THE SECRETARY FOR
BIODIVERSITY AND ENVIRONMENTAL AFFAIRS Thomas E. Lovejoy
DIRECTOR, SMITHSONIAN INSTITUTION PRESS Daniel H. Goodwin
EDITOR, SMITHSONIAN BOOKS Alexis Doster III

THE SMITHSONIAN GUIDES TO NATURAL AMERICA

SERIES EDITOR Sandra Wilmot
MANAGING EDITOR Ellen Scordato
SERIES PHOTO EDITOR Mary Jenkins
PHOTO EDITOR Sarah Longacre
ART DIRECTOR Mervyn Clay
ASSISTANT PHOTO EDITOR Ferris Cook
ASSISTANT PHOTO EDITOR Rebecca Williams
ASSISTANT EDITOR Seth Ginsberg
COPY EDITORS Helen Dunn, Karen Hammonds
FACT CHECKER Jean Cotterell
PRODUCTION DIRECTOR Katherine Rosenbloom

Library of Congress Cataloging-in-Publication Data
Strutin, Michele.
    The Smithsonian guides to natural America. The Great Lakes—Ohio,
  Indiana, Michigan, Wisconsin/text, Michele Strutin; photography,
  Gary Irving; preface, Thomas E. Lovejoy.
      p. cm.
    Includes bibliographical references (p. 254) and index.
    ISBN 0-679-76476-3 (pbk.)
    1. Natural history—Lake States—Guidebooks. 2. Lake States—
  Guidebooks. I. Irving, Gary. II. Title.
  QH104.5.G7S75 1996   95-26065
  508.77—dc20   CIP

How to Use This Book

The SMITHSONIAN GUIDES TO NATURAL AMERICA explore and celebrate the preserved and protected natural areas of this country that are open for the public to use and enjoy. From world-famous national parks to tiny local preserves, the places featured in these guides offer a splendid panoply of this nation's natural wonders.

Divided by state and region, this book offers suggested itineraries for travelers, briefly describing the high points of each preserve, refuge, park, or wilderness area along the way. Each site was chosen for a specific reason: Some are noted for their botanical, zoological, or geological significance, others simply for their exceptional scenic beauty.

Information pertaining to the area as a whole can be found in the introductory sections to the book and to each chapter. In addition, specialized maps at the beginning of each book and chapter highlight an area's geography and geological features as well as pinpoint the specific locales that the author describes.

For quick reference, places of interest are set in **boldface** type; those set in **boldface** followed by the symbol ❖ are listed in the Site Guide at the back of the book. (This feature begins on page **261**, just before the index.) Here noteworthy sites are listed alphabetically by state, and each entry provides practical information that visitors need: telephone numbers, mailing addresses, and specific services available.

Addresses and telephone numbers of national, state, and local agencies and organizations are also listed. Also in appendices are a glossary of pertinent scientific terms and designations used to describe natural areas; the author's recommendations for further reading (both nonfiction and fiction); and a list of sources that can aid travelers planning a guided visit.

The words and images of these guides are meant to help both the active naturalist and the armchair traveler to appreciate more fully the environmental diversity and natural splendor of this country. To ensure a successful visit, always contact a site in advance to obtain detailed maps, updated information on hours and fees, and current weather conditions. Many areas maintain a fragile ecological balance. Remember that their continued vitality depends in part on responsible visitors who tread the land lightly.

C ONTENTS

PREFACE

The Great Lakes region of natural America—Ohio, Indiana, Michigan, and Wisconsin—has been marked dramatically by repeated advances and retreats of great glaciers. Here boreal forest (the great North Woods), eastern deciduous forest, tallgrass prairie, and dune systems both merge and move back and forth in a slow minuet orchestrated by climatic variation and human activity. In these states the impact of people has been very heavy, but, despite massive deforestation and conversion of land to agriculture, a great deal of natural America remains to be seen.

The most dominant features are the Great Lakes themselves, ranging from shallow Lake Erie at 58 feet deep to Lake Superior—seven times deeper and the world's largest lake. It takes only 2.5 years for the water in Lake Erie to be completely replaced, versus 500 years in Lake Superior. It is hardly startling that Michigan means "great water" and Wisconsin "where water meets." The lakes are large enough to be as dangerous as any ocean in stormy weather, and their effect on local weather is so considerable as to be recognized by the term "lake effect." Indeed, it has been estimated that the amount of energy released by the cooling lakes on a single autumn day equals the nation's entire annual energy consumption.

Along the margins of the lakes, mostly to leeward, are impressive dune systems, including (on the eastern side of Lake Michigan) the most extensive and varied freshwater dunes in the world. The Lake Michigan dunes in Indiana—the raison d'être of the first National Lakeshore—are marvelous textbook cases of ecological succession. The dunes farthest from the water are covered with forest, while those nearest the lake are still bare sand. Here such pioneer species as marram grass, with roots extending up to 20 feet, stabilize the system for such ensuing colonists as sand cherry, sea rocket, and beach pea. Occasionally the process is interrupted and the winds blow away sand, revealing "ghost" forests smothered by the initial formations of the dune.

In this region glacial features predominate except for the few areas that the massive ice flows never reached. Among Ohio's most spectacular

---

PRECEDING PAGES: *American poet Carl Sandburg once wrote that the vast, rolling Indiana Dunes "are to the Midwest what the Grand Canyon is to Arizona.... They constitute a signature of time and eternity."*

sights are the glacial grooves in Kelleys Island State Park, 15 feet deep and nearly 100 feet long. But they are pikers compared to a set 30 feet wide and 2,000 feet long, which was destroyed years ago by quarrymen. The region is strewn with eskers (low, narrow ridges); moraines (massive ridges formed where glaciers poured forth meltwaters filled with silt, gravel, and even massive boulders), and kames (cone-shaped mounds—Wisconsin's Kettle Moraine State Forest contains the most perfect and arresting examples in the world). Major portions of the Great Lakes states are covered by till plains formed when the glaciers smeared their internal burden over the landscape.

Also legacies of the ice ages are the region's many lakes, kettle holes formed when a buried piece of glacier finally melted, or depressions caused by the gargantuan powers of the moving ice. Little wonder that one of the main intellectual roots of the science of limnology (the ecology of freshwaters) grew at the University of Wisconsin, where pioneers such as E. A. Birge and Chancey Juday studied Lake Mendota essentially at their front door. At Big Darby Creek in Ohio, 100 species of fish and 41 species of mussels make that drainage one of the top five in diversity in the nation. Over time some of these glacial lakes or ponds fill in and become bogs or fens (like bogs, but with no outlet). Sometimes the bogs conceal surprises, such as the mastodon and the remains of its dinner unearthed in Ohio's Licking County. And, of course, there are rivers, those of the French voyageurs and those of the great internal continental drainage.

Before the glaciers much of this area was a vast inland sea. As a result of this marine heritage, Indiana supplies much of the nation's limestone for construction. For the naturalist, however, the reward is an abundance of fossils, from crinoids to trilobites. Where acidic groundwater has taken its toll on the soft underlying limestone, elaborate cave systems and karst topography have resulted.

For the wildflower enthusiast, the variety of habitats in the region yields a floral treasury: bright yellow celandine poppies at Indiana's Clifty Falls State Park; stemless lady's slipper, pattyroot, and roundleaf catchfly in Lake Katherine State Nature Preserve in Ohio; blazing star, rattlesnake master, and big bluestem in the Hoosier Prairie Nature Preserve of Indiana; and hoary puccoon and wormwood at Michigan's P. J. Hoffmaster State Park. This part of natural America supports trees ranging

---

OVERLEAF: *Spreading oaks and hickories line a cool, shaded trail that climbs through Wisconsin's Perrot State Park. At the top, an open, wildflower-dotted prairie crowns the bluffs overlooking the Mississippi.*

from black spruce to bigleaf magnolia, from buckeye to yellowwood, as well as ferns such as goldie's and resurrection. Northern Michigan boasts elk, wolves, and moose. (On Isle Royale the latter two are the subject of one of the longest of all ecological studies.) There are green salamanders, eastern woodrats, and dapper cedar waxwings, as well as sandhill cranes, trumpeter swans, prairie chickens, and the rare Kirtland's warblers, Karner blue butterflies, and Indiana brown bats.

Human footprints have fallen heavily on the Great Lakes region. John Deere's plow made the prairies and some of the richest soil on earth available for agriculture. A wave of logging swept across the area, taking most of the great white pines with it. By the end of the 1800s, white-tailed deer were extirpated from Indiana—no mean feat, considering how close to pest status they are in many areas of the nation today. Wild turkeys were gone from Ohio by 1900. Improvements for navigation provided the lamprey with access to the Great Lakes, spelling the decline of the lake trout fishery. Today the Eurasian zebra mussel is the most troublesome invasive species, clogging water intake pipes and displacing native mollusks. It is estimated that 131 biological communities are in some state of jeopardy.

Yet much has been done to address the problems perhaps best symbolized by Ohio's Cuyahoga River, which literally caught fire from pollution and helped trigger a revolution in attitudes toward Midwest water quality. The turkeys are back in Ohio, the deer returned in Indiana, and Upper Michigan is again a wild place. This region provides an astonishing profusion of places where one can go to see natural America. Many are not large, but those who apply themselves will find plenty to enjoy. Much of modern America's concern for the natural scene was inspired by the work of two giants, Aldo Leopold and John Muir, both connected with the University of Wisconsin, and the results of this concern can be seen in the region where they studied and taught. So hasten to see what bestirred them, and if you want to experience it thoroughly, be prepared to paddle.

—Thomas E. Lovejoy
Counselor to the Secretary for
Biodiversity and Environmental Affairs,
SMITHSONIAN INSTITUTION

LEFT: *The only tree and shrub species native to all 48 contiguous states, smooth sumac, with its clusters of scarlet seeds, mixes with fluffy yellow goldenrod in a meadow of Wisconsin's Kettle Moraine State Forest.*

INTRODUCTION
THE GREAT LAKES

The Great Lakes region lies at a biological crossroads. Here in presettlement times, the edge of the vast, ancient forest that covered the temperate east met the rolling grassland prairie advancing from the west. Today remnants of these basic habitats still linger. Dense boreal forests thickly blanket the north, and thousands of miles of Great Lakes shoreline encompass intricate dune systems, with their attendant swales, bogs, swamps, and marshes. Together these biomes support some of the most diverse natural communities in the United States.

Encompassing Ohio, Indiana, Michigan, and Wisconsin, this complex region harbors the most extensive freshwater dunes and the greatest concentration of lakes in the world—more than 10,000 along the Wisconsin-Michigan border. The Great Lakes themselves—Superior, Michigan, Huron, Erie, and Ontario—seem lakes in name only. One fifth of the freshwater on the earth's surface is found in the Great Lakes, and Superior reigns supreme as the world's largest lake.

The tides and the capricious, often furious, weather of these immense inland seas affect the states bordering their vast waters. All summer the lakes' 95,000 square miles of water slowly absorb heat. When polar air drifts in during the autumn, they relinquish their heat in explosions of energy termed the "lake effect," which roils the waters, produces fierce winds, and soaks the air with moisture. If it could be harnessed, the energy that the Great Lakes produce on a single fall day would power the nation for a year.

In winter, angry gray waters beat at the shore, often freezing in whitecap patterns. Herman Melville, who sailed on Lake Erie in the early 1800s, incorporated his harrowing experience in the "Town-Ho's Story" of *Moby-Dick.* In that chapter a whaleman says of the Great Lakes, "They are swept by Borean and dismasting blasts as direful as any that lash the salted wave; they know what shipwrecks are, for out of sight of land, however inland, they have drowned full many a midnight ship with all its shrieking crew."

Yet in fair summer weather, few places can seem so tranquil. A huge orange-red setting sun hovers above Superior, suffusing the still cobalt-blue waters with a rich golden glow that reaches to the horizon. Or a morning

---

PRECEDING PAGES: *One of the five U.S. inland seas, Lake Michigan (seen at Nordhouse Dunes) spans 22,400 square miles bordering four states.*
RIGHT: *At Grandfather Falls near its source in upper Wisconsin, the 429-mile Wisconsin River scours potholes in its sandstone bed.*

ABOVE: *In autumn, fiery red sugar maples and other northern hardwoods light up Hiawatha National Forest's 860,000 acres in Michigan's*

mist hangs like an Oriental screen over the shallow, milky waves that lap at a sprinkling of boats on Lake Erie.

Water in its varying forms has long been the defining element in the region's geography. The Great Lakes constitute at least part of the northern boundaries of all four states and surround more than 80 percent of Michigan. Wisconsin's western reaches are delineated by one of the country's greatest rivers, the Mississippi, and the region's southern edge is traced by another, the Ohio, which separates Ohio and Indiana from West Virginia and Kentucky. Rivers, creeks, and streams lace the terrain, and marshes and wetlands flourish on the margins where land meets water. All four states contain prime agricultural acreage, devoted to dairy farms, orchards, and broad fields of corn, grains, and soybeans. Vast forests cover the north, and rolling hills punctuate the south.

The largest area of inland sea on the planet, the Great Lakes are huge stone bowls pouring one into another. Superior's waters, which lie 600 feet above sea level, cascade 22 feet down the Saint Marys River to the Lake Michigan–Huron basin. At the lower edge of Lake Huron, water winds through a series of rivers and lakes to Lake Erie, then on to Niagara Falls, Lake Ontario, the Saint Lawrence River, and the Atlantic. Now a busy commercial route for international shipping and commerce, the shores of the Great Lakes are home to such important U.S. ports as Cleveland, Toledo, Detroit, Gary, Chicago, Milwaukee, Duluth, and Green Bay.

The Great Lakes developed over hundreds of millions of years. In the beginning, a few billion years ago, the collision of the earth's crustal plates

4

relatively unpopulated Upper Peninsula. The vast forests of this region are etched by 5 of Michigan's 16 national wild and scenic rivers.

eventually created high mountains, which eroded even as they rose. Above the present-day states of Michigan and Wisconsin, layer upon layer of lava oozed out to form bedrock so many miles thick that it sagged in the center, creating what became the Lake Superior basin. The huge valleys of early river systems formed the beginnings of the other Great Lakes.

For millions of years, the center of what is now North America was closer to the equator and filled with warm inland seas. The geologic legacy of this era is still evident throughout the four states. Marine shells and skeletons from the prehistoric tropical seas were compacted as layers of limestone, and the muddy deltas where rivers poured in became shale. Sandstone formed from bits of broken rock and sand that the rivers carried from surrounding mountains, and generations of vegetation growing in wet soils became compressed as coal.

All these permutations are apparent at the edges of the Great Lakes region. Sandstone and limestone hills undulate across southern Indiana and Ohio. Western Wisconsin, untouched by glaciers, is edged with ancient dolomite and sandstone hills and eroded bluffs that line the Mississippi River. In Michigan's Upper Peninsula, billion-year-old ridges of igneous rock protrude from the rugged terrain among fir and spruce forests.

The topography of the rest of the region, including the lakes, is relatively recent, the result of four great ice ages. Over a two-million-year period, a

OVERLEAF: *Spring erupts gloriously in southern Indiana with lacy lime-green hardwoods and magenta redbuds, inspiring a row around scenic Lake Wyandotte, part of the Harrison-Crawford State Forest.*

series of enormous sheets of ice, some more than a mile thick, advanced and then retreated over the Northern Hemisphere, especially North America. Each ice age was named for the state most marked by its action: Nebraskan, Kansan, Illinoisan, and Wisconsin. The last, the Wisconsin Glaciation, began 100,000 years ago and ended about 12,000 years ago. During its ponderous advance, great lobes of ice reshaped the land, molding it into its present configuration.

Many distinctive glacial formations are still visible across the Great Lakes states, particularly Wisconsin. Cone-shaped mounds (kames), snaking hills (eskers), canoe-shaped deposits (drumlins), and enormous ridges (moraines) pattern the farmlands and woods. Deep kettle-hole lakes formed when chunks of ice buried in glacial debris later melted.

Glaciers pressed upon the nascent basins of the Great Lakes, deepening and widening them. Like some great tiller of soil, the ice also dragged topsoil from northern areas and redistributed it—along with crushed mineral-laden rock—over the region's midsection, creating what many have called the richest soil on earth. In their to-ing and fro-ing, the glaciers ground the land flat with their great weight, and when the ice finally retreated, its meltwaters filled the holes that the glaciers had gouged, producing thousands of lakes.

Thick boreal forests and cold, wet conifer swamps grew up along the margins of the glaciers. Woolly mammoths, woolly rhinoceroses, saber-toothed tigers, mastodons with molars as long as a human forearm, musk oxen, caribou, and 500-pound giant beavers thrived in these conditions, as did prehistoric peoples.

As the ice retreated, the land began to rebound from the glaciers' weight and is still rising, as much as a foot every hundred years. The climate also warmed, and about 5,000 years ago grasslands extended eastward across the Great Lakes region. When the land cooled slightly, the ancient mesic forests of the southern Appalachians moved north to cover much of the land with towering trees. Tension zones among the boreal forests, more southerly forests, and prairies exist in the Great Lakes region to this day. A bit more rain or temperatures a few degrees higher give a particular ecosystem the opportunity to expand its range.

Hunter-gatherers were the earliest of the peoples occupying the area before the Europeans came. Mound Builders developed societies more than 2,000 years ago, and their farm plots and funerary structures bespeak a settled people. Eventually the region became populated by tribes whose descen-

LEFT: *Along Ohio's Lake Erie shoreline, Mentor Marsh near Headlands Dunes State Nature Preserve features clumps of plumed reed grass, a species which can grow 10 feet high and sink roots up to 30 feet long.*

dants still exist: among them were Potawatomi, Chippewa, and Menominee in the north and Miami, Shawnee, and Erie farther south.

The French, who entered the scene via the northernmost parts of the Great Lakes in the 1600s, were seeking wealth for themselves, territory for their king, and converts for the Catholic Church. They were not interested in settling the land, but other Europeans who breached the Appalachians were. By the late 1700s, settlers had begun arriving in the region, then called the Northwest Territory. The region's southern mesic forests were home to woodland bison, bears, parakeets, and millions—if not billions—of passenger pigeons. In the northern boreal forests lived moose, woodland caribou, elk, fishers, marten, wolves, bears, and many other species now gone. The prairies were a deep sea of bronze and burgundy grasses and myriad wildflowers, and the Great Lakes teemed with whitefish, sturgeon, lake trout, and other native fish.

To the newcomers the wildlife and the endless forests appeared infinite. The swamps and marshes that edged Erie and parts of the other Great Lakes must have seemed interminable obstacles, not freshwater nurseries for a vast array of animals and plants. Believing the land and the lakes limitless, they fished, they cut, they burned, they drained, they leveled, and they planted domestic crops wherever they could.

The magnificent white pine forests that towered over much of Michigan and northern Wisconsin are now all but gone, and Ohio's incredibly diverse mesic forests survive only in patches. Indiana's wet and dry prairies, sedge meadows, and oak openings (sandy ridges) are small jewel-like areas rather than broad fecund bands. As the Great Lakes shorelines were drained, countless waterfowl lost millions of acres of wetlands, and overfishing and pollution from industrial and agricultural runoff decimated the lakes' fish populations.

Although Niagara Falls once posed a barrier to alien river dwellers, bypass canals have allowed lampreys, alewives, and other species to work their way into the Great Lakes. Lampreys, a type of eel, literally sucked the

life out of remaining lake trout, and alewives, part of the herring family, multiplied furiously, choking Great Lakes waters and beaches. Today, some 131 biological communities and species are in trouble, including tallgrass prairie, Kirtland's warblers, Karner blue butterflies, and lake sturgeon.

Yet despite the depredations of the past 200 years, all the region's native habitats still exist. As people recognize their value, these natural areas are increasingly protected, and some are expanding. Prairies have been re-planted or allowed to return to their natural state, and slow-growing white pines are nurtured for future generations to appreciate. Biological and physical controls help regulate lampreys and other lake and river pests.

The region is rich in natural sites, large and small, whose particular beauty and significance have inspired local communities, individual states, the federal government, and private organizations to preserve them. For those willing to search them out, these sanctuaries offer a cornucopia of scenic superlatives: the country's first national lakeshore with its impressive cliffs, the largest waterfall (after Niagara) east of the Mississippi, the only mountain range in the Midwest, and the most extensive freshwater dunes in the world. Here visitors will find world-class wildlife refuges, spectacular gorges, wild rivers, the great North Woods, and a pristine island national park that can be seen only on foot or by boat. Although the Great Lakes region may never again be the primeval place it once was, an astounding diversity of native beauty still rewards those who seek it.

OHIO

PART ONE

O H I O

O hio was once so thickly forested that it was said a squirrel could cross the state without ever touching the ground. It was part of a vast forest that stretched from the Appalachians to the prairies. Unsurpassed among the world's temperate forests for tree size and variety, these woodlands were filled with towering oaks, maples, beeches, pure stands of walnut, and numerous other species—the temperate equivalent of Brazil's rain forest. Accumulating over millennia, leaf debris and other humus on the forest floor made this area one of the most fertile places on earth. And, except for swamps stretching along Lake Erie and patches of prairie, this immense green canopy shaded more than 90 percent of the state and provided centuries of shelter and sustenance to native peoples.

In the 1800s, however, newcomers wielding saws and stump-pullers started changing the look of the land. Early European settlers, untroubled by ecological issues, saw limitless opportunities in the forest, not finite natural resources. Farmers assiduously cleared their acres, burning a treasure's worth of trees in tall piles that lit up the night skies. Loggers harvested timber, and by 1849 Ohio ranked fourth among states in lumber production. By 1900 most of the forest was gone.

Before the land was cleared, black bears and wolves were common. (The 28 streams in Ohio named Wolf are not a case of poetic license.) Ohio's forests also provided roosting and nesting areas for bil-

PRECEDING PAGES: *In Wayne National Forest, the scenic Ohio View Trail winds along the Ohio River, which forms the state's southern border.*

lions of passenger pigeons, perhaps the most abundant bird the world has known. An 1854 event described by Dr. J. M. Wheaton in his *Report on the Birds of Ohio* suggests their numbers: "The light of the sun was perceptibly obscured by the immense, unbroken, and apparently limitless flock which for several hours passed over [Columbus]." Subsequent hunting and habitat destruction so decimated the passenger pigeon that by 1914 only one remained—at the Cincinnati Zoological Gardens. At her death, the species died too.

The majority of those once-towering Ohio forests were no older than the glaciers. The last ice age, the Wisconsin Glaciation, covered northwestern Ohio before reaching its southern limit in the state at the Allegheny Plateau. At that point, about 12,000 years ago, the great glaciers retreated, flooding the rubble-covered land with frigid meltwaters. When plants finally colonized the land, the forests that could survive the cold conditions were boreal spruce-fir. During subsequent climate changes about 5,000 years ago, hot, dry eras encouraged the prairies to move in from the west. Around 2,000 years ago, cooler, moister conditions created an opportunity for the vast ancient forests of the southern Appalachians to push their boundaries northward. When European settlers arrived in Ohio, the land was dominated by beech-maple climax forests, which prefer moister soils. Oak-hickory wood grew in drier sites and mixed mesophytic forests—ash, yellow poplar, black cherry—occupied the rest.

This "recent" history lies atop a thick layer of limestone bedrock formed hundreds of millions of years ago, in the first half of the Paleozoic era. A warm tropical inland sea once covered part of the continent's interior. Eventually shells and skeletons of countless mollusks, fish, and other marine life became compressed as limestone hundreds, even thousands, of feet thick.

When the Appalachian Mountains rose in the east, pressure caused the massive layers of limestone bedrock to bow in the middle, breaking the surface near Cincinnati. The Ordovician-period rock of this well-known exposed structure—called the Cincinnati Arch—is cluttered with fossilized shells, revealing a frozen picture of the life that inhabited warm primordial seas some 500 million years ago. This rockbound still life is one of the attractions awaiting visitors to Ohio's natural areas, which also offer majestic forests, serene rivers, and abundant wildlife.

CHAPTER ONE

SOUTHEASTERN OHIO

Southeastern Ohio's folded hills and hollows, forested mountains hazy with mist, and knobs of fantastically eroded sandstone have little in common with the vast, flat plains that stretch north and west to the shores of Lake Erie. Describing a diagonal line from the northeast corner of the state to the southwest, Interstate 71 roughly separates these two distinct areas. Ohio's split personality was formed about 12,000 years ago, at the end of the last great ice age.

The most recent defining geologic event for Ohio—as for other areas in the Great Lakes region—was the Wisconsin Glaciation. During a 10,000-year advance, glaciers of ice and rock debris, more than a mile thick, pressed upon the land. Like a steamroller, the inexorable grinding weight of these massive ice flows flattened the plains in the northern and western part of the state. Having reached a barrier—the Allegheny Plateau, which marks the westernmost edge of the Appalachian Mountains—the glaciers stopped short of the southeastern corner of the state, which remained untouched.

The 981-mile-long Ohio River forms the eastern and southern borders of Ohio and drains most of the shield-shaped state. Called *O-hee-ya* ("beautiful river") for its big, languid curves, softly sloping banks, and moderate width and current, the river was a perfect highway for native peoples and European settlers alike. Traveling the river, they passed wide, clean sandbanks and saw pelicans, cranes,

---

LEFT: *In Scioto Trail State Park and Forest, dogwoods flaunt creamy blossoms in a spring mist before taller trees leaf out. Native Americans used dogwood bark to treat malaria, contracted in swamps along Lake Erie.*

and wild swans. Europeans found a land covered in great hardwood forests sheltering myriad animals.

As settlers advanced in the late 1700s, bears, wolves, cougars, and other mammals began to disappear from the forests, which soon became farmlands. Today, long stretches of the beautiful river are lined with piles of coal, manufacturing plants, electricity generating stations, and all the concomitant industrial effluvia.

Nonetheless, swaths of southeastern Ohio remain natural and full of wildlife because they were too rugged to subdue with ax and plow. The unglaciated corner of the state contains an incredible diversity of flora, including wild magnolias, papaws, and other southern plants. Poorer agriculturally than the rest of the state, this hilly land is rich in scenic beauty.

Over millions of years, the thick sandstone beds underlying southeastern Ohio have eroded into gorges and a variety of other striking landforms, like those at Hocking Hills, that are the detritus of the once-towering Appalachians. As the mountains rose, streams continuously carried down bits of rock. When it reached slow-moving rivers, the rock accumulated, was compacted, and became the sandstone layers whose wildly eroded forms pattern southeastern Ohio.

This tour of Ohio's southeastern plateau country begins in the far northeast, explores various rivers, and then continues southwest along the big river, the Ohio, to the most southern and mountainous section of the state. A loop north takes travelers to the rock fantasies of the Hocking Hills area, south of Lancaster, and finally to the midsection of the state.

THE FAR EAST

Another river is the natural highlight of the northeastern corner of Ohio. Altered by the glaciers, the **Grand Wild and Scenic River**❖ follows a dogleg course that parallels Route 534 and curves north toward Lake Erie. Where it was blocked by glacial activity, the Grand makes an abrupt 90-degree turn westward, eventually draining into Lake Erie.

OVERLEAF: *American white pelicans, common sights along the Ohio before the arrival of European settlers, use the river as a flyway between Northwest breeding grounds and wintering spots along the Gulf Coast.*

ABOVE: *Anchored by giant sycamores, the Grand, a wild and scenic river, flows between steep bluffs along its western stretch. It then splays into branches that lace the floodplains leading to Lake Erie.*

One of Ohio's oldest and most undeveloped rivers, the Grand was a long-time trade route for Native Americans.

The river's upper portion flows leisurely north through forested wetlands—swamp forests—of maples, swamp oaks, and ash. Here beavers and reintroduced river otters work and play, and black bears, white-tailed deer, eagles, and ducks are among the river corridor's other residents. Beginning at the Harpersfield covered bridge on Route 534, the Grand is designated "wild" where it cuts deeply into Chagrin shale, creating dramatic bluffs that shimmer with waterfalls in spring. Past the gorge, the river heads across floodplains to Lake Erie. Canoe liveries can be found in Geneva and North Canton (the latter also serves Beaver Creek).

Paralleling Ohio's border with Pennsylvania, Route 7 south passes **Pymatuning State Park and Lake,** home to walleye, crappie, and perch. About 60 miles farther south, north of East Liverpool just off 7 on Bell School and Echo Dell roads, is **Beaver Creek State Park❖,** which centers on Little Beaver Creek, the state's first wild river and a national wild and scenic river as well. On its way to the Ohio River, Little Beaver Creek cuts through rounded hills, exposing 300-million-

Above: *Bright red* **Trillium erectum** *(left) uses its carrion scent to attract flies as pollinators. The pileated woodpecker (right) likes to gouge its distinctive rectangular holes in the tall trees of old-growth forests.*

year-old Pennsylvanian-period bedrock laid down during the rise and fall of an ancient inland sea. Thick layers of swampy vegetation from this sea were eventually buried and transformed into the coal deposits underlying much of southeastern Ohio. Later, the contours of this part of the Allegheny Plateau were softened by repeated glaciation. Little Beaver Creek is the only stream valley in the country that shows evidence of all four major glaciations.

On a brisk spring day, the river—not geology—is the focus of attention, its high waters rolling over low banks, its hydraulic power deceptively casual. Although at summer's end the river can contract to a trickle, in spring the waters lap at the legs of river birches, whose graceful moss-encrusted limbs arch over the water. Rising above the birches are tall white-barked sycamores, their broad leaves hiding a panoply of twittering, cawing, and trilling birds. At the center of the park, a pine-covered floodplain extends back from the banks, opening to reveal a preserved nineteenth-century pioneer village. In high water, the river's-edge trail is often flooded, and hikers must stick to bluff trails; ask the park staff about canoe liveries.

About 20 miles farther south, Route 22 leads southwest from

Steubenville to **Salt Fork State Park,** Ohio's largest. Although it is heavily developed, the 20,000-acre park is also being reforested. Many of Ohio's protected lands are being allowed to return to forest, and 30 percent of the state is once again covered with trees. As trees return to Salt Fork, so do wild turkeys, grouse, foxes, and deer.

Southeast of Salt Fork, south of 'Interstate 70 along Route 147 a few miles southeast of Belmont, **Dysart Woods❖** is a fine example of a virgin forest. The largest remnant of southeast Ohio's original forest, Dysart is no manicured park. In the woods, a natural laboratory for Ohio University, trees decompose where they fall. A ridge divides the site, and a trail loops through both sections. Near the edge of one area stands the tallest tulip poplar in Ohio, almost 5 feet in diameter and 130 feet high.

IN AND AROUND WAYNE NATIONAL FOREST

Although much of Ohio has been tamed and crisscrossed by busy highways, about 15 miles south and west of Dysart Woods begins a scenic and gentle roller coaster of a road—Route 26. Forests, fields, covered bridges, and brilliant fall colors abound on this picturesque trip through the easternmost section of far-flung **Wayne National Forest❖,** a checkerboard of private and public land that stretches to the Ohio River. From Marietta, about 20 miles northwest on Route 7, 3 miles past Leith Run, is the **Ohio View Trail,** which offers shady second-growth forests, rock outcrops, streams, ravines, and views of boats on the Ohio River that conjure images from Mark Twain.

24

cut to fire the furnaces that forests in surrounding Zaleski State Forest were denuded. Now protected, the woodlands are making a comeback.

Back at Marietta, Route 60 leads northwest to McConnelsville and another scenic road, Route 78, which winds southwest past **Burr Oak State Park.** At Glouster, go north on Route 13, then east on Township Road 289 about three miles to **Wildcat Hollow❖,** within a second unit of the Wayne National Forest. Like all national forests, Wayne is a mixed-use area where logging and other consumptive uses coexist with hiking and birding. After European-American settlers tried farming and oil drilling to make a living, the land became played out, was returned to the federal government, and entered the national forest system. On its hilly route, the Wildcat Hollow Trail takes hikers past white pine plantations, fields, the detritus of oil drilling, expansive views, and young mixed hardwood forests.

In addition to the three units of Wayne National Forest, Ohio has a state forest system, and at almost 27,000 acres, **Zaleski State Forest❖** is one of the biggest and best. From Glouster, Routes 78 and 278 run southwest to Zaleski and to adjacent **Lake Hope State Park❖,** a pleasant 3,120-acre park just across the road from the Zaleski Backpack Trail. Hikers can combine it with the Olds Hollow Trail to make loops of 1 to 23 miles long. In the marshy area near the trailhead, a chorus of frogs serenades visitors. Farther along, the trail winds through a cathedral pine grove, so-called because the cool, dim interior of the grove is pierced by shafts of light from "windows" in the canopy high above. Devoid of rustling underbrush because of the heavy shade, the grove is hushed. The path descends and then rises again into pines, which, like most oak and hickory, prefer the well-drained soils of

25

LEFT: *Benjamin Franklin's candidate for national bird, the wild turkey is reappearing in Ohio as forests regenerate. At dawn and dusk, cocks with harems of hens in tow stride through meadows at the forest edges.*
RIGHT: *One of Ohio's most botanically rich spots, the Lake Katherine preserve shelters flower-draped cliffs and a placid lake.*

slopes. Oak-covered ridge tops, overlooks, ravines, remnants of human habitation, streams, beaver ponds, and more ridges and hollows follow. Sheltered among the trees of the Olds Hollow Trail lies the graveyard of the town of Hope, which died when the iron-smelting industry declined around the turn of the century. A headstone from 1855 reads, "Remember man as you pass by; As you are now so once was I; As I am now so you must be; Prepare for death and follow me." Just beyond is another relic of Hope, a sunny but incongruous clump of yellow-and-white daffodils nodding in the breeze.

Some 20 miles southwest of Zaleski in Jackson County, which contains the broadest diversity of flora in the state, is one of Ohio's premier preserves, **Lake Katherine State Nature Preserve❖.** Where Route 93 turns southeast in the town of Jackson, continue straight for another block and then make a right turn, west onto State Street (County Road 76). After about two miles, turn right again, and go north onto Lake Katherine Road (County Road 85), which leads to the preserve.

In the botanical cornucopia of Lake Katherine, a number of plants are at their northern limit. Visitors are invariably surprised to round a corner and see, in a sheltered spot, bigleaf magnolia—Ohio's largest. The preserve's more unusual plants include stemless lady's slipper, puttyroot, and roundleaf catchfly. Some of the rare plants may be relics of the ancient Teays River valley, which once stretched from West Virginia to Indiana and was destroyed by glaciation.

Rolling green hills surrounding the preserve belie the layers of underlying sandstone, but streams such as Rock Run carve through the hills and expose rock. Sculpted by water, the graceful lines of these outcrops are colored with dark green moss, light green lichen, and red

stains of iron oxide. Skirts of ferns droop from cracks in the rock, and here and there a partridgeberry vine—its red berries bright against the moss—dangles from soil atop the sandstone.

The Pine Ridge Trail overlooks the hemlock-shaded recesses of Rock Run, where hidden waterfalls can be heard. Thick drifts of shiny-leaved mountain laurel catch the light on a long stretch of the Calico Bush Trail, named for pinkish-white laurel flowers dotted in a pattern resembling calico cloth. Wild turkeys, white-tailed deer, and even the occasional bobcat are among the larger animals roaming the preserve, and in spring, wildflowers light up the forest floor.

Continuing south on Route 93, turn east onto County Road 29 a few miles north of Ironton to the **Lake Vesuvius Recreation Area**❖ of Wayne National Forest. Near the trailheads are the remains of the Vesuvius furnace, built in 1833 and the most efficient iron furnace of its time. Here the trails offer two choices: an 8-mile tree-lined loop around Lake Vesuvius—actually a long skinny impoundment of Storms Creek —and a 16-mile loop branching from

ABOVE: *With a stubby, "bobbed" tail, the bobcat is North America's most common wildcat. It prefers rabbits as prey but if pressed will even eat bats.*

LEFT: *Now serene, Lake Vesuvius in Wayne National Forest was once home to the belching Vesuvius furnace, which produced Union ammunition.*

the lake trail. In autumn, the scene of red, orange, and yellow leaves reflected in the still lake beneath an imposing prow of sandstone evokes the contemplative quiet of a landscape painting. Cool groves of maturing pines, oak-dominated ridge tops, and a billow of mixed hardwoods of various ages give visitors a sense of classic, natural Ohio.

THE EDGE OF APPALACHIA

If Vesuvius whets visitors' appetites for large natural areas, **Shawnee State Forest**❖ is an obvious next stop (follow Route 52 about 30 miles west along the Ohio River and turn northwest onto Route 125 at

ABOVE LEFT: *Boggy limestone soils in the Edge of Appalachia Preserve nurture small white lady's slippers, among the loveliest native orchids.*

Friendship). The largest state forest, Shawnee covers more than 60,000 acres, encompassing an 8,000-acre wilderness area as well as **Shawnee State Park** and a half-dozen lakes. The park and forest are named for the once-dominant tribe of the Ohio Valley, the Shawnee. Although deer and smaller mammals thrive here, in the 1800s black bears, wolves, and otters were still abundant.

Shawnee's maze of hills, hollows, and ravines, characterizing the area as unglaciated Ohio, have earned it the nickname Little Smokies. With its misty layers of ridgelines stacked back to the horizon, not only does Shawnee fit the description, but it is part of the same Appalachian system. In addition to more than 60 miles of hiking trails, 140 miles of narrow roads curl up and down hills and along numerous streams. In spring, blossoming serviceberry, dogwood, and redbud trees soften vistas with white, pink, and plum pastels. Autumn provides a different but equally spectacular palette.

After the wildflowers and understory trees and shrubs have bloomed, the forest leafs out. Oaks and hickories claim the drier ridges, water-loving sycamores hover over the streams, and beeches and maples dominate shaded areas. Shawnee's wealth of tree species also includes white ash, yellow poplar, sweet gum, basswood, black cherry, red elm, and buckeye.

Just west of Shawnee, off Route 125, is the **Edge of Appalachia Preserve❖,** managed by the Nature Conservancy and the Cincinnati Museum of Natural History. The sanctuary is full of remarkable and

anomalous plants with geologic stories to tell. Whereas the rich glacial soils of northeastern Ohio produced rich farmlands and farmers, the thin soils of these hills have made Adams County the state's poorest. The few populated areas look like hardscrabble Appalachia, but the 11,000 protected acres of the Edge are rich in flora and fauna. More than 80 of the more than 900 plant species are rare or endangered, and 20 species of animals—such as green salamanders, certain freshwater mussels, and eastern wood rats (a type of pack rat)—are endangered. The Edge of Appalachia's natural resources are so extensive that four areas of it are in the National Natural Landmark system.

The Edge of Appalachia—where the western edge of the Allegheny Plateau meets the lowlands—owes its broad and unusual diversity to its distinct geologic demarcations, which create all sorts of ecological niches. The uplift's sandstones and shales foster acid soils that in turn support certain types of plant communities. Underlying the lowlands, limestones deposited by shells from ancient inland seas sustain "sweet" alkaline soils and entirely different plant communities.

As the glaciers crept south, plants from boreal forests moved just ahead of them. Because the glaciers stopped here, the Edge is the southernmost limit to the range of white cedar, usually more comfort-

able near the Canadian border. When the glaciers melted and the land dried out, prairie plants moved east, so relict prairie plant communities exist here at the eastern limit of their range. And when Appalachian forests succeeded prairies, plants such as Carolina buckthorn and southern blackhaw moved to the northern limits of their range. No wonder that birds—vireos, tanagers, hawks, warblers, woodpeckers—find the niches of the Edge a good place to linger.

The best way to see the Edge is to arrange a tour by contacting the museum or the Conservancy. The **Lynx Prairie Trail** begins behind the church in the southeast corner. One of ten areas within the Edge, Lynx Prairie is best seen in the full heat of late summer, when sun-loving herbaceous plants have flowered out. Prairies need fire to regenerate, so preserve managers burn overgrown areas when necessary. The reward of one such fire was a splash of gorgeous white lady's slipper orchids in the Abner Hollow area, where dormant plants had been waiting to be freed.

Among Lynx Prairie's profusion of plants—including the world's largest population of tall larkspur—are scarlet paintbrush, purple coneflower, white rattlesnake master, and prairie grasses such as big and little bluestem. Lichen-covered boulders are good places to discover some of the preserve's four types of rare ferns, which include the resurrection fern and the wallrue spleenwort. Even the false aloe, a Southwest succulent that resembles a miniature century plant, has migrated here. Buzzardsroost, a huge limestone promontory favored by vultures, is another part of the Edge that harbors rare prairie flora.

From Edge of Appalachia, Routes 348 east and 23 north lead to **Scioto Trail State Park and Forest❖.** The name means warrior's path, and Route 23 follows a Native American trail from Kentucky hunting grounds to Lake Erie fishing. Also nearby is the sizable Scioto River. Of the 35 tree species on the forested hills, the predominant oaks stage a colorful display in autumn. Scioto Trail is also a good place to see wild turkeys. Extirpated in Ohio by 1900 and reintroduced in the 1950s, they are now thriving, along with ruffed grouse, whose populations increased as forests were cut and replaced by fields.

Take Routes 104 north, 50 east, and 327 north to **Tar Hollow State Park and Forest❖,** named for the now-defunct practice of extracting tar from pitch pine for use as a salve and a wagon-axle lubricant. The centerpiece of Tar Hollow is the Logan Trail, which traces a figure eight up forested hills, down hollows, across streams, and through pine groves. Plentiful deer, birds, and spring wildflowers share Tar Hollow with red-backed and dusky salamanders, as well as numerous other amphibians and reptiles.

HOCKING HILLS

Route 56 east from Laurelville and Route 664 east are the way to Hocking Hills, the best-known scenic area in southeastern Ohio. A spectacular centerpiece among natural areas, **Hocking Hills State Park❖** is to Ohio as Yellowstone is to the National Park System. The park's highlights—Old Man's Cave, Cedar Falls, and Ash Cave—are strung along the perimeter of a quadrilateral formed by Routes 664, 374, and 56.

From about 300 to 150 million years ago, as the Appalachians rose in the east, sand and pebbles rushed down mountain streams to the broad deltas of an ancient inland sea. Over millions of years, these deposits were compacted and then eroded into the fantastic shapes of Hocking Hills' sculpted sandstone. Later, glaciers advancing upon the land stopped six miles short of Hocking Hills. When they retreated, plugs of ice blocked waterways, creating the hourglass-shaped Hocking River. The Wyandot and other tribal peoples called it the Hockhocking (Bottle) River because of its shape.

Water still plays a big role at Hocking Hills. In spring, waterfalls are everywhere around Old Man's Cave: trickling over boulders, spilling down small slopes, and plunging in veils from high stone lips. Steps wind up and down fern-fringed cliffs, around waterfalls, behind boulders, over streams, and past Old Man's Cave, where a nineteenth-century fugitive from Tennessee's Cumberland Mountain lived out his life as a hermit.

Although Hocking Hills' other highlights are only a few minutes by car, the five-mile (one way) Grandma Gatewood Trail links Old Man's Cave, Cedar Falls, and Ash Cave and places these spectacular formations in context while providing a pleasant walk through the woods. The next area—Cedar Falls—was misnamed because pioneers mistook the tall hemlocks shading this dark, luxuriant gorge for cedars. The hemlocks and the Canadian yew dotting some of the more recessed slopes are attractive leftovers—boreal relics from glacial times. As it makes its way

LEFT: *In spring, Hocking Hills State Park, one of Ohio's most picturesque locales, flashes with silvery cascades as dozens of waterfalls sculpt the soaring Blackhand sandstone.*

RIGHT: *A nocturnal insect hunter, the green salamander occupies a narrow, mountainous range that extends from Pennsylvania southwest to Alabama. This well-camouflaged amphibian generally hides during the day.*

down these slopes, Cedar Falls sheets from ledge to ledge in a herringbone pattern, finally crashing dramatically into a large pool at the bottom.

The caves in this area attracted the Adena culture, a mound-building agricultural people who lived in Ohio a couple of thousand years ago. More recent inhabitants used the caves as well, and European-American settlers named the largest Ash Cave because under the curving 700-foot sweep of stone, they found mounds of ashes, presumably from tribal council fires. To one side of the massive overhang that forms the cave, a waterfall plunges 90 feet to a pool below. The surrounding land is swathed in deep green forest, and in winter, when deciduous trees look bare, the waterfall freezes in a gleaming stalagmite of ice.

Hocking Hills is lovely in all seasons. Even nondescript fields are filled in late summer with parti-colored drifts of goldenrod, oxeye daisies, purple ironweed, and other wildflowers. A few miles north of Old Man's Cave along Route 374 lies **Conkles Hollow State Nature Preserve❖,** perhaps the most pristine place within Hocking Hills. A two-and-a-half-mile trail follows the edge of the cliffs that encircle this preserve, and a half-mile trail bisects the gorge bottom.

At the entrance to the hollow, river birches arch with careless grace over Pine Creek, and in spring, pinkish white spring beauties carpet the creek's floodplain. On the cooler, more shaded west rim cliff trail, thick with hemlock and yews, a bedding of needles makes the trail springy. Among the plants that favor the drier east rim are Virginia pine, mountain laurel, and wild hydrangea. From both rims the views

37

are expansive, featuring layered cliffs, delicate waterfalls, and a patch-work of green treetops.

In contrast, the gorge floor, dark under a canopy of leaves and nee-dled trees, seems ten degrees cooler. White, yellow, and purple violets are scattered along the trail, and white starflowers and Dutchman's-breeches mix with ferns and mayapples. In the trunk of a huge tulip poplar, a pileated woodpecker has pecked out its rectangular hole.

A few miles southeast of Lancaster on Route 22, take Beck's Knob Road north a short way to the parking lot for **Shallenberger State Na-ture Preserve❖**. Anchoring this 88-acre preserve are Allen and Ruble knobs, two dense sandstone formations that rode above the glacial ice surrounding them here at the southeastern limits of the last glacial age. The knobs offer views of Ohio's western till plains, and the rich soils at their base support a wide variety of trees and wildflowers.

THE MIDSECTION

Although the midsection of the state is largely devoted to the work of humans, a few places are worth a look. **Blackhand Gorge State Na-ture Preserve❖,** east of Newark off Route 146 and County Road 273, shelters a narrow sandstone gorge carved by the Licking River. Nature is now reclaiming this area long used by people. **Mohican State Park❖,** located within the **Mohican Memorial State Forest,** northeast of Mount Vernon off Route 3, highlights wide and deep Clearfork Gorge, traversed by the Mohican River. The Lyons Falls Trail follows the river, which is lined with great hemlocks and white pines and home to more than 15 species of warblers. About 10 miles southeast of Wooster via Route 250 to Alabama Avenue is the **Wilderness Center,** a private, nonprofit preserve crossed by a half-dozen public trails. The focal point is 30-acre Sigrist Woods—filled with virgin hardwoods, many a hundred years older than the nation. Visitors also enjoy the center's ponds, marshes, creeks, and regenerating prairie.

This section of the state is only a short distance from the shores of Lake Erie, a good starting point for exploring northwestern Ohio.

RIGHT: *Nature has paved the dry, eastern rim of the Conkles Hollow preserve with ocher sandstone, which—despite the mountain laurel and flowering vines—gives this vista a distinctively western ambience.*

NORTHWESTERN OHIO

imming the state's northern border, Lake Erie is northwestern Ohio's most distinctive natural feature. The lake is punctuated by rockbound islands and fringed by dunes and wetlands that shelter thousands of birds. Lake Erie reflects the often fickle Great Lakes weather, changing from a mist-veiled quiet at dawn to sun-spattered blue and cut-glass brilliance at noon. By late afternoon, the wind may whip up whitecaps while dark clouds roll in overhead.

Averaging only 58 feet deep, Erie is the shallowest and smallest of the Great Lakes (Lake Superior is seven times deeper). But Erie, the oldest and deadliest of the five, is the only one that lies on an east-west axis. Storms can rip eastward across it at 100 miles an hour, and more wrecked ships are reportedly buried in its muddy bottom than in any other body of water of its size in the world.

Erie is also the most productive of the lakes, its annual fish catch nearly equaling the combined output of the other Great Lakes. Perch, smallmouth bass, and carp are a few of the 17 main species, which once included the sturgeon, whitefish, and walleye that have been destroyed by overfishing, pollution, and silting from agricultural runoff. Fortunately, water flushes through the lake in 2.5 years—much faster than the approximately 100 years needed to clean Lake Michigan—

LEFT: *One of the few dunes in Ohio not consumed by development, Headlands Dunes on Lake Erie provides welcome landfall for birds migrating south and also defines the eastern range limit of many western plants.*

and thanks to stricter water-quality standards, Erie, once dirtiest of the Great Lakes, is making a comeback.

Before the last ice age, Lake Warren (Erie's precursor) reached much farther south and drained into the Mississippi River. After the glaciers had sculpted the land and withdrawn, the lake waters found a lower outlet in the Niagara River. This new route drained the shallow southern shores, leaving a stretch of marshes and swamp forests 120 miles long and 35 miles wide. Dubbing it the Great Black Swamp, early European-American settlers avoided the dark, flooded forests and their malaria-bearing mosquitoes. A large portion of these wetlands was ditched and drained—with great difficulty—in the late nineteenth century. The remaining section, full of waterfowl, fish, and amphibians, is northwestern Ohio's most biologically diverse area.

South of the Great Black Swamp's remains lie broad till plains, flattened by glaciers and rich with minerals from crushed glacial rock. The glacial till under the fertile topsoil is up to 50 feet thick and blankets a bedrock of limestone. Despite their dense forests, the till plains offered the best soil the new settlers had found and the flattest, most easily worked terrain. Although agriculture and other development eventually claimed 95 percent of these plains, northwestern Ohio is dotted with places where wise land stewards saved a shred of old-growth forest, or a river cut a gorge too deep to tame, or glaciers left a bog too spongy to develop.

Starting on Ohio's northeast shore near Cleveland on Lake Erie, this chapter travels westward along the lake to the northwest corner of the state and then swings eastward through the till plains. From there, a diagonal route to the southwest corner of the state visits gorges, bogs, and scenic rivers before heading toward southern Indiana.

LAKE ERIE SHORELINE

Cleveland calls its metropolitan park system the Emerald Necklace. Established in 1917, the 12 reserves that ring the city encompass 19,000 acres of forests, rivers, and meadows. Particularly appealing are **North Chagrin❖** (east off I-271) and **Bedford❖** (southeast off Route 14) **reservations,** which contain places unlike any manicured urban park. Bedford includes the deep, steep-walled gorge of Tinkers Creek—a national natural landmark—and vistas that equal any others

CANADA

LAKE ERIE

MICHIGAN

Great Black Swamp

IRWIN PRAIRIE STATE NATURE PRESERVE

MAUMEE BAY STATE PARK

Pelee Island

HEADLANDS DUNES STATE NATURE PRESERVE

WOODS NATURE SERVE

Burlington

OTTAWA NATIONAL WILDLIFE REFUGE
CRANE CREEK SP

KELLEYS ISLAND STATE PARK

SHELDON MARSH STATE NATURE PRESERVE

NORTH CHAGRIN RESERVATION

OAK OPENINGS METROPARK

Toledo

Marblehead

Sandusky Bay

Sandusky

Cleveland

BEDFORD RESERVATION

24

15

15   224

224

20

224

SPRINGVILLE MARSH STATE NATURE PRESERVE

224

60

CUYAHOGA VALLEY NRA

271

FOWLER WOODS STATE NATURE PRESERVE

68

75

23

71

13

Big Darby Creek

CEDAR BOG STATE MEMORIAL

Springfield

COLUMBUS

40

BATTELLE–DARBY METROPARK

13

40

JOHN BRYAN STATE PARK

CLIFTON GORGE STATE NATURE PRESERVE

71

22

UESTON WOODS ATE NATURE SERVE

Bellbrook

73

CAESAR CREEK GORGE STATE NATURE PRESERVE

Waynesville

LITTLE MIAMI STATE & NAT SCENIC RIVER

Oregonia

Harveysburg

Caesar Creek

oveland

FT ANCIENT STATE MEM

Little Miami River

350

73

Cincinnati

68

52

RIVER

OHIO

KENTUCKY

NORTHWESTERN OHIO

25   0   25 Miles

25   0   25 Kilometers

in the state. A few miles south is the **Cuyahoga Valley National Recreation Area❖,** a pleasant if tame unit of the National Park System. At North Chagrin, seven miles of trails wind through woods allowed to grow and decay naturally. Brandywine Falls tumbles over scalloped edges of eroded shale, and a small marsh—a mix of cattails, ponds, ducks, and birds—arcs around a nature center.

East of Cleveland off Route 44, near where the Grand River spills into Lake Erie, is **Headlands Dunes State Nature Preserve❖,** the best remaining dune ecosystem in Ohio. From Lake Erie's lapping waters to the trees, Headlands is a study in dune succession. Not far from the water's edge, beach grass and switchgrass invade the beach, anchoring shifting sand with a dense root mat. Sea rocket and beach pea fill niches on the sand, adding more organic material for the willows and cottonwoods that come next. Finally, when the beach is stabilized, oaks take hold. On a quiet morning, when only tiny ruby-crowned kinglets, rufous-sided towhees, and other birds are busy, Headlands provides refuge from the surrounding urban rush, as does adjacent **Mentor Marsh,** with its ten-foot plumed reeds.

On the other side of Cleveland, farther west along Route 2 about five miles east of Sandusky, lies **Sheldon Marsh State Nature Preserve❖,** a good place to see birds heading north during spring migration. One of Ohio's last surviving coastal wetlands, Sheldon Marsh is full of mini-ecosystems. A fat green heron rests alongside a small pond marking the edge of an old field. Planted with red clover, the field has become a butterfly refuge where monarch caterpillars feast on the naturally occurring milkweed. Later, in mid-September, clouds of adult monarchs alight to sip from the clover before continuing their migration south.

Beyond, a flooded forest is noisy with the sounds of woodpeckers, cardinals, and chickadees, and at the edge of the woods, a rust-plumaged brown thrasher flings up papery old leaves as it scrounges on the ground for food. As the land slopes imperceptibly toward Lake Erie, trees stand in increasingly deeper water; in summer, cardinal

---

LEFT: *Flecked with autumn gold, Tinker's Creek Gorge bisects Cleveland's Bedford Reserve, offering steep-walled ravines and colorful views.*
OVERLEAF: *Tall yellow coreopsis brightens Sheldon Marsh, one of the last marshes on southern Lake Erie and a refuge for 300 bird species.*

flowers brighten this shaded woodland swamp with flashy lipsticklike red flower spikes.

In a cove edged with cattails, basking painted turtles cover the exposed end of every half-submerged log, their dark, shiny backs stacked edge to edge like so many coins. Heavyset carp crowd the open waters of the cove, and on the barrier beach separating cove and lake, geese mill about while egrets probe the shallows for edible morsels.

After crossing Sandusky Bay on Route 2, take Route 163 to Marblehead, where a ferry sails to **Kelleys Island State Park❖.** The island's 2,800 acres make it the largest American segment in a 20-island archipelago that crosses the western end of Lake Erie. Only Canada's Pelee Island, about three miles north, is bigger. Kelleys's singular natural feature is its world-famous glacial grooves, where advancing and retreating glaciers scoured a series of trenches 15 feet deep and nearly 100 feet long into the island's limestone bedrock.

During the four ice ages of the Pleistocene epoch, which began about a million years ago and ended with the retreat of the last ice age, the earth cooled and snows did not melt, even in summer. Over thousands of years, the weight of this accumulated snow compressed the bottom layers into ice. As these gargantuan rivers of snow and ice oozed south over North America covering about an inch a day, they engulfed chunks of rock ranging from pebbles to boulders. Researchers believe that the glacial grooves were created when rocks, pushed forward by glaciers, scored the bedrock with troughs, which were eventually broadened by expanding ice.

When picnickers discovered the grooves in the late 1800s, they found a much larger set measuring 2,000 feet long and 30 feet wide each, but these were later destroyed by quarrying. To protect the remaining examples from souvenir hunters and visitors' feet, state officials surrounded the grooves with chain-link fencing.

Not only are the glacial grooves visible evidence of the glaciers' might, but they also display a wealth of fossils from the Devonian sea that covered much of the Midwest 350 million years ago. Underfoot,

---

RIGHT: *About 12,000 years ago, mile-high glaciers ground out deep, 100-foot-long, world-famous rock grooves on Lake Erie's Kelleys Island, which is part of the oldest archipelago on the Great Lakes.*

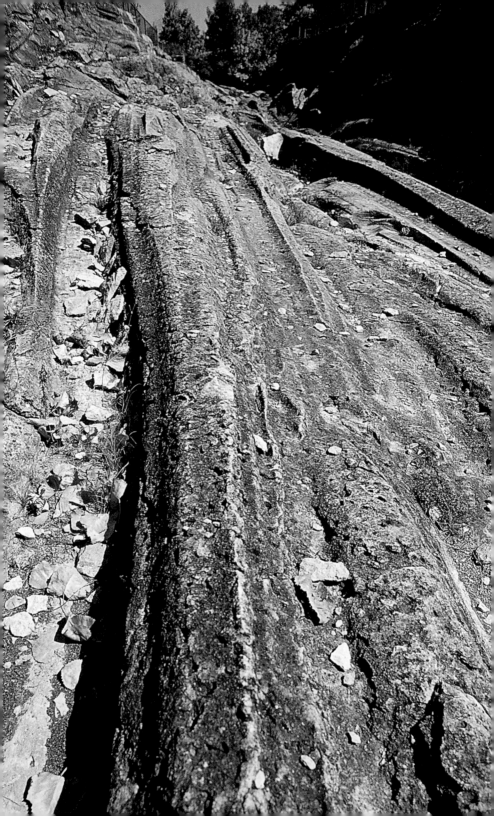

embedded in the limestone, lie fossil remains of corals, brachiopods, gastropods, "sea lily" crinoids, and other marine animals of that period.

Visitors hiking the park's North Shore Trail are likely to encounter black-and-white warblers in spring; lots of cottonwood, buckeye, willow, and redcedar; perhaps a black-crowned night heron at the rock-ledged shoreline; and few other hikers. At dusk, anglers in boats cast for walleye and bass, breaking a lake surface as subtle as raw silk. Cormorants skim the water on their way to Pelee Island, just visible in the misty distance.

At **Crane Creek State Park❖** off Route 2 about 15 miles west of Sandusky Bay, beach and lake activities are eclipsed by nature appreciation. Even before reaching the nature center and bird observation tower, visitors are likely to be welcomed by swooping purple martins and ducks and geese casually crossing the road as if they owned the place. Near the beach, a half-mile-long boardwalk trail with loops and side paths leads visitors alongside 2,000-acre **Magee Marsh Wildlife Area❖** and a world of birds, providing a glimpse of the Lake Erie shoreline before settlement. Although it seems low, the land here is a

At the crossroads of the Mississippi and Atlantic flyways, Magee Marsh (left) is one of Ohio's best birding spots. When fishing, a green heron (above) can dangle by its feet like a trapeze artist. Primarily nocturnal, black-crowned night herons (right) roost in bushes during daylight hours.

hundred feet higher than it was at the end of the Wisconsin Glaciation because mile-high glacial ice so compressed the land that it is still rebounding from that weighty event.

One of the best birding sites in the state, Crane Creek is especially lively during spring migration. Birds from both Atlantic and Mississippi flyways stop at these wetlands to rest before their flight across Lake Erie to Canada. Much of the winding boardwalk is bordered by the dense trees of a swamp forest on one side—great for spotting forest birds—and open marsh on the other—perfect for seeing waterfowl.

Watching the birders can be as entertaining as watching the birds. In the dim early morning—in a scene resembling a bizarre ritual from an Ingmar Bergman film—people of all ages and types slide past one another on the boardwalks with minimal noise and movement, heads craned at the trees and binoculars glued to their eyes. Thrashers, gnatcatchers, cardinals, nuthatches, titmice, warblers, thrushes, and grosbeaks are just a fraction of the more than 300 species recorded here.

In the marsh, muskrat ply the waters around their lodges. Smaller versions of beavers with long ratlike tails, muskrat mound their lodges

51

with grasses and sedges rather than the mud and sticks beavers use. A Canada goose perches on one lodge, and farther out, a marsh hawk glides just above the water, searching. Among the blue irises decorating the water's edge, a fat garter snake coils itself in a bush to await the sun's warmth. Mergansers, pintail, and teal are a few of the ducks scattered throughout the marsh waters.

Next door to Crane Creek is a quite different bird gathering place, **Ottawa National Wildlife Refuge❖.** The national refuges are administered by the U.S. Fish and Wildlife Service, and this one is Ohio's finest. Encompassing more than 8,000 acres of marshes, grasslands, and forest, Ottawa is named for the people who lived in this area and called themselves *adawa,* "traders." Like the European-American settlers who came later, they were daunted by the wetlands and swamp forest, called the Great Black Swamp, covering the western shores of Lake Erie from present-day Sandusky to Detroit.

For wildlife, however, the area was invitingly fecund, sustaining myriad plants, insects, mollusks, and fishes that feed birds; a variety of small mammals; and formerly panthers. One-day marsh counts in the 1970s recorded 35,000 mallard, 46,000 black ducks, 10,000 canvasbacks, 30,000 Canada geese, 80,000 mergansers, 1,000 great blue herons, and tens of thousands of other birds.

Although much of Ottawa is accessible only to wildlife, the refuge includes about seven miles of trails in an area divided into huge shallow pools; the earthen dikes forming the sides of the pools also serve as walking trails. In spring, the pools fill with water, and in summer, Fish and Wildlife Service managers drain the pools, allowing vegetation to grow in the damp mud and thus provide more and varied forage for the wildlife. Summer is a good time to see such wildflowers as water lilies, joe-pye weed, blue pickerelweed, and rose mallows.

Ottawa's spread-out design gives it a more expansive feel than Crane Creek. Terns wheel over the open waters; killdeer shriek from the sidelines; kingbirds light on low shrubs at the edge of a patch of trees; and shovelers, teal, and coots are just some of the ducks pad-

---

LEFT: *Lake Erie's Ottawa National Wildlife Refuge, a magnet for waterfowl, was once part of the Great Black Swamp, which stretched from Sandusky to Detroit. Most of the swamp was drained in the 1800s.*

ABOVE: *Ferocious fighters, mink mark their territory with rank discharges from their scent glands. They live near wetlands such as Ohio's Irwin Prairie where they prey on—and control—muskrat populations.*

dling around. At water's edge, a tall, elegant great blue heron stares over the cattails like a long-legged, impassive runway model. Then, swiftly, the bird stabs the waters and brings up dinner—a fat frog impaled on its beak. In the distance, an enormous eagle's nest fills the crotch of a large tree. Before their numbers plummeted due to pesticide use and habitat reduction, eagles nested all along Lake Erie's southern shores, and today species and habitat protections are helping them make a comeback in northern Ohio.

Although more manicured than wild, nearby **Maumee Bay State Park❖** is a good place for visitors to stay while exploring Crane Creek and Ottawa.

GLACIAL REMNANTS IN THE NORTHWEST

About five miles west of Toledo, just south of Route 20 on Irwin Road, lies **Irwin Prairie State Nature Preserve❖,** perhaps Ohio's premier wet prairie. Irwin Prairie is part of a larger area known as the Oak Openings, which was originally surrounded by the Great Black Swamp. A series of broad sandy ridges, Oak Openings was formed when sand was washed southward from preglacial Lake Warren. In

ABOVE: *Butterflies use the flowers of butterfly weed, a prairie species found at Irwin Prairie, because the plant is poisonous to birds. Monarchs lay their eggs on it to protect their larvae from avian predators.*

some places the sands are 35 feet deep; in others, they lie thinly above a clay bottom. Because water cannot penetrate the clay, a perched water table creates lowlands such as Irwin Prairie. Too wet to support even a swamp forest, it is thick with sedges and wetland grasses. The wet sedge meadow, which attracts waterfowl, state-endangered spotted turtles, and aquatic mammals such as mink, can be viewed from a meandering boardwalk. The drier, sandier areas of Irwin Prairie support oaks and prairie plants rarely found in other parts of the state.

About ten miles southwest of Irwin Prairie, on Wilkins Road just south of Route 2, residents of Lucas County have created **Oak Openings Metropark❖** to preserve a remnant of this unusual ecosystem. Oak Openings takes its name from the sand ridges and widely spaced oaks, which created precious open space within the dense swamp forests. Here, mixed deciduous forests, swamp forests, sandy ridges, open dunes, and prairie provide habitat for more than a thousand plant species, some found nowhere else in the state. Among Oak Openings' abundant species are endangered ear-leaf and Skinner's foxgloves, butterflies, sundews, and salamanders, as well as deer and many birds.

The trees are big and the woods quiet at **Goll Woods State Nature**

Preserve❖, a small, out-of-the-way gem (continue west on Route 2, turn south on Route 66 to Burlington, west on Township Road F, and then south on Township Road 26). The Goll family, who emigrated to America from France in the 1830s, preserved this fertile piece of the Great Black Swamp, one of Ohio's last stands of old-growth forest. Trails take visitors past centuries-old trees, each seemingly more massive than the last. Swamp white oak, ash, and other swamp forest trees grow in the boggy bottomlands. Low sand ridges, some only a foot higher than the bottomlands, are relics of a preglacial lakebed and now support beech and maple.

Ironically, the swamp trees are the instruments of their own demise. The more leaf litter they drop, the faster the swamp fills in and is claimed by beech and maple. In this region of the country, beech-maple forests are dominant because beech and maple seedlings thrive in shade, whereas most other tree seedlings do not. Eventually these shade lovers take over, nurturing successive generations of beeches and maples under their broad, leafy canopies. Occasionally fire clears an area, allowing sun-loving species such as black cherry to move in and begin the process once again.

ABOVE: *Small, elegant, and splashed with round bright yellow dots, the spotted turtle makes its home in wet forests such as Goll Woods.*

LEFT: *In spring, Goll Woods, one of Ohio's finest virgin forests, is carpeted with native geraniums. Their name comes from the Greek for "crane" because the fruit looks like cranes' bills.*

Once Goll Woods was home to bears, elk, bison, and wolves. Now the largest mammals are deer, which flash through the dim forest spotlighted by rays of sunlight penetrating the trees. Spicebush and papaw are among the shrubs occupying the understory, and ferns and wildflowers carpet the forest floor. Fleeting silences are soon filled with the trilling of birds and the hammering of woodpeckers.

THE NORTH-CENTRAL TILL PLAINS

Glacially wrought till plains cover the rest of northwestern Ohio. Take Route 15/224 east from Defiance. About ten miles east of Findlay, head south on Route 23, and west on Township Road 24 to the largest inland wetlands on the till plains: **Springville Marsh State Nature Preserve❖.** Ditched and drained by settlers, the marsh was once part of a much larger ecosystem called Big Spring Prairie. Springville Marsh boardwalks now traverse what is left of that prairie, winding past sedge meadows, cattail marshes, and ponds containing rare fen orchids, lobelia, and gentian. Fertile sedge-peat soils and plentiful water attract numerous birds, mammals, reptiles, and amphibians.

One of the few stands of mature woods left on the till plains, **Fowler Woods State Nature Preserve❖** lies some 50 miles farther east on Route 224. Just beyond Greenwich, go south on Route 13 and then one mile east on Olivesburg Road. Part of Fowler Woods straddles Saint Johns moraine, one of the eroded mounds that still band the till plains. At Fowler Woods, the different types of soils deposited by glacial action support various types of plant communities. A short trail system displays numerous habitats, from well-drained slopes to buttonbush swamp. In the spring, the more than 200 kinds of wildflowers growing here stage a spectacular show.

Just outside Columbus, a wealth of species reside along **Big Darby Creek,** one of the most pristine waterways in Ohio and a state and national scenic river for 82 miles. Big Darby is accessible at **Batelle-Darby Metropark❖,** about 14 miles west of Columbus and 3 miles south of Route 40 on Darby Creek Drive. Among the top five freshwater habitats in the nation, Big Darby and its tributaries are home to more than 100 species of fish and 41 species of mussels. The spotted darter and Scioto madtom are just two of the numerous rare or endangered fish species here, and the aquatic environment attracts herons, mink, and muskrat, among many others. From bluffs and at creekside, trails afford peaceful views of Big Darby. Early national parks, such as Yellowstone and Yosemite, were established mainly for their astonishing features—waterfalls, granite domes, hot pools, and geysers. Today ecologists value the significance of an overall ecosystem, even though it may not inspire visitors to grab their cameras. Big Darby is just such a preserve.

A remarkable anomaly, Ohio's first nature preserve can be found some eight miles north of Springfield, on Woodburn Road a mile west of Route 68. Like much of interest in this region, **Cedar Bog State Memorial❖** is a product of the glaciers. Glaciers do not flow in a neat

ABOVE: *Showy marsh marigolds—a buttercup relative—light up Cedar Bog wetlands. Although it generally resembles a cool, northern Michigan fen, Cedar Bog also contains Ohio's third-largest prairie remnant.*

advance of unbroken ice wall. They move by fits and starts, some lobes progressing faster than others that encounter obstacles. When glacial ice reached Bellefontaine—at 1,549 feet, the highest point in Ohio—it split into two lobes and flowed around this rise. The two lobes, the Miami and the Scioto, met again at what is now Cedar Bog, some 25 miles south, and ground into each other. One had picked up mostly gravel in its icy advance, the other clay. The layering of these two substances traps water, creating Cedar Bog.

Because these wetlands have inlets and outlets, the place is really a fen, not a bog, and the only fen in Ohio where white cedars grow— in dense dark-green clusters. When the glaciers retreated, white cedars, yews, dwarf swamp birches (at their southern limit here), and other northern plants remained because Cedar Bog is fed by cool underground springs. Cedar Bog's ecosystem most closely resembles northern Michigan fens, and the sedge meadows and cedar forests suggest Ohio's appearance at the end of the ice age. In fact, an ice-age mastodon—its stomach full of partially digested sedges and pond lilies—was unearthed in nearby Licking County a few years ago.

In spring, the fen glows with the warm, buttery light of thousands of yellow marsh marigolds, which crowd the boardwalk looping through Cedar Bog's various habitats. Among the many other wildflowers here are large lady's slipper orchids, three varieties of Solomon's seal, swamp candles, and tiny carnivorous sundews. In late summer, queen-of-the-prairie, prairie valerian, coneflowers, and other butterfly-attracting wildflowers dress Ohio's third-largest prairie remnant in a patchwork of color. Later, purple-blue fringed gentians herald the coming of autumn.

Cedar Run, whose cold waters cross the preserve, harbors 18 species of fish, including the rare thumb-sized tongue-tied chub. Although spotted turtles and shy massasauga rattlesnakes live in the preserve, visitors seldom see them. To enjoy all the aspects of Cedar Bog, call ahead and schedule a tour with the site manager.

SOUTHWESTERN RIVER GORGES

South of Cedar Bog and Springfield, just off Routes 72 and 370, **John Bryan State Park❖** contains one of Ohio's most dramatic river gorges, **Clifton Gorge State Nature Preserve❖.** Cut by a river of glacial meltwater at the end of the last ice age and now occupied by the Little Miami River, Clifton Gorge shelters relict boreal habitats where lacy white cedars still grow. Swaying at the edges of the narrow 70-foot-deep gorge, sprays of their dark evergreen branches frame the Little Miami in lush shadowed thickets.

From the rim trails, visitors can look down on quiet pools and boiling rapids as geology shapes the river. Springs seep from cracks in the gorge's rock walls, and in wet weather waterfalls pour over the hardest, least-eroded bedrock. Six layers of sedimentary rock stamp their geologic signatures on the gorge, from Cedarville dolomite near the top to Elkhorn shale at the bottom, representing the Silurian and Ordovician periods, 400 to 500 million years ago, respectively.

Great chunks of dolomite, a hard form of limestone suffused with magnesium, have sloughed off the gorge's sheer walls. Often the

---

RIGHT: *White cedars line Clifton Gorge; the conifer's common name, arborvitae, is Latin for "tree of life," perhaps because tea made from the vitamin C–rich bark saved explorer Jacques Cartier's men from scurvy.*

ABOVE: *At Fort Ancient, the ceremonial mounds built by the Hopewell people 1,500 years ago are now topped by trees and carpeted by patches of mayapple. The site also offers access to the Little Miami River.*

blocks are covered with soft green mosses accented with the white blossoms of Dutchman's-breeches. The hidden brownish blooms of wild ginger and the pinks of hepatica are among colors provided by the 347 species of wildflowers gracing the gorge. Nearby **Glen Helen,** a nature preserve owned by Antioch College, is also worth visiting.

Near its mouth, Caesar Creek presents a benign appearance, although the side walls of the gorge are almost twice as high as Clifton Gorge. **Caesar Creek Gorge State Nature Preserve❖** is some 5 miles southeast of Waynesville, on Corwin Road south of Route 73.

This area has been inhabited for at least 8,000 years, and the latest vestiges of farming are just beginning to fade in the preserve as old fields revert to meadows. Eventually the meadows will blend into the forests of beech, maple, hickory, and oak that border the gorge. In the meantime, preserve managers hope to eliminate such exotics as honeysuckle and multiflora roses planted as hedgerows. Trillium and other forest wildflowers are making a comeback, and beavers have returned.

The trails here are little better than deer paths, and the preserve is not cluttered with signs. The centerpiece is Caesar Creek. Near its confluence with the Little Miami, geese and ducks paddle beside quiet banks. Sparkling in the sunlight, the creek ripples musically over water-rounded rocks, its erosive action laying bare countless fossils

62

ABOVE: *America's first internationally recognized African-American artist, Robert S. Duncanson (1821–72), painted* Blue Hole, Little Miami River *in 1851. Today the Little Miami is a national wild and scenic river.*

embedded in the limestone: brachiopods, corals, and that wildly successful group of marine arthropods called trilobites.

Fossils are also abundant at **Fort Ancient State Memorial❖,** about 10 miles southwest of Caesar Creek on Route 350. River access at Fort Ancient affords the best way to see the **Little Miami State and National Scenic River❖,** the first one in the state and among the first in the national wild and scenic river system. The river has carved 300-foot-high gorges near Fort Ancient, a world-famous Mound Builder site where prehistoric Native Americans constructed mounds that form a celestial calendar. Altogether, the Little Miami flows 105 miles from its headwaters through gorges and woods to a wide floodplain at its confluence with the Ohio River. Canoe liveries are available in Bellbrook, Loveland, and Oregonia, and a hiking/biking path follows an old railroad right-of-way along the river.

A few miles from the Indiana border in Hueston Woods State Park, just southwest of Route 177 on Route 732, lies **Hueston Woods State Nature Preserve❖.** Here the centerpiece is the Big Woods, 200 acres of virgin Ohio forest bisected by an unnamed creek, which shows how most of Ohio once looked. Beyond Hueston Woods, Indiana offers more old-growth forests, areas so thick with giant trees that even in the hot glare of summer they seem cool and dim.

INDIANA

PART TWO

INDIANA

N o neat line marks the transition from forests to tallgrass prairies that occurs in Indiana. The progression has been described as a prairie archipelago: islands of prairie in the surrounding forests that farther west become islands of forest in the surrounding prairie. Fire and especially moisture govern the outcome: A few additional inches of water produce forests; a few less, prairie.

Presettlement Indiana was 13 percent dry prairie, much of it tallgrass and most appearing in the northwest corner of the state. At the beginning of the nineteenth century, European settlers described the grassy landscape as an undulating ocean stretching beyond the horizon. Although some were unnerved by the seemingly endless monotony of grass, others saw in the swaying, feathery vistas rich tapestries of color: bronze, gold, copper, crimson, burgundy, and pale yellow.

At its tallest, prairie grass can dwarf a person. Someone on horseback would have had to stretch up to touch the tops of big bluestem, which can reach as high as 12 feet. Although they looked infinite in the early 1800s, tallgrass prairies predominated in only six states: Indiana, Illinois, Iowa, Wisconsin, Missouri, and Minnesota. Past the hundreth meridian, the so-called Dry Line, mixed and short-grass prairies took over.

Today, where tallgrass prairies once grew, lies some of the richest soil on earth. Thousands of years of grasses accumulated, layer upon thick organic layer, over the deep mantle of till deposited by the glaciers. In a tallgrass prairie, the biomass beneath the ground is even greater than that above ground, and in some places, the topsoil is 30 to 40 feet thick. (By comparison, in the short-grass prairies at the eastern foot of the Rockies, topsoil is sometimes only 2 inches deep.) Not surprisingly, the large fertile till plain that straddles the middle of Indiana—contiguous

---

PRECEDING PAGES: *Golden in the sunset, the Indiana Dunes National Lakeshore on Lake Michigan lies at a crossroads of botanical diversity.*

with till plains in Ohio—is now farmland, specifically corn land.

Although the prairies begin in Indiana, most of the state was once covered by thick beech-maple forests, where early hunter-gatherers made a decent living from prairie bison, woodland mammals, waters teeming with fish, and an abundance of wild plant food. Starting with the last ice age, when hunters roamed the glacial margins seeking woolly mammoths and other game, hunter-gatherer societies populated the well-watered lands of the southern Great Lakes. The woodland mound-building peoples who predominated in Indiana and Ohio about 800 B.C. offer the first look at a more complex society. Mound Builders—the Adena followed by the Hopewell peoples—left huge burial mounds filled with pottery and other funerary artifacts. Cultivating sunflower seeds, pumpkins, and other crops, they were the region's first farmers, and the houses they built were sophisticated for their time and place.

About A.D. 900, Mississippian cultures arrived from the Southwest or Mesoamerica, superseding the Mound Builders and bringing with them the so-called corn-bean-and-squash culture distinctive to peoples from those regions. By the 1600s, the ancient peoples had coalesced into the historic tribes (Miami, Shawnee, Erie) known to French explorers moving south through the Great Lakes and later to European pioneers traveling westward. Although the French probably established the first European settlement at Vincennes in 1727, until Indiana gained statehood in 1816, Native Americans claimed the territory. By the mid-1800s, they had been pushed out by treaties and warfare.

Gone about the same time the native peoples disappeared were most of Indiana's forests and prairies—chopped down and plowed under. With the forests went black bears, river otters, beavers, and bobcat. Land clearing attracted other species, though, and from the south came opossums, eastern moles, and fox squirrels. Through it all, that competent omnivore, the raccoon, has remained.

As elsewhere, natural environments so valued today were left untouched because they were the least desirable lands: shifting, unstable dunes, swamps and bogs, steep inaccessible gorges and uplands, and wild rock-strewn rivers. In Indiana, natural areas form a connect-the-dots C over the state, ranging from the hilly scenic southern third of the state, north to the lush wetlands along the Illinois border, and then to the biologically rich sandy shores along Lake Michigan. All are well worth a visit.

SOUTHERN
INDIANA

In its roller coaster of hills, ridges, bluffs, and gorges, the southern third of Indiana probably contains as much varied topography as the rest of the state combined. The land is dotted with remnants of the forests that once covered this part of the country. Like fingers on a splayed hand, rivers reach south across the bottom of the state, around hills and through steep ravines, to the Wabash and Ohio rivers. As Indiana's southern border, the Ohio is still the graceful river it once was along its entire length.

Southern Indiana can be further divided. If the region were a bed covered by a mantle of topsoil, someone seems to have lifted the covers and stuffed a large, lumpy pillow into the middle of the bed. West and east of this hilly middle are lowlands and plains respectively.

Southeastern Indiana was shaped by the Illinoian glaciation, the third of four great ice ages. Reaching farther south than the most recent glaciers, these ice masses left a till plain over the state's southeastern corner. Because the till here is now so old (more than twice the age of till plains to the north), rivers such as the Whitewater have had time to carve deep ravines forested with oaks and hickories and laced with waterfalls. Visitors to northern Indiana and Ohio a few thousand years from now might find a similarly eroded topography.

In southern Indiana's hilly central section, bedrock, mostly lime-

LEFT: *On the far horizon of Jackson-Washington State Forest is the rolling Knobstone Escarpment that parallels I-65. The knobs are all that remain of ancient hills that once towered above ice-age glaciers.*

stone laid down in ancient seas, rises high enough to have halted the glaciers. This unglaciated lump-under-the-covers is a source of so much limestone that Indiana provides more than 60 percent of the nation's building supply. These hilly uplands also afford the state much of its outdoor recreation and exceptional scenery. On hilltops where soil is too thin to support forests, grassy glades fill the niche.

Over the past two to three million years, water slowly eating away at the limestone has created vast cave networks. The process starts with precipitation, which combines with carbon dioxide in the air and soil to form carbonic acid. Then this weak acid percolates through soil (humus), adding humic acid. When it reaches bedrock, the acidic water slowly dissolves the limestone along the fracture surface. Although glaciers did not traverse these uplands, as ice sheets retreated, their rushing meltwaters found weak spots in the limestone, widening nascent caves. Because limestone is more soluble in cold water than warm, glacial meltwaters were particularly effective at carving caves. Today this area is a Swiss cheese of sinkholes, caves, and underground streams.

In the southwestern lowlands, rivers share the land. The Wabash forms Indiana's western border, the Ohio bounds the south, and the area where these two great rivers converge is full of habitats reminiscent of the Deep South: bayous, cypress swamps, and sloughs.

After visiting the southeastern portion of southern Indiana, beginning in Versailles and Madison, this chapter follows a southerly and westerly course along Interstate 65 and 64, dropping farther south to follow the Ohio River. From these lowlands, the route swings north through the middle of the state to the edge of northern Indiana, ending around the city of Bloomington.

THE SOUTHEAST CORNER

East of the town of Versailles just off Route 50, Laughery, Cedar, and Fallen Timber creeks all meander through **Versailles State Park❖,** Indiana's second largest. Although only the **Fallen Timber Nature Preserve❖** has a trail, the park encompasses three other preserves, one of the state's highest concentrations of preserves. Dawn and dusk are the best times to see white-tailed deer and wild turkeys. Above, turkey vultures cruise the thermals to spot prey below. A fine way to see the park and wetlands wildlife is by canoe on upper Laughery Creek.

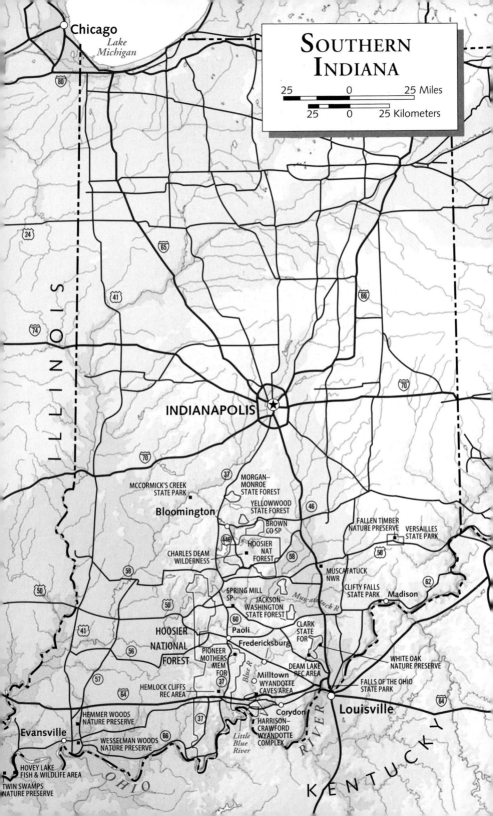

SOUTHERN INDIANA

25   0   25 Miles
25   0   25 Kilometers

Chicago
Lake Michigan

80

ILLINOIS

24

65

41

74

69

INDIANAPOLIS

70

70

McCORMICK'S CREEK
STATE PARK

Bloomington

37

MORGAN–
MONROE
STATE FOREST

YELLOWWOOD
STATE FOREST

46

BROWN
CO SP

446

HOOSIER
NAT
FOREST

FALLEN TIMBER
NATURE PRESERVE

VERSAILLES
STATE PARK

CHARLES DEAM
WILDERNESS

58

50

58

MUSCATATUCK
NWR

CLIFTY FALLS
STATE PARK

Madison

62

50

SPRING MILL
SP

50

JACKSON–
WASHINGTON
STATE FOREST

Muscatatuck R

HOOSIER

41

56

60

Paoli

CLARK
STATE
FOR

NATIONAL

Fredericksburg

DEAM LAKE
REC AREA

WHITE OAK
NATURE PRESERVE

FOREST

57

PIONEER
MOTHERS
MEM FOR

Blue R

37

FALLS OF THE OHIO
STATE PARK

HEMLOCK CLIFFS
REC AREA

64

37

Milltown

WYANDOTTE
CAVES AREA

Corydon

Louisville

64

HEMMER WOODS
NATURE PRESERVE

66

HARRISON–
CRAWFORD
WYANDOTTE
COMPLEX

RIVER

Evansville

WESSELMAN WOODS
NATURE PRESERVE

Little
Blue
River

KENTUCKY

HOVEY LAKE
FISH & WILDLIFE AREA

OHIO

TWIN SWAMPS
NATURE PRESERVE

LEFT: *In spring, Clifty Falls spills 70 feet over limestone cliffs that once formed an ancient seabed; the stream then tumbles three miles farther to the Ohio River.*

RIGHT: *Young raccoon observe the world from the safety of a tree limb. Born in the spring, by fall these omnivores are on their own, using agile hands and ready intelligence to forage nearly anything.*

About 25 miles farther south, just west of Madison, Route 56 hugs bluffs above the Ohio River as it enters **Clifty Falls State Park❖.** Visitors looking east toward the historic river town can readily understand why the Ohio was a highway for native peoples and European-American settlers alike. In the opposite direction, monster power-plant stacks pierce the sky, adding an eerie sci-fi feel to the otherwise peaceful scene.

On their way to the Ohio River, Clifty Creek and its tributaries have cut through limestone and shale, exposing some of the oldest bedrock in the state. The harder rock sends water rippling down shale slopes and plunging over ledges in Clifty's myriad waterfalls. Although the park provides plenty of overlooks, the best way to see its natural beauty is by taking the rugged three-mile Number Two trail that runs south along the west bank of the canyon and switchbacks down to the creek bottom. In spring, the soil along this trail exudes moisture, which trickles, spills, and curtains toward the canyon bottom. The south-facing switchbacks, in particular, are crowded with white-flowered nodding trillium, purple larkspur, bright yellow celandine poppies, and along every seep and stream, jack-in-the-pulpit and Solomon's seal. Beneath bare branches dotted with hints of green, budding wild hydrangea and the unfolding fans of buckeye leaves add substance to the understory.

No obvious trail leads up the creek bed. Rock hopping is the way to go—exercising caution on slippery stones, especially during spring runoff. The dappled light, the burbling stream, and the ever-changing rock sculptures and cliff outcrops are worth the wet feet. A close look at the rock reveals clusters of fossils—more than 400 million years old—that nearly cover the surface. Around the bend, dropping in elegant, lacy veils, is Clifty Falls.

Other trails pass through woods and upland fields where a leggy white-flowered plant seems to dominate. A bane of park managers, this uninvited exotic from Europe is garlic mustard, which is displacing native perennials throughout the Great Lakes region and similar North American habitats. Both red foxes (perhaps long-ago transplants from England) and gray foxes as well as deer and a variety of birds, inhabit the park.

North on scenic Route 7, then east on Route 50, lies one of Indiana's only two national wildlife refuges, located east of Seymour. Five short loop trails cluster in 7,700-acre **Muscatatuck National Wildlife Refuge❖,** whose wetlands teem with waterfowl. A self-guided auto tour, trails, and abandoned lanes showcase much of Muscatatuck, the Piankashaw tribe's word for "land of winding waters."

Beginning near the visitor center, the **Chestnut Ridge Trail** circles a flooded bottomland forest where blue flag irises and white-flowered arrowheads poke up through still, shallow waters. The chestnuts that gave the ridge its name are gone, decimated throughout the United States in the early part of this century by a fungus introduced from Asia. Once dominant in eastern forests, chestnuts provided valuable food for bears and other wildlife as well as excellent timber. Although researchers are studying resistant varieties of chestnut and organisms that attack the fungus, bears no longer roam Indiana, and oaks have replaced chestnuts on the ridge.

In spring, the woods near the Richart Lake Trail are carpeted with pinkish-white spring beauties, pretty complements to the flitting blue-gray gnatcatchers. The fields are full of warbling meadowlarks; herons pick through the marshes; and shovelers, coots, blue-winged teal, and other ducks glide through the open waters.

SOUTH-CENTRAL INDIANA

The Muscatatuck River divides **Jackson-Washington State Forest❖** (some 10 miles southwest, off Route 250) into two units. In the northern section, a trail leading from Knob Lake to the top of Pinnacle Peak provides a fine panorama of the countryside and of the "knobs"— unglaciated Mississippian Age (362 to 322 million years ago) rock—that parallel I-65 to the east. Starve Hollow Lake and Beach are part of the state forest complex, and a number of trails loop through the wooded hills bordering the lake. The nearby **Hemlock Bluff Nature Preserve** is home to a grove that includes the state's largest hemlock, a tree rarely found this far west.

South along I-65 and the Knobstone Range, between Scottsburg and New Albany, **Clark State Forest**❖ encompasses a 2,000-acre backcountry wilderness area; seven small lakes supporting bluegill, largemouth bass, and channel catfish; and more developed recreation. Within the forest, a short self-guided trail loops through the **White Oak Nature Preserve**❖, an oak-hickory woods with an understory of blueberries and wildflowers such as brassy orange hawkweed, shooting stars, and the pink-and-yellow flowers of goat's rue.

All the sights at **Falls of the Ohio State Park**❖ (Exit 0 from I-65, then right on Riverside Drive) are along the banks of the Ohio River in Clarksville. In late summer and autumn the river is low, revealing one of the largest exposed Devonian fossil beds in the world. The 400-million-year-old fossils encased in the limestone include more than 600 different species, most of them discovered here first and studied by paleontologists from around the world. Fossilized coral beds measure about 150 feet thick, and almost any rock shelf displays countless fossils: delicately whorled nautiluslike shells, coral colonies 6 feet across, crinoids, snails, and layers of large and small shells encrusted in the rocks like dusty old jewels.

ABOVE: *Native blue flag irises dot the wetlands along Muscatatuck's Chestnut Ridge Trail;* flagge *is Middle English for rush or reed.*

OVERLEAF: *From the Hoosier Heritage Trail (Route 66), travelers get a bird's-eye view of the Ohio River as it meanders past farm fields and the verdant Harrison-Crawford State Forest beyond.*

John James Audubon, who lived in the area from 1807 to 1810, made more than 200 sketches of 14 resident bird species. Today, at one time or another, about 265 avian species still frequent Falls of the Ohio: Sandpipers scurry across patches of sand, gulls and terns wheel overhead, herons and egrets pick in the

ABOVE: *Gray-barked beech trees overlook Lake Wyandotte in Harrison-Crawford State Forest. The lake borders one of Indiana's finest rivers, the Blue, whose aqua tint originates in underground springs.*

tidal pools created by rising and falling river waters, and ospreys fish the waters. More than 125 species of fish include shovelnose sturgeon, longnose gar, and paddlefish—prehistoric species all. A visitor center helps interpret both ancient and modern wildlife.

West on scenic Route 62, past picturesque Corydon, Harrison-Crawford State Forest, Wyandotte Woods State Recreation Area, and Wyandotte Caves Area have been joined to form the **Harrison-Crawford Wyandotte Complex❖,** an area rich in natural wonders. Because these 24,000 acres are reclaimed from abandoned farmlands, the vast and peaceful woods are at most 60 years old. The 30-mile Adventure Trail loop passes through all three parts of the complex. On the west edge of the forest, the Post Oak Nature Preserve Trail presents a wealth of oaks—post, white, chestnut, blackjack, scarlet, and black— and circles an upland glade full of prairie plants such as bluestem grasses, coneflowers, and false dragonhead.

Most other trails begin in Wyandotte Woods. The Cliff Dweller Trail winds along creek bottoms, climbs bluffs, and everywhere is surrounded by the limestone that makes southern Indiana one of the largest

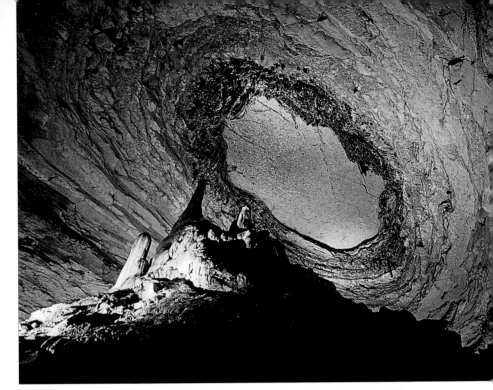

Above: *Hundreds of caves pock the limestone of southern Indiana. Big Wyandotte Cave's high-ceilinged Rothrock Cathedral features delicate crystals, mammoth pillars, and a 130-foot-high underground mountain.*

karst-riddled areas in the country. (Karst is a limestone area that includes sinks, short underground streams, and caverns created by the solution of limestone in water.) Whorls of club moss patch the floor of the young forests overlooking Potato Run and soften the steps of deer, which flip their white tails when alarmed and flee down the slope.

The Blue River, the first included in the Indiana Natural and Scenic Rivers System, flows placidly through the state forest past bluffs, cave entrances, and birdlife before spilling into the Ohio River. The Blue's 11 river miles between Route 462 and the Ohio include five access sites, and outfitters are located upriver in Milltown and Fredericksburg. At its best in spring, the nearby Little Blue River, accessible to the west at I-64, is another of Indiana's most natural and pristine streams.

Big and Little Wyandotte caves show visitors what lies beneath Indiana's southern uplands, where more than 700 caves pock the subterranean landscape. Cave systems are created when weak natural acids dissolve the limestone, and geologists believe that **Wyandotte Cave** was further enlarged by an underground tributary of the Blue River. Numerous large and small rooms and miles of interconnected passageways

LEFT: *Where the Wabash and Ohio meet, wetlands such as Twin Swamps harbor great blue herons, which remain motionless as they stalk fish.*
RIGHT: *This lithograph, created from an 1833 painting by Swiss artist Karl Bodmer, depicts swamps near New Harmony, Indiana. Vultures, vines, and giant sycamores emphasize the primeval nature of the frontier.*

have been mapped in the Wyandotte system. Visitors can take tours of any length, even serious spelunking trips. To protect stalactites, which grow only one cubic inch every 150 years, and stalagmites, which take twice as long, Indiana has established a strict defacing law. Even touching a cave formation is illegal because body oils can keep deposits from forming for years.

Within the caves, stone draperies glittering with gypsum fold against the walls like the set of a Dracula movie. Both Big and Little Wyandotte contain huge pillars, each thousands of years old, that resemble giant saguaro cacti. In Rothrock Cathedral, a capacious subterranean cavern, Monument Mountain rises more than 130 feet—the highest underground mountain in the country.

At the micro level, Helictite Garden displays one of the best helictite formations in the country, each crystal twisting itself into a small, deformed claw hanging from the cave roof. In Little Wyandotte, only 12 to 15 feet below the surface, hollow soda-straw formations and stalactites follow dripping seam lines, showing the cracks between rocks.

The most intriguing wild creatures are Big Wyandotte's 15,000 endangered Indiana brown bats, which lodge near rivers in the summer. Bats eat about 2,000 insects per bat per night, but this useful service is destroying them. The insects they eat are often loaded with pesticides, which become concentrated in the bats' bodies, hindering reproduction and even poisoning them. In Little Wyandotte, a few cling to crevices in the cave walls. With wings tucked up, each furry, soft brown bat is the size of a baby's palm.

SOUTHWESTERN LOWLANDS

Leading south and west into the lowlands from I-64 at the town of West Fork, Route 66 (Hoosier Heritage Trail) winds scenically through Hoosier National Forest and along the Ohio River. In Evansville, off Boeke Road, 200-acre **Wesselman Woods Nature Preserve❖** is one of Indiana's finest hardwood remnants. Some two dozen tree species, including sweet gum and tulip, are represented here, many of great size. The forest's canopy is high, making Wesselman a good place to see and hear a variety of songbirds, especially during migration in early May. Adjacent to the woods and its trails and boardwalks are a prairie and manmade pond.

At the low-lying southwesternmost tip of the state via Routes 62 and 69, **Twin Swamps Nature Preserve❖** and **Hovey Lake Fish and Wildlife Area❖** present habitat unusual in the Midwest—a bald cypress swamp, once common along the Ohio and Wabash rivers. A trail through Twin Swamps's oak flatwoods forest leads to a boardwalk for viewing the swamp and birds such as the golden prothonotary warbler. True to its name, Twin Swamps contains an overcup oak swamp as well as the cypress swamp. Here the water-loving overcup is at the northern edge of its range, as are swamp cottonwood, mistletoe, and pecan. The area is also home to eastern mud turtles rare in Indiana.

81

Adjacent Hovey Lake is known for turtle migrations across roads and fields in the late spring, a good time to visit only for those un- bothered by clouds of insects. In more comfortable early spring or mid-autumn, visitors can witness the bird migrations. Full of bluegill, largemouth bass, crappie, and catfish, Hovey Lake is a fine setting for birdlife: Canada geese, migrating cormorants, wood ducks, black ducks, and mallard; bald eagles, ospreys, and other hunters; and long- legged waders such as herons.

North of the intersection of I-64 and I-164 on Route 57 is **Hemmer Woods Nature Preserve❖,** whose fine old-growth hardwoods are now rare in Indiana. Here tall sycamores, river birches with ribboned bark, sweet gums, cherry bark oaks, tulip poplars, and others fill a bottomland ecological niche.

HOOSIER NATIONAL FOREST AND WESTERN UPLANDS

Hoosier National Forest, the only one in Indiana, is divided into four units, each containing a few destination areas. To reach **Hem- lock Cliffs Recreation Area❖** from I-64 at West Fork, take Route 37 north about three miles, turn left onto a county road leading west and south for about four miles, and follow national forest signs to the un- prepossessing parking lot.

At Hemlock Cliffs the forest is thick with dark-needled hemlocks and leafy hardwoods, and natural bridges and rock formations add a touch of drama. A loop trail follows the 150-foot-deep sandstone canyon back to a cliff, where a waterfall is found in wet weather, and a side trail goes to Hemlock Caverns, an overhang used by people 10,000 years ago that provides a real feeling of prehistoric Indiana.

Farther north on Route 37, a mile or so south of Paoli and the in- tersection with Route 150, lies the small parking lot for another section of Hoosier National Forest. **Pioneer Mothers Memorial Forest❖** is an 88-acre triangle of old-growth woodland wedged between these two highways, and sometimes the noise of tractor trailers penetrates the edges of the forest. A virgin timber tract, Pioneer Mothers has re- mained untouched since the Cox family purchased it in 1816. In the

RIGHT: *Lavender dwarf irises light up the moody slopes of Hemlock Cliffs Recreation Area in Hoosier National Forest. Intensely fragrant, these lovely woodland plants thrive among the acid-loving hemlocks.*

JUGLANS squamosa
Shell bark Hickory

JUGLANS nigra
Black Walnut

ABOVE: *In the first illustrated catalog of native North American forest trees (1810–13), French botanist André Michaux published colored plates of the shellbark hickory (left) and the black walnut (right).*

1940s, the forest almost fell to a lumber company, but the Indiana Pioneer Mothers Club helped save the old-growth trees for inclusion in the national forest, where they are a living museum representing the immense forests that once covered much of Indiana.

In this research area for natural succession, saplings struggle toward the light in small open areas where a huge giant has fallen, and old, limbless snags serve as apartment houses for a variety of birds and animals. The majority of the forest is filled with large, sometimes huge, trees—oaks, walnuts, beeches, cherries, and others—some hundreds of years old. An oak standing near the memorial to the Pioneer Mothers probably predates Columbus's discovery of North America. In spring, when unfolding leaves tinge bare branches with light green, the forest floor glows with the purple-blues of larkspur and violets and the whites of rue anemone and that queen of the forest, trillium. Elsewhere, the broad umbrella foliage of mayapples spreads a foot above the forest floor.

Old-growth forest, remarkable caves, and an authentic pioneer village

LEFT: *In Pioneer Mothers Memorial Forest, vine-clad beeches, walnuts, and other old-growth trees survive in a splendid virgin forest.*

LEFT: *Flocks of cedar waxwings, whose calls sound like hisses, cruise Indiana's woodlands searching for their favorite serviceberries.*

RIGHT: *Surrounded by vinca, a nonnative ground-cover, tall sprays of wild phlox adorn slopes near Donaldson Cave in Spring Mill State Park.*

are preserved at **Spring Mill State Park❖,** about 15 miles farther north on Route 60, just east of Route 37. Packing a lot of natural and cultural history into little more than 1,300 acres, the park includes two outstanding nature preserves: Donaldson Woods and Donaldson Cave. George Donaldson, an eccentric Scotsman who bought the property in 1864, intended to preserve every tree and flower in the face of enthusiastic land-clearing practices. Although his heart was in the right place, park managers now struggle to eradicate nonnative vinca, which Donaldson planted in his garden. The vine subsequently spread to many parts of the park.

In **Donaldson Woods,** the Scotsman preserved a piece of authentic Indiana. This virgin forest is a land of big trees: a time-immemorial mix of ashes, tulip poplars, and the usual denizens. Interestingly, records show a change in the balance between beech-maple and oak-hickory communities. Since the first half of the century, mean temperatures have dropped about two degrees and precipitation has risen about two inches—just enough to give beech-maple the edge over oak-hickory. The big woods attract woodpeckers, nuthatches, titmice, chickadees, and numerous other birds. Spring flowers include blue phlox, Solomon's seal, rue anemone, and trout lilies with their yellow recurved petals; less shaded parts of the park sustain butterfly weed, nonnative day lilies, and wild bergamot.

Donaldson Woods hints at a subterranean feature of the unglaciated uplands. The trail winds through forest so pocked with sinkholes that the trail builders seem to have found the only stable ground in a collapsing landscape. Indeed, those unaware that the land beneath is a warren of caves might think these woods an ancient battlefield filled with healing bomb craters. On the contrary, the sinkholes are active.

Formed when rain combines with atmospheric carbon dioxide, carbonic acid slowly dissolves the underlying limestone, creating a small

depression. As the weak acid that collects in the depression combines with acids produced by decaying tree roots and other vegetation and becomes more concentrated, the sinkhole expands. Eventually the sinkhole can collapse and break through the roof of a cave, becoming a cave entrance. A collapsed sinkhole has opened a karst window at Bronson Cave and also at Twin Caves, where an underground stream flows through a tunnel-like cavern. For a small fee, the park offers a short boat ride through the milky green waters of Twin Caves.

Donaldson Cave presents itself with high drama. A sparkling teal-blue stream rushes from the cave's stony portals to bisect a forested ravine. Directly above the cave mouth, dry, limy soils support shooting stars, bird's-foot violets, and other "sweet soil" flowers. Visitors can explore a bit by themselves or, accompanied by a park naturalist, go farther into the cave, which houses bats and blind crayfish. Not generally seen is the five-inch-long northern blind cave fish, an endangered species discovered and studied here.

Waters flowing within the park's two major cave systems feed Spring Mill Lake, where visitors can boat and fish for the trout that thrive in the cave-cooled waters. The preserved village and mill are also of interest. Spring Mill is one of six Indiana state parks that have an inn within their boundaries, so that visitors can stay overnight and walk in the woods all day without ever getting into a car. During summer weekends, however, the park is extremely popular.

LEFT: *Emerging spring foliage cloaks the soft folds and ridges of the 13,000-acre Charles Deam Wilderness in Hoosier National Forest.*
RIGHT: *One of North America's most widely distributed mammals, the beaver shapes streams and lakes with its dams, working mainly at night.*

Indiana's only designated wilderness area is also in Hoosier National Forest. The **Charles Deam Wilderness❖** can be reached by taking Route 37 north, Route 50 east, Route 446 north, and Tower Ridge Road east for just over six miles. These forests are not old, but they are big, and the most noticeable sounds are birds and the wind. Here hikers can forget the dozen items on the daily to-do list and jettison the clutter that sneaks into daily life.

Deam Wilderness commemorates Charles C. Deam, a drugstore owner who was advised to take walks to improve his health. The rambles inspired Deam to collect thousands of plant species, write four books on Indiana plants, and in 1909 become the state's first and foremost forester. This national wilderness area, a tree, a lake, and 50 plants are named in his honor.

Much of Deam Wilderness, at its colorful best during autumn, is truly wild. Only 35 miles of the myriad trails are marked, although the well-used ones—such as Hickory Ridge—are obvious. For serious exploring, a topographic map and compass are essential. Many of the trails ride the backs of narrow ridges past lush, bristling pine plantations and then oaks, hickories, maples, tulip poplars, even persimmons, with sumac and dogwood forming the understory. Old-timers forage here for crenelated morels and other edible mushrooms.

A few trails afford views of **Monroe Lake**—actually Indiana's largest impoundment—which is accessible from boat ramps at Hardin Ridge and other state recreation areas. Like all reservoirs, Monroe Lake has molded itself to the landscape rather than shaping the land. Nevertheless, it is big enough to raise whitecaps and to harbor peaceful coves away from the main boat traffic.

ABOVE: *A colorful patchwork of red and gold in autumn, Brown County State Park becomes a crystal rhapsody in winter. The park's Ogle Hollow protects some of the northernmost stands of rare yellowwood trees.*

On the northern side of Monroe Lake, east of Bloomington on Route 46, **Brown County State Park❖**—Indiana's largest—is the centerpiece of a scenic county. In autumn, the park's nearly 16,000 acres blaze with reds, oranges, and golds, attracting quantities of attention and people. With its huge rounded hills and great misty vistas, Brown County State Park conveys a sense of size and height. In spring, park roads are lined with the airy white flowers of serviceberries, the dark limbs of redbuds bejeweled with amethyst blossoms, and lacy boughs of flowering dogwood.

Of the nine trails wending through the park, the Ogle Hollow Nature Preserve Trail showcases the yellowwood tree, rare throughout its range. Although the yellowwood's bark resembles that of a beech, its lovely and fragrant flowers are more like wisteria blossoms. The preserve also includes papaws, spicebush, black cherry, walnut, and, along the stream bottom, sycamores. Before sections of Indiana were clear cut, old river-bottom sycamores were among the largest trees east of the Rockies—some swelling ten feet in diameter. In summer, ferns fill empty spaces on the forest floor.

In Ogle Hollow and elsewhere in the park, deer are abundant.

ABOVE RIGHT: *Once nearly extirpated in the Midwest, white-tailed deer are flourishing again. Hunting restrictions and the absence of natural predators such as cougars have now led to an unhealthy overabundance.*

Eliminated from Indiana by the end of the 1800s, deer were reintroduced early in the 1930s, not long after the park was established. Without the mountain lions (also called cougars or pumas) and other predators necessary to control its numbers, however, the deer population has exploded. Seventy percent of the park shows damage from deer browsing, and the hungry animals even take a big bite out of the spring wildflower display. Yet, because there are so many of them, the deer are often malnourished. Also common at Brown County, flocks of wild turkeys—comprising a couple of males and up to 22 hens—are a delight rather than a population management problem.

The 16-mile Ten O'Clock Line Trail, one of a dozen state trails following historic routes, connects Brown County State Park with **Yellowwood State Forest❖.** Nearby too is the fine spring wildflower display at Selma Steele Nature Preserve. From Yellowwood State Forest, Route 37 leads to **Morgan-Monroe State Forest❖.** Morgan-Monroe's Scout Ridge Nature Preserve boasts a rich variety of flora, from understory shrubs such as maple-leaved viburnum to many types of ferns.

From Morgan-Monroe, **McCormick's Creek State Park❖** is a short jaunt back down Route 37, then northwest on Route 46. The first of

ABOVE: *Lush native wildflowers and ferns crowd McCormick's Creek State Park. Cinnamon fern, which can grow to five feet, is distinguished by the rusty-colored stalks that hold its spores.*

RIGHT: *Above McCormick's Creek, the umbrellalike leaves of mayapples herald spring. Scientists think the plant may have anticancer properties.*

Indiana's state parks, McCormick's Creek is a natural showpiece, especially the canyon and its waterfalls. The creekbed and the canyon walls are eroded limestone, now mostly covered with verdant growth. The best way to see this part of the park is to follow the trail that meanders back and forth along the creek up to Echo Canyon and the falls.

Each bank offers its special treat. On one, rue anemone, Dutchman's-breeches, and squirrel corn completely cover the forest floor with nodding white flowers and lacy foliage. On the other, masses of bluebells and their large oval leaves color the understory with opalescent greens and blues. Upstream, the sheer canyon walls close in until they reach the dramatic cascade at Echo Canyon Falls.

In summer, ferns flourish: delicate maidenhair, dark and shiny ebony spleenwort, evergreen walking fern—to name just a few. Of the more than 150 bird species frequenting the park, cardinals, cowbirds, nuthatches, brown creepers, catbirds, all sorts of warblers, and a variety of woodpeckers are easily seen. Mid-May brings migrating songbirds, and in late summer the fields-reverting-to-forests are full of butterflies.

The **Wolf Cave Nature Preserve** contains classic climax beech-maple forest. Large, well-spaced trees shade trillium and other understory plants in a woods perfectly still except for a small rippling stream. Sinkholes hint at the formation of limestone caves, and a natural bridge and the shallow, hemispheric opening of Wolf Cave at the lowest part of the preserve are examples of geologic etching.

From McCormick's Creek, northern Indiana and the rock fantasies of Turkey Run State Park are only a short drive away.

CHAPTER FOUR

NORTHERN INDIANA

Northern Indiana was once a verdant natural patchwork of prairie, wetland, and forest. Today, however, travelers flying by on Interstate 80 along the state's northern border may be forgiven for thinking that only an artificial landscape of flame-spewing industrial chimneys and endless cornfields remains. In fact, on the dune-sheltered shores of Lake Michigan, within sight of Gary's smokestacks, North American ecology began. In the 1890s, Henry Chandler Cowles, later a professor at the University of Chicago, began his pioneering study of dune succession at what is now Indiana Dunes National Lakeshore and laid the foundation for modern ecology. And, for those willing to look beyond the freeway, northern Indiana still possesses a wealth of peaceful wetlands, canopied forests, and a phantasmagoria of carved sandstone canyons.

This portion of the state can be divided into four natural regions: Lake Plains, prairies and wetlands, a rich central till plain, and scenic sandstone gorges. The Lake Plains, a narrow brow of land beginning behind Lake Michigan's dunes, are low sediment terraces deposited by a vast predecessor of Lake Michigan. Highways such as Route 12 often follow these ancient embankments. The Lake Plains are home to a strange and wonderful mix of wildlife, including the white tiger beetle and plants found here and on the Atlantic coast, but nowhere in between.

LEFT: *In the shadow of Gary's steel mills, the Indiana Dunes National Lakeshore shelters bogs, prairie, forest, and dunes. With nearly 1,500 plant species, the dunes are incredibly rich in biotic diversity.*

Just below the Lake Plains, filling the northwest corner of the state, are the remnants of Indiana's prairies and wetlands. Ice age meltwaters created wide river basins running southwest, much as the Wabash River does now. Broad, moist valleys like the Kankakee Basin contain fine sands and alkaline soils that are perfect for vivid, flower-filled prairies.

Before drainage projects began in 1884, more than 50 percent of this region was wetland, mostly wet prairies and cattail marshes like today's Jasper-Pulaski and Willow Slough wildlife areas. Trumpeter swans lived in Indiana, and cranberry bogs attracted the lovely copper-gilded "bog copper" butterfly. Until the 1830s, bison roamed the state's dry prairies.

In the northeast corner, the Wisconsin Glaciation left a jumble of moraines, kettle-hole lakes, kames, and eskers that make the land look as though giants had been toying with it. (Kames are cone-shaped mounds of debris left by melted glaciers; eskers are long, sinuous mounds of debris.) Kettle lakes, such as those in Chain O'Lakes State Park, were formed when mammoth chunks of glacial ice embedded themselves in the glacial till. When the glaciers retreated, the ice chunks melted, creating deep steep-sided lakes.

Traveling the broad midsection of Indiana, called the Tipton Till Plain, feels like crossing a vast plateau beneath a huge 180-degree bowl of sky unblemished from horizon to horizon. As the glaciers retreated, they spread their burden of sand, rock, and clay evenly and thickly across the state's midsection. This deep, fertile mantle—material the glaciers scraped from northern regions in their progress south—gives the Midwest a vital legacy, its rich soils.

In the southwest section of the till plain, streams have cut through to bedrock, carving scenic canyons such as the ones at Turkey Run and Shades state parks. Beginning in these sandstone canyons, this chapter's exploration of northern Indiana continues north along the state's western border and cuts across the wetlands section to the northeast corner. From there, it travels west across the top of the state, ending at the Lake Plains and the Indiana Dunes.

SANDSTONE CANYONS

Nature and dreams meet in the folded, tilted, tangled canyons and uplands of **Turkey Run State Park❖,** some 65 miles west of Indianapolis on Route 47. Like a half-dozen other Indiana state parks, Turkey Run

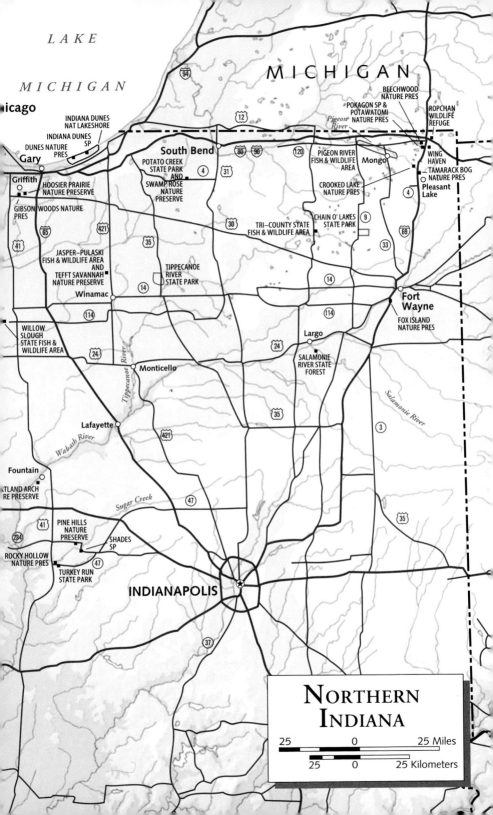

ABOVE: *As though flung by giants, massive blocks of tumbled sandstone dwarf visitors to Rocky Hollow Falls Canyon. This magnificent rock*

centers on its inn, nature center, and recreation facilities such as tennis courts and swimming pools. The best part of the park, however, lies across the suspension footbridge that spans Sugar Creek.

On the other side is the sandstone maze of **Rocky Hollow Nature Preserve❖,** a rock fantasy seemingly designed by perspective-bending artist M. C. Escher. Looming canyon walls narrow the trail, often leaving space for little more than a trickle of water and a band of rock on either side. In these dim recesses, hemlocks take hold, shading the preserve with their lacy needles. In the heart of summer, the leaves of beeches and maples cast the canyon in aqueous green light, creating a cool refuge on even the hottest days. In spring, the stream is broader and the rock bank narrower. Where the canyon widens, the trail seems to disappear—and the only way out is a watery one: up a gently terraced little waterfall.

Spring is also a good time to spot birds in the old-growth uplands above Rocky Hollow. The red crests of pileated woodpeckers flash in the deep quiet, and cardinals, chickadees, goldfinches, and numerous other avian residents streak among the big trees. A fallen giant's massive earth-clotted roots form a wildflower nursery of violets, rue anemones,

labyrinth lies at the geologic heart of Turkey Run State Park, which contains trails trod for centuries by the native Miami people.

and ferns. Wildflowers and mossy logs are scattered through the woods.

A fine way to see Turkey Run and nearby Shades State Park is by canoeing sycamore-lined Sugar Creek, which eventually feeds into the Wabash River. Quiet water and white water transport canoeists beneath a long covered bridge and past sandstone cliffs and bluffs, sandy banks, and clouds of swallows. The inn can provide information on canoeing, which is extremely popular on summer weekends.

Lying along Sugar Creek, upstream from Turkey Run, **Shades State Park**❖ (take Route 47 northeast, then 234 west) is bedded with sandstone. The sandstone was laid down during the Pennsylvanian period (270 million years ago), when ancient river systems carried sand and pebbles toward a shallow sea whose shores lay in what is now eastern Illinois. Ceded by the native Miami people to the U.S. government in 1818, this land was spared an agricultural destiny because its soils were too thin and its topography too rugged. Once called Shades of Death because a warrior allegedly killed a settler and a wife murdered her evil husband here, the park's name has been shortened to Shades to suggest its thick, leafy summer canopy.

From the picnic area, trails wind up and down, past waterfalls, to

LEFT: *Sandhill cranes have distinctive red skin patches on their foreheads. They are easy to tell from herons in flight: Cranes hold their necks straight out, while herons tuck theirs in.* RIGHT: *Migrating sandhill cranes perform elaborate courtship dances in the marsh-side croplands of Indiana's Jasper-Pulaski refuge.*

Prospect Point, a high bluff 210 feet above Sugar Creek, where hawks and vultures lazily circle on thermals. Below, golden sandbars cushion bends in the river, and behind, wild black cherry, prized for its fine wood, grows in the heavily shaded woods. Black cherry bark has been inelegantly described as resembling burnt cornflakes, but to the tree's admirers it looks more like a black-tile mosaic.

Just north of the park entrance on Route 234 is the parking lot for **Pine Hills Nature Preserve❖.** In aerial views of Pine Hills, narrow gorges and backbone ridges twist like snakes across the landscape. The four bony ridges, 70 to 100 feet high, were carved by hairpin bends in streams—some of the best incised meanders in the eastern United States. Walking across Devil's Backbone, its sheer drop-offs harboring northern relicts such as white pine, hemlock, and yew, is like negotiating a tightrope.

Route 234 continues west to Route 41, running north to Fountain, Indiana, a few miles west of the highway on County Road 650N. In town, signs direct visitors to tucked-away **Portland Arch Nature Preserve❖,** whose highlight is the state's most famous natural sandstone bridge, carved over millennia by shallow, rippling Bear Creek. The self-guided trail leading to the arch is a pleasure in its own right.

Beneath a canopy of walnuts, pines, maples, elms, and oaks, dappled sunlight illuminates spring wildflowers: delicate anemones, spring beauties, violets, mayapples, trilliums, and fat white Dutchman's-breeches. Flowering understory trees include witch hazel, redbud, dogwood, and spicebush. Watered by tiny rivulets, a variety of ferns form hanging gardens in cliff-face crevices. One of the preserve's rare plants is Canada blueberry, which grows nowhere else in the

100

state. Another is wintergreen, a standout with glossy green leaves, spicy fragrance, and red autumn berries.

Northwest Wetlands

The northwest corner of the state contains Indiana's remaining wetlands, including 9,000-acre **Willow Slough State Fish and Wildlife Area❖,** north on State Line Road from Route 114, near the town of Morocco. The area encompasses a range of habitats: open water, marshes, prairie remnants, and sandy, oak-dotted hills that originated when glacial winds blew fine sands south.

Routes 14 and 421 lead east and north to the state's premier wetlands, **Jasper-Pulaski Fish and Wildlife Area❖** (the main entrance is a mile west on Route 143). Jasper-Pulaski is one of the best places in the country to view migrating greater sandhill cranes. In March, on their way from wintering in Florida and Georgia to summer nesting grounds in the Great Lakes region, 8,000 cranes stop and feed in fields and croplands set aside for them next to shallow marshlands where they roost. Their numbers double in October, when most of the country's eastern crane population stops at Jasper-Pulaski.

101

LEFT: *Controlled burns at the Tefft Savanna preserve keep its native grasslands from becoming overgrown and allow drifts of wild blue lupines to flourish.*

RIGHT: *Colorfully patterned in red and yellow, painted turtles bask together on a river rock. North America's most widespread turtle,* Chrysemys picta *begins as a carnivore and matures into an herb eater.*

These three-and-a-half-foot-tall wading birds have blue-gray plumage accented by a red cap of bare skin. Cranes mate for life and renew their bonds each spring in extraordinary ritual dances, bowing and leaping like ballet dancers tuned to an intricate interior choreography. By the 1950s, wetlands destruction and human proximity had caused the sandhill crane population to fall to less than a thousand, and in the 1970s, the U.S. Fish and Wildlife Service classified them as threatened. Protected places such as Jasper-Pulaski, however, have helped the cranes increase their numbers, and today the population is once again healthy.

Besides observation towers, Jasper-Pulaski offers open waters for boating, canoeing, and fishing for carp, bullhead, catfish, bass, and bluegill. Boaters share the waters with coots, buffleheads, mergansers, pintail, and mallard, and on bits of island rising in the shallows, Canada geese build big nests of straw. Giant cottonwoods shade dry fingers of land that reach into the marshes, where the backs of turtles glisten on every wet log. In these seemingly endless wetlands, where horizontal vistas stretch far beyond the visible canvas, time slows down, and human visitors feel like spies in a placid, unchanging scene. Here, water and the panoply of species it nurtures spark thoughts of life's beginnings.

Just down the road and within Jasper-Pulaski, **Tefft Savanna Nature Preserve❖** makes a dry contrast. The preserve is a prime example of the sand savannas that typically formed near wetlands in this part of the state. Carried by wind and water from glacier margins, these sands were

ABOVE: *Wood ducks (the male is shown above) nest in tree cavities above the water at Tippecanoe River State Park. When ducklings jump from the nest at their mother's call, the water provides a soft landing.*

RIGHT: *In the Fox Island preserve, a trail traces the ridge of an old dune system. Marshes and bottomland forest adjoin the forested dunes, which attract numerous songbirds.*

either dispersed as sand plains or accumulated as the rolling dunes at Tefft. Eventually black oak took hold, as well as sassafras and bigtooth aspen. Understory plants include black huckleberry, bracken fern, wild lupine, and a number of species rare in this area.

About 20 miles directly east of Jasper-Pulaski, just off Route 35, **Tippecanoe River State Park❖** features the river that meanders across the midsection of northern Indiana and empties into the Wabash. The Tippecanoe is full of oxbow sloughs, created when a hairpin curve in a waterway is "stranded" because later flows cut a more direct path, leaving a swampy wetland in the hairpin. Tippecanoe's oxbows are one of the best places in the state to see wood ducks, which nest in tree snags near the sloughs. With dark, long-feathered heads elegantly etched in white and eyes outlined in brilliant red, wood ducks are among the most visually dramatic birds in North America. In slow motion on enormous wings, great blue herons rise from the sloughs and river shallows where they fish and fly to their nesting area in a remote part of the park. Muskrat happily paddle Tippecanoe's wetlands along with beavers and mink, which are less typical in Indiana parks. Deer and foxes roam throughout the park, but ground squirrels prefer the prairie remnants.

Each of the two nature preserves within the park—Sand Hill, which shelters sand prairie and oak woods, and Tippecanoe River, which showcases bottomlands and sloughs—can be reached by a loop trail. Another good way to see the site or the river is by canoe. Liveries can be found south of the park in Winamac and Monticello.

THE NORTHEAST

Bordering another of the big rivers that feed the Wabash, **Salamonie River State Forest❖,** south and east via Route 31 and 24 and Route 524 at Lagro, preserves the only surviving sizable forest in northern Indiana. Two attractive waterfalls are within sight of Salamonie River's trail systems, and the forest presents a fine display of spring wildflowers. The Birdhouse Trail provides a good show of jewelweed, black-eyed Susans, and other summer flowers, as well as the purples and golds of autumn asters and goldenrod.

Farther east along Route 24, south on Ellison Road, and east on Yohne Road lies **Fox Island Nature Preserve❖,** near Fort Wayne. Fox Island is actually morainal material from the last ice age surrounded not by water but by swampy soils. Black oak rules dune-top forests with an understory of hazelnut, dogwood, bittersweet, and maple-leaved viburnum—classy plants all. White oak, walnut, and black cherry live on the slopes, and willow and sycamore inhabit the moist soils. These varied habitats shelter an array of small mammals and more than 200 species of birds.

A fine introduction to the glacial imprints found all over northeastern Indiana is provided by the **Tri-County State Fish and Wildlife Area❖,** about 40 miles northwest of Fort Wayne via Routes 30 and 13. Kettle-hole lakes (formed from embedded ice chunks that melt, leaving a water-filled depression) and gravel beds are the most obvious glacial signs. Among the area's high and dry sections of oak-hickory slopes and rolling fields, the best is **Grieder's Woods Nature Preserve.** Six of the nine natural lakes scattered through the preserve have been subsumed as open water within surrounding Flatbelly Marsh. Because the destruction of wetlands had left waterfowl, amphibians, and mammals such as muskrat and beavers with so few places to live, the narrow, meandering marsh was created in 1963 to expand their habitat.

Wyland Lake, outside the marsh, is deep and perfectly round—a classic kettle shape. In summer, stocked trout swim beneath waters edged with sedges and blue-flowered pickerelweed. In names such as Wood Duck, Ruddy, Goldeneye, Scaup, Bufflehead, Heron, and Grebe, Tri-County's ponds indicate just a few of the species of ducks and wading birds seen here.

ABOVE: *Muskrat ply the waters of Indiana wetlands. Like beavers, they build lodges, but theirs are smaller and constructed of cattails.*

LEFT: *Ringed by water lilies, Little Finster Lake at Chain O' Lakes State Park is separated from its twin kettle lake by the ridge of an ice-age kame.*

The ice age story continues at **Chain O' Lakes State Park❖,** some 15 miles east of Tri-County just off Route 9. The focus of this narrow park is a series of lakes that curve through the park's center like a beaded necklace unclasped on a table. Eight of the 11 kettle-hole

OVERLEAF: *The sun rises over Lake Lonidaw at Pokagon State Park. This quiet tamarack-fringed spot is mistshrouded one moment, sunny with dragonflies the next.*

lakes form the beads on this chain, linked with channels created by glacial meltwater. In spring, renting a park canoe is one of the best ways to see this aquamarine necklace and its attendant wildlife (the channels between lakes become overgrown in summer).

Shoreline trees canopy the channel between Weber and Mud lakes, creating a cool green tunnel. Deer come down to the banks to drink,

107

Found at Pigeon River, coyotes (left) are expanding their range eastward. Golden black-eyed Susans (above) grow on Indiana prairies but are being pushed out—along with other natives—by spotted knapweed (right), an invasive European plant.

muskrat paddle by, painted turtles slip into the water at the sound of a canoe, and a blue heron fills the tunnel with its great blue-gray wings. Just after the glaciers retreated, the land that is now the park contained many more kettle lakes, which over millennia have filled in with muck and peat. Park trails lead through these areas, and where they are shaded by trees, orchids grow. The self-guided nature trail that loops around Little Finster Lake displays another glacial oddity. Big and Little Finster lakes would be one larger lake if they were not separated by a kame—a cone-shaped mound of earth formed when gravel and other glacial debris are deposited by a glacier.

Even the park's gravel pits, which look as though a dump truck had dropped a load of gravel, are glacial leftovers. Although small, the park is crossed by three different watersheds, an unusual phenomenon that is the result of glaciers muscling waterways into new channels. Nearby **Crooked Lake Nature Preserve❖** protects one of Indiana's deepest and cleanest lakes and a shoreline bordered by wooded slopes and a host of wildflowers. The trails that loop through the preserve are all peaceful, the marshes full of life.

110

Pokagon State Park❖, near the intersection of Interstates 80 and 69 in the far northeastern corner of Indiana, contains terrain that is a classic example of the moraine-and-kettle region. The park lies within Steuben County, which contains more lakes—120—than any other county in Indiana. Within and around Pokagon are a number of nature preserves.

The park takes its name from Simon Pokagon, a nineteenth-century Potawatomi chief who ceded tribal hunting and fishing lands stretching all the way to Chicago—a million acres—to the U.S. government for three cents per acre. **Potawatomi Nature Preserve❖** displays the best of these woods, lakes, and marshes, which include plant communities unlike those found in the rest of the state. The preserve's morainal ridges are covered with familiar oak-hickory stands mixed with maple and black cherry. Water drains from the moraines to the depression at the center of the preserve—a small and lovely kettle lake called Lonidaw. On a summer Tuesday, when the weekend crowds have departed, the loudest sounds here may be the buzz of a dragonfly, the white noise of croaking frogs, and the rustle of cattails that skirt the lake.

Just behind the cattail marsh is a swamp filled with trees at home in more northerly climes. Visitors are surprised and delighted to see black ash; yellow birch, the sturdiest of the birches; and that anomaly among evergreens, the tamarack, which loses its needles each autumn in a flurry of gold. Seen from a small wooden dock, a red-winged blackbird perches atop burnished cattails ringing the soft cornflower blue of Lake Lonidaw against a backdrop of feathery green tamaracks and expansive sky. The lake is named for Pokagon's wife, who loved nature. Appropriately, because the lake is certainly the soul of this forest, her name is said to mean Spirit of the Woods.

The crest of a knobby kame called Hell's Point affords another good vista—over marshes, sedge meadows, and wet forests that were probably lakes hundreds of years ago. The trail between Lake Lonidaw and Hell's Point shows how leaf debris and other organic materials can fill in a wet area with rich, boggy muck. Yellow marsh marigolds light the trail in spring, and sometimes the path is flooded by beavers busily building dams. In winter, cross-country skis offer a fine way to see the park. Just a few miles from Pokagon are Beechwood Nature Preserve, Ropchan Wildlife Refuge, and Wing Haven,

111

natural areas managed by **Acres Land Trust❖.**

Routes 120 and 3 lead east and south to **Pigeon River Fish and Wildlife Area❖.** The meandering Pigeon River is bordered by bogs, fens, sedge meadows, marshes, swampy woods—every manner of wet transition between water and land—environments that attract a wide variety of wildlife. Although partially created by impoundments, Pigeon River's wetlands look natural enough, as Canada geese nest on tiny islands protected by water from foxes. Just about every type of fish caught in northern Indiana can be found here, and migrating ospreys fish in the wetlands, as do kingfishers and a variety of herons. Grouse, quail, pheasant, and wild turkeys range through the reserve, along with badgers, beavers, moles, raccoon, weasels, three species of squirrels, coyotes, and deer.

Besides every type of wetland, the area preserves dry prairie covered with plants such as orange butterfly weed, purple-pink monarda, yellow potentilla, yarrow, and sumac. At the other end of the scale is **Tamarack Bog Nature Preserve❖,** the state's largest tamarack swamp. Tamarack Bog flaunts a full succession of habitats: clear sandy-bottomed streams; marshes choked with water lilies and arrowhead; tamarack bogs where wildflowers cluster beneath the tamaracks, dwarf birches, alders, and other boreal plants. The best way to see this natural area is by boat, and outfitters can be found in Mongo and Pleasant Lake. Nearby, along the Michigan border, flows the Fawn River, one of the clearest in the state and a smaller version of the swift and wild Michigan rivers farther north.

The **Swamp Rose Nature Preserve,** southwest of South Bend, is about 60 miles farther west along Route 4 in **Potato Creek State Park❖.** Here water is becoming land. Over the centuries, silting and plant growth turned the natural lake to marsh. Now, filling with swamp roses, yellow marsh marigolds, and the clean spears of blue flag irises, the marsh is becoming shrub swamp. This eutrophic process ultimately creates moist woodlands such as those on the terrace adjacent to Swamp Rose.

LAKE PLAINS

A sweep across Route 30 to the far northwestern corner of the state, almost at the Illinois border and then north on Route 6, leads to the small

ABOVE: *Black-and-white warblers, which glean bark for insects, migrate through Hoosier Prairie spring and fall.*
LEFT: *A male American goldfinch surveys the scene; this colorful songbird, a denizen of Hoosier Prairie, feeds on thistles and seeds.*

town of Griffith. Along Main Street, just east of Kennedy Avenue, is the parking lot for **Hoosier Prairie Nature Preserve❖**—a place that shines in mid- to late summer. Visitors arriving at other times of year might mistake Hoosier Prairie for abandoned industrial lots: The scruffy stalks of withered grasses and wildflowers look a bit lonesome surrounded by train tracks and industrial plants. Despite their unlikely location, these 400-plus acres preserve Indiana's largest prairie remnant and more than 300 native plants.

Dense cream-colored bush clover, fringed purple spikes of blazing star, geometric green heads of rattlesnake master, bright yellow goldenrod, and big bluestem grasses are just a few of the grasses and wildflowers that light up this colorful quilt of tallgrass prairie. Preserve managers also literally light the site in controlled fires because prairies must burn regularly to remain healthy.

Lake Michigan's predecessors left swells of sand and swales between them, and today sedge meadows and marshes fill the low swales and rare dry-sand prairies and black-oak savannas cover the swells. Hoosier Prairie is a biotic cornucopia of habitats and wildlife, attracting foxes, deer, mink, warblers, song sparrows, woodcocks, and many other species, which can be seen from the self-guided trail. To the north the nearby **Gibson Woods Nature Preserve❖** protects a rare example of ridge-and-swale topography.

From these preserves, a short hop north and east to Route 12 leads through the city of Gary to **Indiana Dunes National Lakeshore❖**—one of the state's preeminent natural areas and the birthplace of ecology. When Henry Chandler Cowles, a significant figure in the history of ecol-

ogy, organized a 1913 plant geography trip for European scientists, the sites they asked to visit were the Grand Canyon, Yellowstone, Yosemite, and Indiana Dunes. Although it lacks the grand vistas and soaring geologic formations of the first three, Indiana Dunes compensates for its dearth of larger-than-life drama with unparalleled biological diversity and moods of subtle beauty. The national lakeshore—which includes **Indiana Dunes State Park❖** and **Dunes Nature Preserve❖**—encompasses more than 14,000 acres and 1,442 plant species—the third-largest number in a National Park System area and the first in biotic diversity per acre.

Bogs, swamps, marshes, oak savannas, forests, and the complete dune environment: Indiana Dunes harbors most ecosystems found in the eastern United States. Within this crossroads live relicts of colder, glacial times, plants usually found in Canada's boreal forests: Paper birches flourish in cool, damp areas, and jack pines prefer sandy swells where kinnikinnick spreads thick, glossy leaves at their feet. Dogwoods and tulip poplars, usually more comfortable in the southern Appalachians, thrive on warmer parts of the lakeshore. Sugar maples and oaks have claimed their niches, and even prickly pear cactus, an immigrant from a hotter, drier postglacial period, has found a home here. From foredunes and blowouts to forested

ABOVE: *Orange-flowered hoary puccoon grows among feathery bluestem grasses in the prairie habitats of Indiana Dunes.*

LEFT: *Bare dunes are first colonized by grasses; then shrubs and trees further anchor the drifting sands, eventually creating forested dunes.*

OVERLEAF: *A world away, the distant Chicago sky line is often visible from the shore of the Indiana Dunes across the southern end of Lake Michigan.*

dunes and swales, Indiana Dunes runs the gamut of dune systems.

Then there's the lake and its many moods: a bland and overcast gray-green one day; bright, brisk, and steely blue the next; benign and milky under warm summer skies; and fearsome in winter, with blue-black waters raging at frozen whitecaps along its edge.

The park area is not a contiguous strand. Beginning in the 1800s, iron ore shipped from Minnesota and Michigan created a need for refineries and steel plants, and the southern shores of Lake Michigan, near burgeoning Chicago, seemed a good site. The city of Gary, to the west of the dunes area, was part of the result. So Indiana Dunes, designated by Congress in 1966, twists around steel companies and a few small communities.

The natural lay of the land changes as it nears Lake Michigan. About six miles from the lake are the rolling hills of the oldest glacial moraines. Pinhook Bog, a former kettle-hole lake full of rare flora, lies in this outer region. Younger moraines form a ragged line closer to shore, and between the old and young moraines lies the bottom of a large preglacial lake now crossed by the Little Calumet River. The site also contains a heron rookery.

Closer to Lake Michigan, rows of dunes parallel the shoreline. The oldest are forested, usually with oaks. Between the rows are swales: low wetland areas such as Cowles Bog. On the front lines, facing the lake, are West Beach, Mount Baldy, and the other dunes, formed when sand is washed south by lake currents and deposited along the lake's southeastern shores. When northwesterly winds try to sweep the beach sand farther south, trees and other vegetation block the way and trap the sand as dunes.

The West Beach Trail offers a guide to dunal succession, from bare sand to colonizing marram grass. The roots of a single marram grass plant can spread 20 feet in all directions, anchoring sand so that other grasses, flowers, and shrubs such as sand cherry and wild grape can take hold. These plants add humus, increasing the soil content for trees such as cottonwoods and eventually black oaks.

The boardwalks of the Cowles Bog Trail lead past the dark, mucky waters of this fen. (A fen, unlike a true bog, contains moving water, and Cowles is supplied by underground springs.) Bulbous skunk cabbage crowds the boardwalk, and birches form clumps near water and willows. As it climbs the back of a dune and heads toward the beach, the trail passes Indiana's only stand of northern white cedar. Along the way, wrens, towhees, kingfishers, cardinals, and others fly in and out of the trees, and a deer dashes behind a rise at the sound of footsteps.

Miller Woods showcases interdunal ponds and the herons, buffle-

Encompassing many habitats, the Indiana Dunes support a great diversity of plants. Showy wood lilies (above right) bloom against a tamarack's deciduous needles. The lavender large blazing star (above left) is a denizen of dry woods and clearings. With tight cones that open after the heat of a fire, the boreal jack pine (left) is actually at the far southern edge of its range here.

heads, and other waterfowl that frequent them. The Paul H. Douglas Center for Environmental Education provides glimpses of residents that visitors rarely see, such as odd-looking soft-shell turtles. And Pinhook, a true bog, is full of plants uncommon in Indiana: sphagnum moss, leatherleaf, and predatory sundews and pitcher plants.

Because dunes are too fragile for foot traffic, most dune walks are confined to park trails and boardwalks. In a few places, however, visitors can enjoy the singular pleasure of struggling up shifting, grainy slopes and then leaping down the soft sand in exhilarating ten-league strides as they race toward the summer-warmed waters and easy swells of Lake Michigan—a perfect introduction to lower Michigan and its dune-stacked west coast.

119

MICHIGAN

PART THREE

MICHIGAN

Michigan means "great water," and the state is surrounded by it. Upper and lower Michigan are bordered by four of the five Great Lakes—all but Ontario. With more than 3,200 miles touching the lakes, Michigan has the longest freshwater shoreline in the United States, and only Alaska has a longer total coastline. The retreating glaciers did not leave a neat division here between land and lake: More than 3,000 islands—big, little, whole archipelagoes—fringe Michigan's shorelines. Glacial meltwaters also spawned more than 120 major rivers in Michigan and filled low-lying spots with more than 11,000 lakes. As a result, Michigan residents are reportedly never more than six miles from some body of water.

The Upper Peninsula, known as the UP, is a long hook of land attached to the northeast corner of Wisconsin and defined on its northern shores by one of the world's largest lakes—Superior. Gitche Gumee, the Shining Big-Sea Water of Henry Wadsworth Longfellow's *Song of Hiawatha*, is more than 400 miles long and 1,333 feet deep, occupying 31,800 square miles of surface area. If spread over the continental United States, Lake Superior water would cover the country to a depth of five feet.

Whereas Lake Erie's flush time is a mere 2.5 years, water takes approximately 500 years to move through Lake Superior. Fortunately, Superior experiences far less pollution than Lake Erie, and also in contrast to Erie, Superior supports the smallest number of fish because it is so cold. Superior is connected to the lower lakes by the Saint Marys River, whose boiling rapids drop 22 feet from Superior to Huron. Lake Huron forms lower Michigan's eastern border just past the "thumb" of the mit-

---

PRECEDING PAGES: *Topped by North Woods forests, the rainbow-striped sandstone at Pictured Rocks juts into wave-tossed Lake Superior.*

ten-shaped peninsula. Huron's waters contain the two largest bays in the Great Lakes, Canada's Georgian Bay and Saginaw Bay, which is rich with marshes and wildlife.

Near Detroit, the Saint Clair River, Lake Saint Clair, and the Detroit River carry the current of the Great Lakes from Lake Huron to Lake Erie. Michigan's short Lake Erie shoreline—contiguous with Ohio's—was once part of the notorious, now-drained Great Black Swamp. The western shores of lower Michigan and the southern shores of the Upper Peninsula are washed by Lake Michigan and fringed by the most sweeping freshwater dunes in the nation.

Until European settlers arrived during the 1800s, dense coniferous forests and northern hardwoods covered most of Michigan, and moose, caribou, wolves, mink, marten, otters, and beavers were just a few of the creatures inhabiting the forests and waters. The Huron, Chippewa, Ottawa, Potawatomi, and other tribes gathered wild rice, hunted game, and fished for the plentiful whitefish and sturgeon.

Beginning in the early 1600s, French explorers and voyageurs traveled to Lakes Huron, Superior, and Michigan by way of northern rivers, avoiding Niagara's cataracts and hostile Iroquois. The wealth of wildlife in the North Woods kept voyageurs and fur traders busy for decades—until the wildlife was depleted. In the early 1800s, when the Northwest Territory was being divided into states, Michigan and Ohio almost came to blows over which should possess the mouth of the Maumee River. As recompense for giving the Maumee to Ohio, Michigan got the Upper Peninsula when it became a state in 1837.

The logging era of the late nineteenth century stripped Michigan of many virgin forests, and between habitat loss and hunting, more than 260 state plants and animals are now endangered. Despite such pressures, much of Michigan still looks and feels wild. More than a dozen of its dark, fast rivers rushing into the Great Lakes are part of the National Wild and Scenic River System. In the far north, immense forests still cover the land. And, as wilderness is allowed to blossom, plants and animals are returning to their former habitats, filling Michigan with extraordinary variety and those who visit with the joy of the wild.

OVERLEAF: *In the late 1800s, Mortimer Smith captured the timelessness of a snowy Upper Peninsula forest in this detail from* **Winter Landscape.**

LOWER MICHIGAN

L akes Huron and Michigan nearly match in width, length, and surface area, and geologists often think of them as a single, structural lake basin. But a mammoth, mitten-shaped mound of bedrock, known as Michigan's lower peninsula, has intruded between these Great Lakes waters for a long, long time.

Before European settlement in the early 1800s, lower Michigan was forested from shore to shore (except for patches of prairie in the south), and modest strands of beach traced the Huron shoreline. Michigan's western shoreline, however, sets the state apart. Beginning at the southern end of Lake Michigan and reaching north, the western shoreline shelters the most extensive and varied freshwater dunes in the world—high, golden mountains of sand, mounds rippling in vast ranks to the horizon, and grand swaths of forested dunes, whose soft, sandy floors are carpeted with ferns and mushrooms the size of salad plates.

The dunes begin when prevailing westerly winds scour sand from beaches, propelling it eastward. Blocked by trees, the wind-driven sand drops at the feet of the forests and begins accumulating in drifting piles. Over time, the dunes move inland, row after row running parallel to the shore. Occasionally, they engulf a stand of trees, creating a ghost forest—a grove of lifeless silvery trunks protruding from the sand like mournful sentinels. Although Michigan's dunes reach

---

LEFT: *P. J. Hoffmaster State Park's 1,000-plus acres along Lake Michigan display quintessential dunes. Marram grass, sea rocket, and seaside spurge are among the first plants to colonize and stabilize the sands.*

miles back from shore and some stand 200 feet high, most are geologic newcomers, only 3,000 to 4,000 years old.

In the eighteenth century, the forested southern section of lower Michigan differed substantially from the less fertile northern half of the peninsula. An imaginary line extends from Saginaw Bay, in the crotch of Michigan's thumb, to the mouth of the Grand River on the western shore. South of this line, the glaciers left a fairly flat till plain with low moraines. Because this part of Michigan is relatively warm and its soils are rich, the hardwood forests that covered Ohio and Indiana predominated here too. Beech-maple forests claimed the moist, loamy areas, and oak-hickory woods thrived on the drier ridges. European settlers knew that it was great country for agriculture. It still is. Today this region produces large blueberry and tulip crops as well as about 80 percent of the country's tart cherries. Most of the state's industries, cities, and population are located here as well.

Because glaciers carried much of northern Michigan's fertile topsoil farther south, a high sandy plain now dominates the interior, whose highest point—1,725 feet above sea level—is near Cadillac. Coniferous forests, especially giant white pines, populated the sparse soils.

Although settlers were unable to farm this soil-poor region, between 1848 and 1898 the lumber culled from northern Michigan's old-growth forests netted four billion dollars—more than all the gold taken from California in those years. During that period, Michigan was dotted with 800 lumber camps, and the timber harvested could have covered the entire state with an inch of wood flooring. By 1900, with nothing left to cut, lumber companies moved on to Minnesota and eventually the Pacific Northwest. Today the second-growth forests and abundant rivers and lakes make this region a haven for outdoor recreation.

To explore lower Michigan, this chapter follows the dunes up the scenic western shore of the state to the wetlands north of Traverse Bay and then travels south along Lake Huron. Finally, the route heads north through the middle of the state, where woodlands still thrive, toward the Upper Peninsula.

OVERLEAF: *Silvery branches lace the airiness of budding beech trees in Warren Woods. The native beeches produce a thick leafy canopy each year and retain their smooth gray bark into old age.*

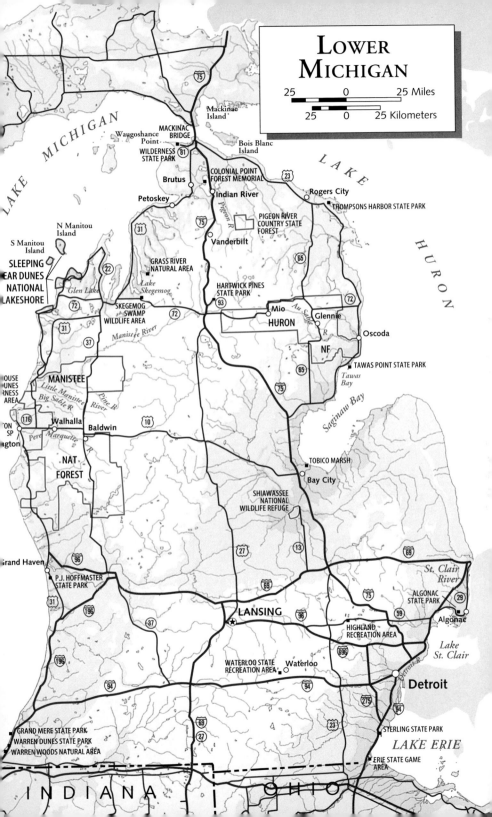

LEFT: *The barred, or hoot, owl produces hair-raising screams and frequents forests such as Warren Woods.*
RIGHT: *A showy northern wildflower in the dogwood family, bunchberry bears creamy flowers in the spring and bright red berries in the fall.*

SOUTHERN MICHIGAN DUNESCAPES

Although **Warren Dunes State Park❖** is a popular dunes destination, the real gem there is an old-growth forest a few miles from Lake Michigan. From I-94, south of the park, take Sawyer Road (Exit 12) west to Three Oaks Road, then south a few miles to Elm Valley Road, and west to **Warren Woods Natural Area❖.** In the heat of a Midwest summer, discovering Warren Woods is like entering a cool, dim room. So thick is the leaf cover that even the air seems colored green. The place has presence. The trees soar, dwarfing visitors. Warren Woods is a deep, dark Hansel-and-Gretel woods—the last of its kind in Michigan.

This virgin beech-maple climax forest towers over a 3.5-mile trail that crosses and then parallels the Galien River for part of its length. Above, abundant vertical living space makes the forest one of the best spots in Michigan (especially before the trees leaf out in spring) to see birds, including warblers, flycatchers, barred owls, and woodpeckers, particularly pileated woodpeckers, which are most at home in old-growth forest.

Warren Woods is a four-season area. In autumn, the red and orange maples, yellow beeches, and scarlet oaks paint a vivid scene. With winter snow on the ground and outlining the trees, cross-country skiers can see the woods at their quietest and most open. Most of the land around Warren Woods was cleared for farming in the late 1800s. Luckily, a storekeeper named E. K. Warren, who had made a fortune on his lightweight, affordable turkey-feather corsets, decided to buy—and preserve—what is now Warren Woods. His contemporaries found the idea of spending money to keep trees from being cut down particularly amusing.

Just north of Warren Dunes, at the John Beers Road exit off I-94,

then south on Thornton Drive, **Grand Mere State Park❖** preserves a classic example of interdunal lakes, as well as diverse wetlands and pockets of prairie. The wetlands and three small lakes that are the park's centerpiece were once part of a bay in a much larger Great Lake. Over time, sand spits cut off the bay, then dunes covered the sand spits, and the bay shriveled to small lakes.

Because the swamps remain cool even in summer, hemlock, tamarack, and white cedar trees live here, farther south than their usual range. Bluebead lilies, bunchberries, and other handsome northern flowering plants make their home near more expected flowers such as trilliums and marsh marigolds. Grand Mere's prairie areas sustain gentians, coreopsis, and lady's tresses, plus bluestem and other grasses, and its wide range of habitats and more than 400 plant species attract a variety of birds, including meadowlarks, tanagers, vireos, thrushes, warblers, hawks, a slew of ducks and shorebirds, and even loons.

The dunes take center stage at **P. J. Hoffmaster State Park❖,** north on I-94, I-196, and Route 31 past Grand Haven and then west on Pontaluna Road. The park's 1,000-plus acres showcase all the functions of dune ecosystems. Before exploring, visit the **Gillette Sand Dune Visitor Center,** appropriately nestled at the foot of a soaring dune, the prime interpretative center of dune ecology for the Michigan park system. It was named for Genevieve Gillette, who helped establish the state park system and two of its jewels: Hartwick

Lower Michigan

ABOVE: *Protected in Michigan, the wood turtle lives along the state's rivers but suffers from habitat loss.*
RIGHT: *The Pine River meanders through 500,000-acre Manistee National Forest, which encompasses a huge chunk of western Michigan.*

Pines and the Upper Peninsula's Porcupine Mountains.

From the visitor center, a path meanders through dunes forested with beech, maple, oak, and hemlock to the foot of a staircase. More than 150 steps lead breathless visitors to the crest of a dune and a vista that defines the breadth and depth of Michigan's dunes: Undulating waves of forested barrier dunes, back dunes, foredunes, and the sandy troughs in between roll out toward the water. Beyond, at the horizon, Lake Michigan's broad blue profile, spotlighted by satiny pools of sunlight, extends to a strip of sky.

Low, silvery mounds of wormwood and the fuzzy stems of hoary puccoon, topped by bright yellow flowers, grow in the troughs between the dunes. Fluttering in the wind like elegant ornamentals are panicles of loose, delicate sand reed grass, which actually helps stabilize the dunes so that shrubs and trees can take hold. Wild bittersweet vine wraps around the trees, displaying its striking orange-and-scarlet fruits in fall. Beautiful bittersweet has been so heavily poached that its numbers in the wild are low, and it is now protected in Michigan.

After a long, hot hike, visitors can immerse themselves in Lake Michi-

134

gan. Vicious riptides are rare in this warm, gentle ocean without the salt, and near the shore, soft lake-bottom sands slope up toward sandbars.

NORTHWEST BEACHES AND SHORES

Covering a vast area northeast of Hoffmaster, **Manistee National Forest❖** abounds in places to camp, hike, boat, and fish. One of the best places to explore is the renowned Pere Marquette River. Neither a big river nor a wild and crazy river, the Pere Marquette moves in tight twists and turns past wildlife in the water, on the banks, and in the air. It is also a world-class fly-fishing stream for steelhead, brown trout, and salmon. The Pere Marquette flows 100 miles under a green canopy of forest. Route 37, which parallels Route 31 inland, leads to Baldwin and a number of Pere Marquette outfitters.

The most natural section lies between Lower Branch and Walhalla, where the river forms tight meanders and wildlife is everywhere: fish flashing as they rise for insects, deer coming to drink, turtles sliding off logs into the water, black-and-orange orioles darting between trees, a flock of cedar waxwings roller-coastering on the air, a great

135

blue heron intently fishing, and a gang of vultures flaunting an attitude. Swooping low, they reveal naked red heads, designed for dipping into carrion without gore clinging afterward.

Sometimes the banks are thickly forested, and sometimes they are sandy slopes where wood turtles nest. Occasionally they are open and filled with goldenrod, wild bergamot, and a host of other wildflowers that sweeten the air. Before emptying into Lake Michigan, the Pere Marquette forms a marshy lake ideal for waterfowl, but only knowledgeable boaters can negotiate its confusing, plant-clogged channels. Like other waterways on this side of lower Michigan, the Pere Marquette is an "extended" river. Formerly, glacial meltwaters made the lake basin fuller. As the Great Lake shrank, rivers had to extend their channels. Where they were blocked by dunes, they backed up and formed lakes before cutting a channel to Lake Michigan.

Other fine rivers running through Manistee National Forest include the Little Manistee, the Little Muskegon, and the Manistee. The **North Country National Scenic Trail,** which wanders 3,200 miles from New York's Adirondack Mountains to the Missouri River in North Dakota, provides hiking and cross-country skiing in the forest; about 20 miles south of Baldwin is the **Loda Lake Wildflower Sanctuary,** rife with wildflowers, forests, marshes, swamps, and dunes.

Back at the lakeshore, **Ludington State Park❖** lies just north of the town of Ludington off Route 116. The park visitor center is the best place to get oriented, and the Skyline Trail boardwalks provide a fine overview of the park as they loop around the tops of dunes.

One of the largest parks in lower Michigan, Ludington offers 5.5 miles of Lake Michigan beach, plus dunes, conifer and hardwood forests, Hamlin Lake, and the Big Sable River. Bass, walleye, northern pike, bluegill, and even muskie inhabit Hamlin Lake, and salmon and trout frequent the river and Lake Michigan. The park contains miles of trails, and visitors can canoe on the Big Sable River. Although most of the land along the river is privately owned, wildlife disregard property lines. An even greater variety of species—muskrat, beavers,

---

RIGHT: *The nation's only dune wilderness, Nordhouse Dunes offers incomparable beach solitude along with hushed, pristine forested dunes. Its interdunal wetlands are the most extensive on the Great Lakes.*

ABOVE: *The ghost forest at Sleeping Bear Dunes National Lakeshore tells of relentlessly shifting sands. As winds sweep across Lake Michigan,*

ducks, and other waterfowl—can be found at Hamlin Lake. Along its notched, southwestern shores, a canoe trail wanders into a maze of coves and marshy areas full of birds and animals escaping the developed lakeshore beyond the park.

Ludington's lengthy Lake Michigan shoreline allows visitors to find quiet spots on the beach. Lying on warm sands with the lake beyond lapping slowly back and forth under the summer sun is the perfect therapy for a cluttered brain. In autumn, brisk winds, choppy blue-gray waters, and bleached sand can inspire visitors to stride into the wind. Those who stride far enough north will reach the picturesque Point Sable Lighthouse (not open to the public).

Unlike Ludington, its northern next-door neighbor is not busy in the summer. **Nordhouse Dunes Wilderness Area❖,** part of Manistee National Forest, is accessible by parking at the Lake Michigan Recreation Area or taking Stiles Road north from Route 10 in Ludington, doglegging onto Quarterline Road, and then following Nurnberg Road six miles west to the Nordhouse parking lot.

The only nationally designated dunes wilderness area in the country, Nordhouse Dunes is wild and almost untouched. Inexorably, in the spreading sands, marram grass, followed by sand cherry, grape, and poison ivy, takes hold, preparing the dunes for trees such as cottonwood and—at this latitude—jack pine. Inhabiting the poor soils of the

138

*mountainous dunes grow up along the shore. The dunes then advance
inland, overwhelming the forests and leaving dead sentinels behind.*

Canadian taiga (moist, subarctic forest), jack pines were probably the
first trees to appear after the glaciers retreated. They are also among
the first trees to return to northern woods after a fire, which triggers
the opening of their cones. Viable cones may hang on a jack pine for
years awaiting a fiery disaster to start the regeneration process.

Within the extensive forested Nordhouse Dunes, maps and a compass are useful because trails are obvious but not signed. The springy
forest paths are shaded by jack, red, and white pines plus oaks, beech,
and maples. Spring wildflowers are abundant, and later in the year,
glossy wintergreen vines trail among unfurled ferns. The extraordinary
fungi here come in an amazing array of shapes and colors: huge yellow-and-white mounds like lemon meringue pies, patches of red and
yellow, white with red polka dots against green moss, orange frills like
the fluttering gills of a fish, and immaculate whites. Interdunal ponds
are scattered about in low spots, crowded with water lilies, tamarack,
and other vegetation that attracts fish, amphibians, and waterfowl.

Emerging onto open sand to enjoy a long-awaited view of the
lake and shoreline populated only by gulls and sandpipers, visitors
may feel like the first people to reach this beach.

Routes 31 and 22 lead north along the lakeshore to **Sleeping Bear
Dunes National Lakeshore❖,** the only national park area in lower
Michigan. In addition to beaches and dunes, Sleeping Bear encompasses

139

bluffs, lakes, rivers and creeks, forests, and two islands. The main visitor center is in the small town of Empire, and the seven-mile Pierce Stocking Scenic Drive provides a good visual introduction to the park.

Beech-maple forests are interspersed with old farm fields returning to the wild, and in autumn these leafy dells turn brilliant colors. Although beeches and maples are the dominant species, basswood, three kinds of pine, yellow and paper birch, white cedar, elm, ash, and oak all inhabit Sleeping Bear. Balsam fir, that aromatic pioneer tree of the north, also begins to appear here. Although wolves, cougars, elk, and moose have been driven from this part of Michigan, a few coyotes and bobcat remain; visitors usually see raccoon, squirrels, and deer.

The Lake Michigan Overlook, high on a slope, presents a giddy view of the sandy, 460-foot plunge into the vast waters below. The panorama also takes in clear, blue Glen Lake, formed when a sand spit enclosed a bay; Sleeping Bear Dune, actually a glacial sand dune perched atop a tall bluff; and North and South Manitou islands. According to Chippewa (Ojibway) legend, a mother bear and her two cubs were driven across Lake Michigan by a raging forest fire. After reaching shore, the mother climbed onto the bluff to await her cubs; but the exhausted young ones drowned and lie just offshore as North and South Manitou islands.

Once heavily forested, Sleeping Bear is now a blowout dune, created when wind or fire strips the vegetation anchoring a dune. Then the wind gouges a hole at the weak section of the dune, throwing sand to the sides and behind. Eventually, the hole becomes a huge bowl-like cavity with arms reaching out on either side. The excavated sand at Sleeping Bear reveals a ghost forest—old trees buried by the sand.

Sleeping Bear was a landmark for Chippewa, Ottawa, and Potawatomi—the People of the Three Fires—and for early French explorers. Later, a lighthouse on South Manitou guided sailors and lumbermen traveling these waters. Besides providing the only natural harbor between here and Chicago, 220 miles away, South Manitou features an 80-acre tract called Valley of the Giants, which shelters America's largest white cedar tree and such rare ferns as green spleenwort. Both North and South Manitou, which have their share of old fields and structures, are now managed as wilderness. Both islands are accessible by ferry from Leland. For divers with a historical bent, **Manitou Passage Underwater Preserve,** partially within national lakeshore waters, contains some 50 ships that sank here between 1835 and 1960.

SWAMPS, MARSHES, AND LAKESHORE POINTS

A complete contrast to Sleeping Bear, **Skegemog Swamp Wildlife Area❖** lies about 35 miles east via Route 72. Beyond Williamsburg, go east briefly on Hill Road and north on Route 597 (Rapid City Road) for 2.5 miles to the Skegemog Swamp parking lot, which is perfumed by wild chamomile. The trail starts at a bit of fern-floored woods and then follows an abandoned railroad grade for a mile to the swamp boardwalk.

Skegemog is a study in subdued greens and browns: Sprays of scaly green white-cedar needles keep the interior dim and cool, and occasional tamaracks add their gray-green airiness. The edges of the narrow stream that feeds this flooded forest are covered with watercress. Occasionally, the shadowed tannic-brown floor of the swamp is brightened by the showy pinks and purples of orchids flaunting their colors. The wildflowers compete with insects for attention. At a bench built into the boardwalk, one visitor commented, "Look, a bench where you can *have lunch*—and *be lunch*." Bring insect repellent.

The short boardwalk trail emerges from the swamp at a raised platform overlooking sedges, cattails, scattered cedars, and open water dotted with lily pads. Beyond this marsh is Lake Skegemog proper, also a wildlife area; visitors can explore these wetlands by canoe from the lake. Black bears, river otters, mink, ospreys, bald eagles, badgers, and loons are just a few of the resident species.

From nearby Rapid City, take Route 593 north, then 618 east to Grass River Natural Area Road. Striated with vertical bays, long thin lakes, and fingerlike peninsulas, this region looks as though a giant took an enormous rake to it. **Grass River Natural Area❖** centers on the river, which flows from Lake Bellaire into Clam Lake. Adjacent sphagnum-sedge bogs support carnivorous sundews and pitcher plants. Boardwalks and trails provide fine views of the preserve's sedge mead-

---

OVERLEAF: *Sunset burnishes Waugoshance Point in Wilderness State Park.*
One of the most evocative spots on the Great Lakes, the moist meadows
are ringed by conifers and the northern reaches of Lake Michigan.

141

ows, marshes, cedar swamp, and forests. Ospreys and otters fish these waters, also home to swans and a variety of ducks.

The best stand of old-growth red oak in lower Michigan is the centerpiece of the **Colonial Point Memorial Forest❖.** To see these giants, take Shoreline Route 31 about 55 miles north and turn east at Brutus. Where Brutus Road becomes Indian Point Road, look for a trail leading south into the preserve. Colonial Point fills the end of the peninsula jutting into Burt Lake. Although pines, birches, maples, hemlocks, and other species are scattered through the forest, the towering oaks predominate. Majestic trees almost 150 years old have barely reached middle age. The oldest stand of red oak here survived not only the logging but also logging-era fires that raged through northern Michigan in the late 1800s.

At the top of the Lower Peninsula, on a finger of land reaching into Lake Michigan, lies **Wilderness State Park❖.** Take Route 31 north, then Country Road 81 and Wilderness Park Drive west to the second-largest but perhaps wildest state park in lower Michigan. Wilderness's 7,500 acres offer all sorts of recreation and three mainland natural areas, including spectacular Waugoshance Point.

Hemlocks and leafy hardwoods form a thick bower over the road to Waugoshance Point, eventually dropping away to reveal open meadows and a narrow line of evergreens concealing sandy strands along the lake. At the shoreline, wildflowers and arching sand reed grass cluster near small pools where green pickerel frogs splash. Views to the edge of the point are rimmed with cedar and spruce, which rise above flat rock outcrops and hide the point's interior meadows. The remote, moody beach invariably seduces visitors into long, leisurely walks.

The wildness of the point also attracts endangered and rarely seen piping plover. Because piping plover avoid developed areas, Wilderness State Park is one of the few places in lower Michigan where these shorebirds still nest. During nesting season, park staff limit access to beaches where plover lay their eggs.

Behind the lines of conifers edging the point are broad, wet meadows filled with orange paintbrush, yellow-flowering potentilla, the striped white flowers of grass-of-parnassus, sedges, and other plants. The point is the place to hear the voices of warblers and see hawks swooping low over the trees, black cormorants winging toward the water, and Canada geese, terns, and ducks congregating along the shore. In a green, marshy part of the meadow, a great blue heron stands on one long leg, suspended in sunlight. Large monarch butterflies flirt with flowers, and dragonflies in a rainbow of iridescent colors drone lazily at eye level.

Within the forests are deer, rarely seen black bears, and red squirrels that scold noisily from the trees. Wetlands around the Big Stone and Red Pine trails show signs of beavers. After a big show of spring wildflowers, brilliant scarlet cardinal flower and purple bee balm appear along Stone Creek. A less pleasant sight is purple spotted knapweed, not because it is unattractive but because it is an alien species from Europe stealing native wildflower habitat up and down Michigan's dunes and shorelines and in much of the United States. Altogether, about 20 exotic plant species, including baby's breath and purple loosestrife, have made major pests of themselves in Michigan's parks.

The southwestern beaches of Wilderness State Park are full of small dunes rolling back to forested dunes, a pleasant miniature version of Ludington and often less crowded than the more developed parts of the park. Quaint Cross Village, near the park, complements the trees, cliffs, and Lake Michigan beaches, and Route 119 between Cross Village and Petoskey is particularly scenic. Farther south, the getaway mansions of Chicago's rich, perched on rolling hills, counterpoint the natural.

EASTERN SHORES

From the northern tip of Michigan at Mackinaw City, follow Route 23 south about 75 miles along Lake Huron past Rogers City, then east on Old State Road to gravel roads leading into **Thompsons Harbor State Park❖.** The gates blocking these roads are less than two miles' walk from Lake Huron itself.

Missing from the Lake Huron shoreline are the immense dunes thrown up by prevailing winds on the western side of the state. Thompsons Harbor presents more subtle beach types: underlying limestone intruding on the shore as cobbles, and forest, conifer swamps, marshes, and beach pools bedded with marl among the other habitats. In this little-used park, blue dwarf lake iris, a threatened species that grows only on narrow strips bordering the Great Lakes, produces its largest population. Other rare plants found only in the Great Lakes re-

LEFT: *Wilderness State Park is one of the few nesting areas of endangered piping plover, which lay their eggs in the sand of beaches.* **RIGHT:** *Thompsons Harbor once gave refuge to ships on Lake Huron. Now it protects Houghton's goldenrod and other rare plants.*

gion, more than 100 bird species, and a quiet 7.5-mile shoreline are highlights of Thompsons Harbor, which once served merchant ships traveling Lake Huron.

About 50 miles farther south, **Huron National Forest❖,** occupying the bulge between Thunder and Tawas bays, offers plenty of natural wonder and ways to see it. The Island Lake Nature and Wakeley Lake trails are two good choices. The jewel of the forest, however, is the **Au Sable River** corridor. The graceful Rivière aux Sables—River of Sands, named by French explorers—was among the first Michigan rivers included in the National Wild and Scenic River System. The Au Sable's tributaries begin about where Route 27 bisects the state lengthwise, and the river then flows southeast to its confluence with Lake Huron. Although most of the river corridor appears natural, the South Branch and the section between Mio and Glennie are particularly scenic. The Au Sable is also renowned for its brown trout.

This section of the Au Sable corridor is managed as a protected area for Kirtland's warblers. About 660 pairs of Kirtland's warblers exist, and many of them nest near the river. The yellow-breasted Kirtland's are a classic case of bird decline paralleling habitat destruction. They nest in large tracts of young jack pine, then winter in the Bahamas. Jack pines are pioneer trees in northern burned areas, and when fires occurred naturally, young jack pines were common. Because logging and fire suppression have decimated the Kirtland's habitat, the Forest Service cultivates tracts of young jack pines, which are harvested and then replanted to keep tree populations young and Kirtland's populations extant.

From the McKinley bridge downriver, the Au Sable's width and current are moderate, allowing canoeists to focus on river's-edge marshes, shrub swamps, and the wildlife inhabiting these wetlands. In

lower latitudes, the standard wetland shrub is willow. Close to boreal climes, tag alders begin appearing, as they do here. Boaters share the river with deer, beavers, porcupines, wild turkeys pecking in the dirt, and a variety of other animals. The riverbanks vary from low and green with white cedar, aspen, and ash to sandy bluffs topped with pines. The U.S. Forest Service can provide a list of canoe liveries, and for those who prefer to see the river on foot, trails line the banks.

Another good way to explore the Au Sable is to drive along River Road, a 22-mile national forest scenic byway along the river's southern bank that begins on Route 65 at Loud Pond. Downriver, the Eagle's Nest Overlook provides scenic views of the river and a chance to see the pair of bald eagles that usually nest nearby. Another stop is exquisite Iargo Spring (the name refers to white pines), the site of Chippewa powwows, which was later acquired by European-American settlers.

A mixture of stairs, boardwalks, and platforms lead down the steep bank past dark hemlocks, through the spring area, to the river's edge. Spilling in smooth sheets over small log dams, the spring flows placidly through evergreens and hardwoods out to the river. This broad marshy curve of the Au Sable is full of stumps and tiny white-cedar islands that seem so artistically placed that they resemble a Zen garden in the still, reflective water. Lingering here, visitors can see ducks,

LEFT: *The Au Sable River flows from Michigan's forested central ridge to Lake Huron. Once a classic voyageurs' river, the Au Sable still attracts many canoeists.*
RIGHT: *The northern pitcher plant inhabits Michigan bogs and must ingest insects because the anaerobic soil where it grows is so lacking in vital nutrients.*

terns, hawks, and other birds. The Au Sable ends ignominiously at Lake Huron in a crowded marina that runs right through the town of Oscoda.

Farther south on Route 23, just before the town of East Tawas, take Tawas Point Road east to **Tawas Point State Park❖,** called the Cape Cod of the Midwest. On a wild, windy day, when gulls scream and waves beat at the edge of Lake Huron, this hook of sand curving in toward Tawas Bay seems to front a vast ocean lacking only the salt spray. Perhaps that is why the French, the first Europeans in these parts, named the Huron *Mer Douce,* "sweet water."

To see the best of Tawas Point, take the Sandy Hook Nature Trail, beginning near the lighthouse. The trail passes staghorn sumac and quaking aspens on higher sandy ground and red-twigged dogwood and rushes in wetter areas, as well as a variety of pastel-colored wildflowers. Watch for poison ivy, which likes to help colonize beach areas. The ponds, and the trees and bushes around them, are busy with small flocks of cedar waxwings, kingfishers, kingbirds, bluewinged teal, and more than 200 other avian species, including rare red-knots and piping plover. The point is also a migration stopover for many species taking the shortcut across Saginaw Bay. At the end of a warm day, Tawas Point's two-plus miles of beach are a luxurious and refreshing conclusion.

North of Bay City, about 55 miles farther south on I-75, take Exit 168 (Beaver Road) five miles east to **Bay City State Recreation Area** and the entrance to **Tobico Marsh❖,** the largest remaining wetlands along Saginaw Bay and a national natural landmark. From the Saginaw Bay Visitor Center, a trail circles through woods to the marsh, where observation towers provide overviews and a boardwalk provides a closer look. Deer, beavers, mink, muskrat, and more than 125 species of birds

149

LEFT: *Pines, with deep taproots that allow them to thrive in sandy soils, line the beach at Tawas Point State Park, a fine site for birding on Lake Huron.*
RIGHT: *A female belted kingfisher watches for prey. Common at Tawas Point, kingfishers spot the fish and then hover above or plummet directly from a tree to pluck their hapless catch from the water.*

inhabit Tobico. The best time to visit is during spring or fall migration, when thousands of waterfowl arrive. A few species rare to Michigan nest here, including ruddy and redhead ducks and yellow-headed blackbirds.

Shiawassee National Wildlife Refuge❖, the only staffed national wildlife refuge in the lower peninsula, is south of Bay City and Saginaw via Route 13, then west on West Curtis Road. Four rivers converge here: the Flint, Cass, Tittabawassee, and Shiawassee. The Chippewa named the latter two, and evidence dates human communities in the area to 7,000 B.C. The rivers leave the refuge as one: the Saginaw, the largest yet shortest river in the state, which drains one sixth of lower Michigan.

The refuge's 9,000 acres of wetlands, croplands, and floodplain forests attract great numbers of waterfowl during spring and fall migrations: more than 25,000 Canada, blue, and snow geese; 50,000 ducks, including black, mallard, pintail, teal, shoveler, and canvasback; and hundreds of tundra swans. Bald eagles live in the refuge along with beavers, deer, foxes, and other mammals.

A natural getaway for people in nearby Detroit is offered by the **Highland Recreation Area❖** about 55 miles southeast, east of Route 23 off Route 59. **Haven Hill Natural Area,** the old Edsel estate within Highland, preserves every type of forest found in southern Michigan. Oak and hickory dominate the hilly glacial moraines, while beech and maple proliferate in flatter territory, and elm, ash, and basswood rule the hardwood swamp forests. Conifer swamps are filled with white cedar and tamarack. In spring, rue, mayapples, native geraniums, and other wildflowers are the stars, yielding center stage in autumn to the trees, which mount a fine show of color. Summer can be close and buggy, and winter cross-country skiing is often compromised by the smell and sound of snowmobiles. Haven Hill Lake attracts numerous waterfowl, including the occasional glossy white trumpeter swan.

Routes 59 and 29 lead east some 55 miles to **Algonac State Park❖,** which occupies a critical point on the Great Lakes. Ships from Superior, Michigan, and Huron must pass through the Saint Clair River, connecting Lake Huron to Lake Saint Clair, and the Detroit River to reach Lake Erie. Algonac, near the mouth of the Saint Clair River, witnesses some of the world's busiest water traffic. Visitors here can watch every sort of vessel, from international freighters to local walleye trollers.

Algonac also preserves a few remnants of the lake plain prairies that covered large portions of southern Michigan. In mid- to late summer, Algonac's prairies glow with feathery seed heads of bluestem grasses, purple spears of liatris, goldenrod, purple ironweed, and about 300 other species. Another attraction is the huge old oaks that survive on Algonac's sandy oak-savanna ridges.

Devoted to wetlands, **Sterling State Park❖,** some 25 miles south of Detroit and east on Dixie Highway from I-75, is Michigan's only state park on Lake Erie. The area bordering Lake Erie once embraced a broad swath of wetlands, but more than 70 percent of Michigan's lakeshore wetlands are gone. Consequently, Sterling's four lagoons and the marshes around Sandy Creek Outlet are particularly attractive to migrating birds. Canada geese, blue-winged teal, and mergansers commonly stop here, and great blue and black-crowned night herons stalk the waters. About 15 miles farther south, just north of the Ohio state line, **Erie State Game Area❖** encompasses about twice as many wetlands and is one of Michigan's prime birding locations.

MICHIGAN'S MIDDLE

Like northwestern Indiana, southern Michigan was left with a jumble of moraines, bogs, outwash plains, and kettle-hole lakes when the glaciers retreated. Near the town of Waterloo, about 10 miles west of Ann Arbor off I-94 on Kalmbach Road, **Waterloo State Recreation Area❖** contains probably the southernmost example of a black spruce bog—a former kettle-hole lake that has filled in over millennia. The bog is studded with species rare to this part of the state: tamarack, chokeberry, blueberry, and a native of arctic regions, the evergreen leatherleaf shrub. Be

ABOVE: *Stately native pines, which once covered most of northern Michigan, were logged by the millions in the 1800s. Today they are regenerating in Pigeon River Country State Forest, as is Michigan's only elk herd.*

careful of the poison sumac that grows in wet areas.

Running along the spine of the state, Routes 127 and 27 lead 150 miles north to I-75 and Route 93 to **Hartwick Pines State Park❖**, the largest in lower Michigan. The park's virgin white pine forest gives visitors a breathtaking view of how much of Michigan looked until the 1800s. A high, dense canopy keeps the understory open and the ground springy with fallen needles. The hundred-foot-high forest—along with visitors' awe of these great trees—dampens noise, and the place feels much like California's celebrated giant redwood groves. Astonishingly, goliath white pines such as these once covered more than 28,000 square miles—half of Michigan's land area—making the majestic white pine the logical choice for state tree.

In spring, parts of the park are carpeted in wildflowers, but the floor of the 49-acre virgin forest is largely clear because the canopy allows in so little light. Occasionally, wind fells some trees and provides opportunities for struggling maple seedlings, which can add a few feet of new growth per year. In contrast, the Monarch, the largest white pine in the virgin grove, grows only $\frac{1}{32}$ of an inch per year. Almost 4 feet in diameter and 155 feet high, this giant has lived more than 300 years.

Park staff believe that the life of one old stump, once a white pine as big as the Monarch, was shortened by human traffic. Too many people walking around the foot of a tree compacts soil, thus cutting off oxygen

ABOVE: *The most abundant mammal in lower Michigan forests, the white-tailed deer flips its white "flag" tail to warn others of danger.*
RIGHT: *Ablaze with vivid autumn color, Mackinaw State Forest on lower Michigan's northern tip provides a scenic introduction to the immense woodlands of the Upper Peninsula.*

needed by the roots. Staying on the trail in a heavily used park such as Hartwick Pines can mean the difference between a tree's life and death.

Within the virgin grove, a replica of a lumber camp helps visitors envision Michigan's logging era, when more than a billion white pines were cut and the state led the nation in lumber production. Other areas of the park include lakes, rolling hills (moraines), and the quiet, glassy beginnings of the East Branch of the Au Sable River. The Au Sable Trail winds through young stands of pine bedded with blueberry, both flourishing in the sandy, gravelly soils that glaciers deposited in this part of Michigan. Groves of white-barked paper birch, fields filling in with ferns, and a white-cedar swamp are other highlights.

An eight-mile scenic drive, on a narrow dirt road that keeps visitors close to the woods, offers a bigger picture of the park. In areas charred by vast forest fires that spread across Michigan decades ago as a result of relentless logging, groves of rugged pioneer jack pine prepare the land for white pine, this area's dominant species, as wild turkeys scurry through the park's deciduous forests.

The home of Michigan's only elk herd is **Pigeon River Country State Forest❖,** some 25 miles farther north on I-75 and then 12 miles east of Vanderbilt on Sturgeon Valley Road (forest headquarters is another mile north on Twin Lake Road). Logged into the early part of this century, Pigeon River Country's forests are relatively new. Although logging continues and oil and gas production caused a huge

154

outcry when they began in the 1970s, protecting wildlife habitat is a major concern in this part of the Mackinaw State Forest.

In 1918, 24 elk (which had disappeared due to logging) were reintroduced at three sites, and by 1927, the three herds combined numbered at least 300. Because predators such as wolves have disappeared, the present herd of 1,100 is maintained by limited hunting. Black bears, bobcat, bald eagles, ospreys, and pine marten, reintroduced to Pigeon River Country in 1985, are all currently thriving. Inspiration Point is a good scenic overlook, and across the road and a bit north is a trail leading to an elk-viewing area (when planning a visit, remember that elk are crepuscular and best seen at dawn or dusk).

Pigeon River Country's northern hardwood forests—white and jack pines, aspen, lowland hardwoods, conifer swamps, and grassy openings—support myriad wildlife, including deer, bears, coyotes, woodcocks, and ruffed grouse. Following the Pigeon River for miles and wandering past several lakes, the Shingle Mill Pathway offers one way of seeing Pigeon River Country. Although the Sturgeon River, which parallels the Pigeon, is reputedly the swiftest, most challenging canoeing river in lower Michigan, the Pigeon's slower pace through the forest provides lingering views of wildlife.

Interstate 75 continues north to the Mackinac Bridge and across the straits to the Upper Peninsula, some of the wildest country in the contiguous United States.

CHAPTER SIX

UPPER MICHIGAN

Nowhere is America wilder than on Michigan's Upper Peninsula, the realm of moose, wolf, and loon—northern species that avoid populated places—and boreal forests stretching to the horizon. All but a couple of the state's 150 waterfalls are here, along with thousands of lakes, named and un-named, that lie hidden within coniferous forests of balsam, pine, and spruce. A dozen or so wild and scenic rivers tumble toward the Great Lakes, and the Porcupine Mountains form the only real mountain range in the Midwest. Michigan's Upper Peninsula feels like the top of the world: northern skies, northern air, and winters buried under many feet of snow. Here the wild takes precedence over the settled.

Ninety percent of the Upper Peninsula is forested and half is public land, including the largest state forest system in the contiguous United States. From the low-lying eastern half, the peninsula rises to mountains and tablelands in the west. Most of the scattered towns cling to the coasts. Like a long, gnarled finger pointing into Lake Huron, the Upper Peninsula divides Lakes Superior and Michigan. On this claw-shaped chunk of land, Archean rock, some of the world's oldest, is laid bare.

On its northern shores is Superior, a lake of legends and fearsome power where the *manitous* (spirits) of the Chippewa are said to hover ever near. Stories of sailing ships and freighters sunk by Lake Superior

---

LEFT: *Etched by the gold of the setting sun, the sandstone rock terraces at Lake Superior's Pictured Rocks National Lakeshore echo the autumn colors of the surrounding maples, oaks, and other hardwoods.*

are legion. Father Jacques Marquette, who traveled the region in the 1670s with explorer Louis Jolliet, found Lake Superior as brutal as it was beautiful. Storms on the lake, Marquette wrote, seemed "to be living in the heart of a hurricane."

French explorers and Jesuits who had begun surveying the land for material bounty and converts earlier in the seventeenth century were staggered by the breadth of land and lake and the wealth of wildlife. Voyageurs, adopting the light, elegant birch-bark canoes of the Chippewa, began reaping this wealth in mink, marten, and especially beaver pelts—indispensable in Europe for men's top hats. When the voyageurs first arrived, more than ten million beavers lived in the North Woods. By the 1800s, few were left.

Beginning in the mid-1800s, copper mining boomed in the far north on the Keweenaw Peninsula, and led to the discovery of iron in Michigan's Gogebic Range. During this period, lumbermen denuded U.P. forests, and although the land is now covered with second-growth forests, huge virgin trees are hard to find. Not long ago, a Chippewa was commissioned to build a replica birch-bark canoe, which could be as large as 30 feet long and 7 feet wide. To find a paper birch big enough to fit the specifications, he had to search a thousand miles.

After mining declined on the Upper Peninsula, the inhabitants headed elsewhere, and today the U.P.'s population density is half that of Texas. Its most valuable resources are pristine lakes, plunging rivers, and vast boreal forests filled with mink, moose, wolves, foxes, deer, bears, and dozens of other species.

Traveling through the Upper Peninsula, this chapter begins at the north end of Mackinac Bridge, heads west along the northern half of the peninsula, and then dips south to the Lake Michigan shores at the U.P.'s narrow neck. From there, it returns to the Lake Superior side, continuing to the state's northwestern corner to the Keweenaw Peninsula and Isle Royale National Park.

EASTERN U.P.: WHITEFISH, TAHQUAMENON, AND SENEY

Before entering the Upper Peninsula proper, kayakers and other boaters should consider investigating the state's **Island Explorer Trail,** which wanders along the northern shoreline of Lake Huron as well as the bays and channels of Saint Marys River leading to Sault

UPPER MICHIGAN

25 Miles
25 Kilometers

CANADA

LAKE HURON

Drummond Island

HARBOR ISLAND NATURE PRESERVE

SOO LOCKS

LAKE SUPERIOR STATE FOREST

Sault Ste Marie

75

St. Marys River

123

28

Whitefish Point
WHITEFISH POINT BIRD OBSERVATORY
Paradise
TAHQUAMENON FALLS SP
Whitefish Falls SP
Whitefish Bay

2

BETSY LAKE RESEARCH NATURAL AREA

LAKE SUPERIOR STATE FOREST

77

Tahquamenon R.

Grand Marais
Grand Sable Lake

Seney

Fox R.

SENEY NWR

Manistique R.

94

Garden Peninsula

149

PALMS BOOK STATE PARK

183

FAYETTE SP

Munsing
PICTURED ROCKS NATIONAL LAKESHORE

HIAWATHA NATIONAL FOREST

509

Whitefish R.

LAKE MICHIGAN

ESCANABA RIVER STATE FOREST

94

Rapid River

2

41

S U P E R I O R

L A K E

NATIONAL PARK

Eagle Harbor

26

Keweenaw Peninsula

41

ESTIVANT PINES SANCTUARY

LITTLE PRESQUE ISLE TRACT (ESCANABA SF)
Marquette
Sugar Loaf Mtn

550

ESCANABA RIVER STATE FOREST
Hogsback Mtn x
Champion

41

VAN RIPER SP

Lake Michigamme

CRAIG LAKE STATE PARK

Michigamme R.

ESCANABA RIVER STATE FOREST

Menomimee River

Houghton

26

45

Ontonagon

Big Carp River

PORCUPINE MTNS WILDERNESS SP
Porcupine Mtns
Summit Peak x

Presque Isle R

2

Watersmeet

535

SYLVANIA WILDERNESS

W I S C O N S I N

45

Sainte Marie and Lake Superior. Linking state parks and forests, this innovative water trail allows intrepid travelers to see wildlife and natural treasures not readily accessible and experience Great Lakes waters where the big ships cannot go. Boaters on the trail may share the waves with otters, but not with freighters. Based on Lime Island in the Saint Marys River across from Canada's Saint Joseph Island, the Explorer Trail takes in Drummond, Les Cheneaux, and other islands, plus lots of shoreline. Next to Drummond, **Harbor Island Nature Preserve❖,** whose long arms enclose a bay, is full of conifer swamps, oak forests, and wildlife.

Also worth a visit is Sault Sainte Marie, a city older than Philadelphia. Although not a natural area, the Soo Locks, through which huge ships pass, put Lake Superior into perspective. Connecting Superior to Lake Huron and the other Great Lakes, the first Soo Locks opened to ship traffic in 1855. They were needed because the natural connection, the Saint Marys River, drops a roiling 22 feet, which forced Chippewa and early European travelers to shoot the rapids or portage. Today more than 12,000 ships slide through the most recent version of the locks, and thousand-foot-long freighters carry iron ore and grain east through the Great Lakes to the Saint Lawrence Seaway and the Atlantic Ocean.

Thousand-footers that look unshakable at the Soo become specks on Lake Superior's vastness. Autumn lake storms, packing 70-mile winds and piling waves 30 feet high, can turn mighty ships into broken toys. In 1975, a fierce storm off Whitefish Point plunged the 729-foot *Edmund Fitzgerald* to the bottom of the lake with all its crew.

Just south of Sault Sainte Marie, take Route 28 west, then Route 123 and Whitefish Point Road north of Paradise to **Whitefish Point Bird Observatory❖.** Behind rocky beaches curving to a narrow spit washed by Lake Superior, a broad swath of sand leads to shrubs full of warblers, sparrows, and other small birds. Pines further anchor the sand, and a hawk observation station rests atop dunes rising above the trees. Now a refuge for raptors, this spot once witnessed wholesale slaughter as hunters took advantage of a federal bounty on birds of prey. The observatory, which includes a lighthouse and a small visitor center, is active in bird research and protection.

In April, northward-bound bald and golden eagles and northern goshawks—the classic raptors of boreal forests—as well as migrating

Above: *Dunes and conifers at Whitefish Point Bird Observatory offer welcome landfall for millions of migrating birds. When fierce Lake Superior storms sweep through, adjacent Whitefish Bay is also a haven for ships.*

Cooper's, sharp-shinned, red-tailed, and broad-winged hawks, soar overhead. In May, swans, herons, loons, scoters, sandpipers, gulls, and many more reach the point, and warblers and other birds of the woods make their way from Central and South America along the Midwest flyways. As the birds start south in fall, their numbers at Whitefish Point are even more spectacular. Dozens of rare and rare-to-the-area species have been sighted here.

Of the 230 species sighted at Whitefish Point, raptors wing through in the greatest numbers—up to 23,000 some springs. Because they avoid flying over open water, raptors follow the Great Lakes shorelines as far as they can. At Whitefish Point, the Upper Peninsula narrows to a thin slice of land that is less than 20 miles from Ontario across the mouth of Lake Superior's Whitefish Bay.

From the town of Paradise, Route 123 runs southwest to **Tahquamenon Falls State Park❖.** Here the smell of balsam wafts by, as it does often on the Upper Peninsula, perfuming the air with its clean, resinous scent. At nearly 36,000 acres, second only to Porcupine Mountains Wilderness State Park in size, Tahquamenon Falls State Park centers on its famous cascades. The second largest falls east of the Mississippi (Niagara Falls is number one), Upper Tahquamenon Falls draws visitors from all over the Midwest during the summer. In autumn crowds disperse, and the brilliant maples and beeches color the forests in every shade of the red-to-yellow spectrum. Winter brings its own magic as cross-country skiers glide quietly through the woods and the falls sparkle with edgings of ice.

Above the park, the Tahquamenon River is stained a tea color as it flows through peaty coniferous swamps and past forests whose understories are dense with blueberries. Henry Wadsworth Longfellow set part of his *Song of Hiawatha* along the banks of the Tahquamenon, which means Marsh of the Blueberries.

Where it thunders over a 200-foot-wide lip of rock at the upper falls, the Tahquamenon explodes in a kaleidoscope of earth tones: cream, yellow, ocher, and copper. Watching the falls' shifting tones is as mesmerizing as gazing into a fire. If the upper falls present drama, the lower falls provide grace. Here the river splits, tumbling casually around a small wooded island. For a modest fee, visitors can row over to the island and stroll the trail around it. Below the falls, the seething waters disperse in masses of foam and flow between gorge walls crowned by verdant forest. Other trails—unevenly maintained depending on the funding available to state parks—wind through beech-maple old-growth forest into groves of giant white pines and eastern hemlocks.

Farther north into the park, dauntless travelers can make their way to **Betsy Lake Research Natural Area❖.** Northern pike and perch lie below the surface of a lake surrounded by a wilderness of sandy ridges and a muskeg of sedges, sphagnum, bog laurel, and tamarack. These ridges and boggy, low-lying flats are the bed of former Lake Algonquin, a larger predecessor of Lake Superior. Blackflies can be pesky in the summer.

One of the best refuges in the Midwest can be reached via Routes 28 west and 77 south. **Seney National Wildlife Refuge❖** is fecund with wetlands, forests, and 200 bird, 50 mammal, and 26 fish species. Although Seney's more than 95,000 acres encompass many habitats, water is never far from the surface. About half of Seney is covered by the **Manistique Swamp,** a marsh-muskeg mix containing tamarack and

RIGHT: *Upper Tahquamenon Falls, the Midwest's largest cascade, roars over Cambrian sandstone at the rate of 2,000 gallons per second. Longfellow's Hiawatha built his canoe along quiet sections of this river.*

black spruce swamp forests. Designated wilderness, about 25,000 acres of this wild, difficult terrain are home to timber wolves, moose, bald eagles, coyotes, foxes, bears, deer, muskrat, beavers, and others. Three species of grouse—the spruce, ruffed, and sharp-tailed, reside within Seney's borders. The refuge also provides the nation's best habitat for woodcocks, birds shaped like croquet balls with long bills.

Within the wilderness area lies **Strangmoor Bog Research Natural Area.** Strangmoors—"string bogs"—occur only in boreal climes, and Seney's is one of the continent's southernmost. Patterned like bleachers stepping down to a gym floor, the remains of ancient beach ridges with newer, sandy crossbars and intersecting swales attract a wide range of plants, including pitcher plants and other unusual species.

As in lower Michigan, most of the U.P.'s original stands of white pine were cut. What remained was often ravaged in the 1800s by wildfires or blazes set to clear the debris. Development companies tried to drain the area for agriculture, but farmers found that the soil could not support cultivation; after the farms failed, Seney reverted to the government for back taxes. Except for its white pines, Seney has recovered and is now a haven for myriad birds. Just off the highway, the area near the visitor center—surrounded by a maze of large artificial but natural-looking pools—is by far the most accessible.

164

LEFT: *With its swamp forests and muskeg (rare this far south), Seney National Wildlife Refuge is one of the nation's most wildlife-rich sanctuaries. The narrow, conical trees on the horizon are balsam firs, whose fragrance pervades Michigan's scenic Upper Peninsula.*

RIGHT: *The long, convoluted windpipe of the trumpeter swan is responsible for its distinctive call. These large birds, which mate for life and live 20 to 30 years, are making a comeback at Seney with the help of humans.*

Routes through Seney include the Manistique River, which is open to canoeists. A short nature trail loops around one pool, and a self-guided auto tour winds past many of the pools, displaying some of Seney's best waterbird habitat. Cross-country skis are an option in winter, but bikes may be the best way to travel the refuge's 100 miles of roads. (Canoe and bike rentals are available in nearby Germfask, on Route 77.)

Those on foot can walk a short distance from the visitor center to see small flocks of cedar waxwings gobble red serviceberries from trees heavy with fruit, while woodpeckers bang on bark. An osprey swoops low over a pool where a bittern points its brown-and-tan–striped neck skyward, intent on appearing to be a reed.

After habitat destruction reduced their numbers, Canada geese were reintroduced in 1936 and have made a strong comeback—at the Seney Visitor Center they are as common as gulls around a fishing boat. Canada geese nest at Seney, as do black ducks, wood ducks, teal, mergansers, sandhill cranes, and other waterbirds.

Less common are Seney's spectacular trumpeter swans. With their snowy plumage and immense eight-foot wingspan, the world's largest waterfowl are astonishing to behold. That they exist here at all is astonishing too. Trumpeters were extirpated from Michigan in the late 1880s: their wetlands drained, their skins made into powder puffs, and

165

their feathers plucked to adorn hats. By the early 1900s, trumpeters were found only in Canada, Alaska, and remote areas of Montana, Idaho, and Wyoming. In 1991, ten swans were released in Seney, and their numbers are growing. Long necks held gracefully erect, they float in the pools with dignified elegance. More often, their stout white-feathered bottoms are topmost as their showpiece necks probe for tasty underwater weeds. While trumpeters dive and preen, mated pairs of loons glide sedately by, and a soft-shell turtle lifts its long, rubbery neck above the water.

The refuge's eagle observation deck is usually a fine place to spot young and mature bald eagles, which sometimes build a few nests in their territory and rotate among them from year to year (each massive nest can weigh up to two tons). Visitors who take their eyes off the wildlife will find Seney's wildflowers and flowering shrubs worth noticing too.

Ernest Hemingway fished in **Lake Superior State Forest❖,** which extends north and south of Route 28. Nick Adams fished here too in Hemingway's story "Big Two-Hearted River." Although the Two-Hearted River is nearby, the one in the story was probably the Fox. Visitors can fish or canoe either of these state-designated "natural" rivers or hike along the 28-mile Fox River Pathway, which begins near the town of Seney and follows the Fox nearly to Pictured Rocks National Lakeshore. In addition to the river, stands of pine, wild blueberries, and a satisfying peacefulness, the pathway reveals some of the wholesale logging that occurred in the 1800s.

PICTURED ROCKS NATIONAL LAKESHORE

Route 28 leads some 35 miles west to Munising and headquarters for **Pictured Rocks National Lakeshore❖.** Although the Pictured Rocks are its deservedly celebrated feature, this country's first national lakeshore is not a one-note song. Along the shoreline of this narrow park, which meanders about 40 miles beside Lake Superior between Munising and Grand Marais, lie not only its namesake rocks but also miles of beaches, lakes, waterfalls, forests, wetlands, and Grand Sable Banks and Dunes.

Grand Sable Banks, rising nearly 300 feet above the beach at the eastern end of the park, were formed when retreating glaciers

ABOVE: *In late autumn, a snowstorm makes a dramatic approach to Pictured Rocks National Lakeshore and the pancake layers of Miners Castle, a sandstone pinnacle towering nine stories above Lake Superior.*

dumped loads of sand and gravel. Then wind lifted and deposited sand atop the banks, creating the shifting Grand Sable Dunes, one of the nation's best examples of perched dunes. The path to the dunes begins at Sable Falls and passes meadows, woodlands, and Sable Falls. Shifting in the wind, the marram grass that covers much of the dunes catches light like a flock of birds turning on the wing. Against the rippling grasses, yellow tansies and purple-flowering sand peas glow. Behind the banks is Grand Sable, a kettle-hole lake, and farther west, behind Twelve-Mile Beach, forests of white birch and pine support ferns, blueberries, lichens, and wildflowers.

Recessed in a small tree-shaded gorge near the west entrance of the park, slender Munising Falls spills gracefully from a sandstone lip, filling the gorge with moisture that nurtures hanging gardens along the rock walls. Before the tree leaves unfurl, hepatica, violets, Dutchman's-breeches, and other wildflowers paint the forest floor. Although Pictured Rocks may look picture-perfect, as in many areas spotted knapweed, vinca, and other alien plants are invading.

At the western end of the park is Sand Point Marsh, where ancient beach ridges bracket wetlands. At the entrance to the marsh, traversed

by a sturdy boardwalk built by the Youth Conservation Corps, a shadowed white-cedar wetland is filled with a mix of balsam fir, red maple, paper birch, and even white pine. Beyond the cedars, the area opens up, and the boardwalk is crowded by a typical northern shrub swamp: red osier dogwood; sweetgale, which has aromatic leaves like its bayberry cousins; and Labrador tea, whose waxy, fragrant leaves often substituted for tea during the Revolutionary War. Where the marsh dries out periodically, sedges take over. At any ecotone, however, the line between plant groups can shift depending on conditions.

The ponds at Sand Point Marsh are edged with marsh herbs, black spruce, tamaracks, and alders, the latter attracting yellow-throated warblers. Crossbills congregate around spruce trees, cracking open cones with odd-shaped bills that work like nutcrackers. Black bears ramble through snacking on blueberries, and pine marten, honey-colored cat-sized weasels that live in the trees, are making a comeback. The most obvious signs of wildlife are the engineered waterways where ferns, white arums, orchids, and other plants have been munched back. These beaver-built water lanes allow the paddle-tailed rodents to cruise easily through marshes choked with vegetation.

The **Pictured Rocks** are the centerpiece of this remarkably diverse and scenic place. They are best seen by boat, and of the commercial trips offered, the last one of the day is the most spectacular, when the setting sun washes the rocks in soft light. Two hundred feet at their highest, the Pictured Rocks are sheer sandstone cliffs capped by limy sandstone, with a fringe of forest along the top. Leached out by water, copper and iron within the rock stain the cliffs blue-green and red-orange respectively. Those simple facts belie the luminous beauty of these colored bands and fanciful water-carved rock formations. Miners Castle, a jutting point of white sandstone, is tessellated like a castle, and water has hollowed its tan sandstone base in shallow caves. Farther along, great blocks of polished white rock sheared off the cliff face lie in the water like the ruins of a Greek temple. Indian Head Rock is sacred to the Chippewa, and Battleship Row resembles the in-

---

LEFT: *At rest, Lake Superior shimmers peacefully. In a storm, waves cresting at more than 30 feet pound at Pictured Rocks promontories, creating arches. The spectacular cliff face is crowned by conifers.*

domitable prows of a line of Navy flagships. Everywhere, curtains of color cascade down the rocks: white edged by sky blue, velvet browns, mossy greens, rust reds, orange-and-black stripes. Thunder Cove is splashed with mother-of-pearl pink, onyx, copper, charcoal, salmon, and a spectrum of other colors. Waterfalls spill into the lake, and natural arches span the waters.

CENTRAL U.P.: LAKESHORES, WATERFALLS, AND NORTH WOODS

From Pictured Rocks, take Routes 94 and 2 south to Thompson, then Route 149 north to **Palms Book State Park❖,** where the attraction is a huge pool called Kitch-iti-kipi (Big Springs). The largest spring-fed pool in the state, Kitch-iti-kipi is about 200 feet across and 40 feet deep. The bottom is bedded with limestone, and underground springs pour 10,000 gallons per minute through cracks in the bedrock. On a large raft, visitors can pull themselves to the middle of the pool and view the world beneath these limpid waters, resembling an enormous aquarium populated by drowned trees and large trout. Pine-rimmed shores and mossy banks complete the scene.

South onto the Garden Peninsula on Lake Michigan via Routes 183 and 483 lies **Fayette State Park❖.** Besides preserving a late-nine-teenth-century company town from the U.P.'s iron-smelting period, the park offers abundant natural beauty. Above the hook-shaped point that forms Snail Shell Harbor rise hundred-foot white limestone cliffs seemingly sculpted of marble. Behind the cliffs, forests of north-ern hardwoods and conifers cover most of the park. Trails lead through the woods to water's edge at the hook, where sandy beaches stretch along Lake Michigan's Big Bay de Noc.

Another way to see this midsection of the U.P., which is less visited than the Lake Superior side, is on foot via the **Bay de Noc–Grand Island Trail** within **Hiawatha National Forest❖,** the route followed for centuries by the Chippewa portaging canoes between Lakes Michigan and Superior. Beginning east of the town of Rapid River and 1.5 miles

---

RIGHT: *Evergreens surround a pond in Hiawatha National Forest, whose two units occupy the eastern Upper Peninsula and include forests, rivers, and the shores of three Great Lakes: Superior, Huron, and Michigan.*

north on H05 (Route 509), the trail continues north for another 40 miles across the U.P.'s narrow neck almost to Munising on the Superior lakeshore. Paralleling the Whitefish River, it passes through pines and aspens along its southern section, then winds into beech-maple forest. Heading in the same direction, Routes 41 north, 94 east, and Dorsey Road north lead to **Laughing Whitefish Falls State Scenic Site❖.** This 960-acre area centers on the lovely 30-foot falls. At the bottom, water cascades another 70 feet over thin layers of sandstone. The falls and river are surrounded by forests of hemlock and white pine, along with maples and other northern hardwoods. White cedar and black spruce occupy their usual place—the wet spot at the bottom of the falls.

After continuing west on Routes 94 and 41 to Marquette, visitors can stop along Route 550 just north of town to enjoy the **Little Presque Isle Tract❖** of Escanaba River State Forest. Once managed almost solely for timber production, public forests today reflect increasing concern for resource protection and recreation. Within Little Presque Isle's 3,000 acres lie Lake Superior beaches and Harlow Lake, as well as trails to ponds, scenic overlooks, Sugar Loaf Mountain, and the highest point of this area, Hogsback Mountain. Also within the far-flung **Escanaba River State Forest❖,** Shakey Lakes is a hard-to-reach but verdant savanna along the Menominee River.

Moose country and **Van Riper State Park❖** are about 30 miles west on Route 41, just past Champion. Geared toward recreation, the south side of Van Riper is known for walleye and northern pike fishing in Lake Michigamme. Across from the park entrance and just east of the Peshekee River, however, unpaved roads lead to hilly backcountry and lowlands scattered with lakes and bogs—perfect moose habitat.

Until mining and logging destroyed their habitat and settlers killed them for meat, moose were plentiful on the Upper Peninsula. Unlike moose, which live in deep boreal forests and wetlands, deer like forest margins, the habitat created by logging. As they moved into former moose territory, white-tailed deer brought with them brainworm, a parasite that rarely affects deer but is deadly to moose. Deer dispersed

LEFT: *Framed by tall hemlocks and delicate maples in autumn dress, lacy curtains of water plunge over Laughing Whitefish Falls, a state scenic site with one of the prettiest cascades in the Upper Peninsula.*

the parasite through the ecosystem, and as the deer population grew, moose declined.

After the forests near Van Riper recovered from the logging era, Michigan's wildlife managers decided to reintroduce moose. Beginning in 1985, in cooperation with Ontario, they trapped and air-lifted about 60 Canadian moose to the area northwest of the park. In less than five years, the moose population had tripled.

Often standing more than six feet high at the shoulder, moose spend hours up to their bellies in vegetation-clogged ponds, slurping up water lilies and other aquatic plants. The lakes and rivers around the Peshekee River are thus good places to spot these large mammals, but don't look too closely: Moose can be dangerous.

Van Riper also serves as a gateway to Michigan's most remote park, **Craig Lake State Park❖,** a few miles farther west on Route 41, then about six miles north on Craig Lake Road. Difficult to reach and full of wildlife and lakes, this North Woods wilderness centers on its namesake lake, which is rimmed by granite cliffs and dotted with a half-dozen islands. Visitors with canoes can follow marked portages connecting the main lakes.

THE KEWEENAW PENINSULA

Route 41 proceeds northwest onto the Keweenaw Peninsula. This curved spit of land, jutting into Lake Superior, resonates with history and the feel of a remote outpost of civilization. Its spine of Precambrian rock is a remnant of earth's earliest terrain, discharged from the molten center when the planet was barely formed. Flecked and occasionally loaded with copper, the peninsula was first mined by Paleo-Indians a few thousand years ago. In the 1840s, a rush of miners consumed with copper fever wrested 11 billion pounds of the metal from the Keweenaw and made the peninsula one of the most ethnically diverse places in the nation. Keweenaw copper mining eventually declined, and by 1968 the last mine had closed.

RIGHT: *Migrating hawks are often seen above Keweenaw Peninsula. The red-tailed hawk (top left) is a solitary soarer; the broad-winged hawk (bottom right) migrates in huge flocks, or kettles. The sharp-shinned hawk (top right), preys on small birds, while the larger northern goshawk (bottom left), hunts grouse, ducks, and snowshoe hares.*

Now, full of grand but often empty brick buildings, copper-boom towns languish. Handsomely flanged smelting stacks, symbols of prosperity in their fumy prime, divide the sky in silence. A sign on a store near Calumet reads "Last Place on Earth Antiques." That's wrong: The last place is about 30 miles down the road at the tip of the peninsula.

Because it protrudes into Lake Superior, the Keweenaw catches lots of lake moisture and is deluged by more than 16 feet of snow each winter. On a summer evening, however, when ducks fly low over the lake and the setting sun paints each knobby island and strand of sand in rose tones, the Keweenaw is warm and serene.

In addition to following Route 41 to land's end, two other roads present different but equally evocative views of the peninsula. As it hugs the northern coastline, Route 26 is crowded with scenic spots. Brockway Mountain Drive, which branches from Route 26 past Eagle Harbor, rises higher above sea level than any other road between the Rockies and the Appalachians. The panoramic views encompass Lake Superior; Copper Harbor, Michigan's northernmost community; and the peninsula's interior. Four small nature preserves—two coastal plant

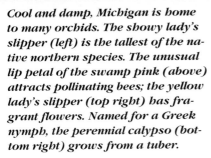

Cool and damp, Michigan is home to many orchids. The showy lady's slipper (left) is the tallest of the native northern species. The unusual lip petal of the swamp pink (above) attracts pollinating bees; the yellow lady's slipper (top right) has fragrant flowers. Named for a Greek nymph, the perennial calypso (bottom right) grows from a tuber.

refuges, the **Brockway Mountain Sanctuary,** and the **James H. Klipfel Memorial Sanctuary**—protect parcels of the peninsula's singular terrain and a number of endangered and threatened plants. Thousands of migrating hawks and other raptors follow the peninsula to land's end.

Three miles south of Copper Harbor, follow the signs about a half mile to the unassuming entrance of **Estivant Pines Sanctuary❖.** Winding through the big woods, an unmanicured trail leaves the impression that people are small, temporary visitors. Among red oaks, red maples, and paper birches, balsam scents the air, and a tangle of white cedar and black spruce fills low, wet areas. Nature is allowed to take its course here, so saplings fight their way to light, the rotting trunks of huge, fallen trees become nurse logs for future generations, and the dappled light is suffused with the color of dense greenery.

OVERLEAF: *Caribou Island is one of dozens flanking Isle Royale, a national park and the largest island in Lake Superior. Boreal forest and colorful lichens cover the ancient igneous rocks along Caribou's shore.*

177

LEFT: Moose, the largest creatures in the deer family, arrived at Isle Royale in the early 1900s. The animals thrive on vegetation found in the many ponds.

This remnant forest also harbors some of the state's oldest and largest white pines. Almost 150 feet high and half a millennium old, these stately giants soar in undisturbed, little-known grandeur at the northern edge of the nation. Noisy pileated woodpeckers, northern goshawks, black bears, and coyotes are just a few of the wild inhabitants of Estivant Pines.

ISLE ROYALE NATIONAL PARK

Copper Harbor and Houghton are Michigan's embarkation points for the boat trip to **Isle Royale National Park❖**. Covering some 500,000 acres, the park includes the main island as well as about 200 smaller ones. The largest island in Lake Superior, Isle Royale is closer to Canada but became part of the United States under the 1783 Treaty of Paris. Benjamin Franklin allegedly included the island because he believed it was rich in copper, and ancient pits indicate that copper was mined here in prehistoric times. Archaeologists estimate that Paleo-Indians extracted 500 million to 1 billion pounds of copper from pits dotting the Upper Peninsula, and nineteenth-century miners attempted copper mining on Isle Royale as well. Today the island's greatest riches are its natural beauty and pristine environment.

Isle Royale is accessible by seaplane and ferry, but the ferry does not take cars because none are allowed on the island. (Reservations are essential.) Besides a tent or cabin, the only place to stay is the national park lodge, which is usually booked early in the year. Not surprisingly, Isle Royale is one of the most remote and least visited parks

Right: *Wolves live in tightly bonded family packs in which only the head male and female breed. On Isle Royale, these predators have a closely balanced relationship with the moose population.*

in the national system. (Yellowstone has more visitors on a summer day than Isle Royale receives in a year)—a plus for those who make the effort to go.

The ferry trip takes at least four to six hours, affording ample opportunity for visitors to contemplate Lake Superior itself. Although fogs often blanket the water in morning and evening, when the sun shines and the air is still, the lake looks glassy. Despite the sun, the water, which averages 39 degrees Fahrenheit, is never warm. "Superior, it's said, never gives up its dead," reads a verse from the song "The Wreck of the Edmund Fitzgerald" by Gordon Lightfoot. Because the frigid waters do not allow gas to form, bodies that sink to the cold depths of Lake Superior stay there.

Once on Isle Royale, visitors can take reasonably priced interpretative boat trips and day hikes or backpack the 40-plus miles from **Rock Harbor Visitor Center** at the northeastern end of the island to **Windigo Visitor Center** at the southwestern tip. The island is composed of the same Archean rock that shaped the Keweenaw, and both areas are part of a thick crust of volcanic bedrock that extruded as lava, layer by molten layer, more than a billion years ago. As layers accumulated, the middle of this 50,000-foot-thick crust sagged under its own weight, creating the beginnings of a basin. Millions of years later, eroded by rivers and scraped by glaciers, this sagging syncline filled with water and became Lake Superior, its edges—Isle Royale and the Keweenaw among them—cresting above the water.

As on the Keweenaw, a bony spine called the Greenstone Ridge anchors Isle Royale. Along the island's edges, smaller islands and fjordlike bays all echo the long thin lines of Isle Royale. In the morn-

181

LEFT: *The haunting cries of the common loon, a bird that nests on unspoiled waters, echo throughout Isle Royale. A superb swimmer, the loon has powerful paddling legs set so far back that it has trouble walking.*

RIGHT: *One of four lighthouses at Isle Royale National Park, the Menagerie Island lighthouse, operated by the Coast Guard, was built in 1875 to warn sailors of the shallow water and treacherous reefs that surround the island.*

ing the island's margins are a mist-cloaked dream country where loons wail crazy, plaintive songs in the bays and black ducks and cormorants wing by, heard but only vaguely seen.

Later, when sunshine burns off the mist, a walk out to Scoville Point at the northeastern end near Rock Harbor passes through stands of paper birch, white spruce, and balsam, which yield the swampy spots to black spruce and the more than two dozen types of orchids that grow on the island. The floor of this boreal forest is bedded with large-leaved aster; bunchberry, which is a dogwood relative with creamy white flowers and autumn red berries; and pipsissewa, which has shiny evergreen leaves and pink flowers. At the other end of the island, thicker soils support maples and yellow birches.

Where the trail reaches the lakeshore, plants that grow in dry, thin soils take over. Low junipers spread across the rocks, and gray reindeer moss mingles with green-leaved blueberries to create intricate patterns of light and dark. As waves beat against the rocky, cove-etched shore and the smell of big water permeates the air, Superior seems more ocean than lake.

Isle Royale makes a perfect natural laboratory, a self-contained system that allows scientists to study the workings of an ecosystem. Recognized as an International Biosphere Reserve, Isle Royale is the site of the longest continuous mammal study in America, focusing on the balance between moose and wolves. When copper prospectors arrived in the mid-1800s, woodland caribou, lynx, and coyotes lived here, but moose and wolves did not. The caribou were probably hunted out by prospectors, and moose may have swum over from Canada in the early

1900s. A few decades later, in about 1949, timber wolves crossed from Canada on an ice bridge and flourished, preying on the moose and providing an ecological balance.

Yew and mountain ash flourished in the substory before the arrival of the moose, which ate the plants to extirpation; thimbleberry and large-leaved aster have since taken their place. Beavers have helped the moose population by creating more ponds, thus providing more pond vegetation, the mainstay of the *Alces alces* diet. With no predators, the moose population exploded to 3,000 by the 1930s. Having exceeded their food supply, they began starving to death and were down to 200 animals within a decade. Now wolves help keep the moose population in check by culling the weak and the old. Although wolves avoid humans and are rarely seen, moose can often be found at the natural salt lick at Hidden Lake. There visitors may encounter moose but are more likely to find rare orchids, irises, and higher up, fine views of Canada.

WESTERN U.P.: THE PORCUPINE RANGE

Back on the mainland, travel southwest to Ontonagon and then take Routes 64 and 107 to **Porcupine Mountains Wilderness State Park❖,** at 63,000 acres Michigan's largest by far. The park is the country as it was, the way the Chippewa and earlier people experienced it. Few other places in the Great Lakes area—actually the whole Midwest—are so wild or so big. To the Chippewa, who named them, the mountains looked like the rounded backs of crouching porcupines covered with quills. Supporting one of America's most extensive old-growth hardwood forests, the Porkies are among the handful of true mountain ranges between the Appalachians and the Rockies.

Sugar maple, basswood, and yellow birch form the dominant community, and large stands of hemlock and white pine cover the slopes. Sometimes called the Asbestos Forest, the Porcupines rarely burn extensively because the land is too cold and wet. Instead, they experience massive blowdowns, such as the ten million board feet of timber that a tornado once leveled.

Viewpoints at Lake of the Clouds and Summit Peak display the big picture. Seen from the top of a 1,300-foot escarpment, **Lake of the Clouds,** one of the most celebrated scenic spots in the state, is a sapphire set in emerald forests. Chockablock with volcanic and conglomerate rock, the escarpment is backed by a forest of pygmy maples that eke out a meager living in the thin soils. Far below, the Big Carp River offers a fine destination as it cuts a serpentine path through the trees.

The view from the Summit Peak tower provides an even better sense of the breadth and remoteness of the Porkies and the great inland sea they border. On exceptionally clear days, Wisconsin's Apostle Islands are visible to the southwest. Having seen the park from above, visitors can immerse themselves in it by following trails that lead to Lily Pond. In summer and fall, mushrooms in fluorescent yellows and reds edge the forest floor, and sugar maple shades the ferns and wildflowers. Yellow birch—its curls of peeling bark polished the color of old, yellowed satin—adds its distinctive elegance.

ABOVE: In winter the porcupine, a vegetarian, eats tree cambium and antlers, such as this set shed by an elk.
BELOW: Plentiful in the Porcupine Mountains, wary black bear cubs quickly learn to climb trees to avoid danger.

Ringed by balsam spires and towering white pine, Lily Pond and its surrounding marshes probably look as they did thousands of years ago. Sedges, grasses, cattails, pink swamp milkweed, and orchids crowd the fringes of beaver waterways and ponds. Creamy white water lilies float below a perfectly arced beaver dam, and only the plucked banjo-string sounds of green frogs engaged in desultory chorus break the silence.

OVERLEAF: A 1,300-foot escarpment overlooks the Big Carp River in Porcupine Mountains Wilderness State Park, a spectacularly scenic area with the region's largest forests and highest mountains.

185

ABOVE: *Bigtooth aspens and other trees flank more than 26 miles of Lake Superior shoreline in the Porcupine Mountains. About a dozen rivers*

Besides beavers, the Porcupine Mountains are home to plenty of black bears and deer, as well as fishers. Members of the weasel family, fishers are larger, darker versions of marten and one of the few animals that hunt porcupines successfully. Except for their hold in the Porkies, fishers had all but disappeared in Michigan, but with protection they are making a comeback.

The Lake Superior Trail parallels the park's 26-plus miles of shoreline, affording splendid views of Lake Superior and its shorebirds. The trail passes the park's Presque Isle River, a salmon and steelhead stream shaded by hemlocks, birches, and maples. As it rushes toward Lake Superior, the river tumbles over ledges of volcanic rock stacked like Scrabble tiles—the hard, upturned edges of the Lake Superior basin. The geologic events that formed the basin created dancing waterfalls and sinuous water-carved rock hollows near the river's mouth.

About 35 miles southeast, Route 2, a thin ribbon of highway dividing the endless forests of the far north, leads to the **Sylvania Wilderness❖** within **Ottawa National Forest❖** (the entrance is a couple of miles west of Watersmeet on Route 535). Because the Sylvania section is designated national wilderness, motorized traffic is

drain into the icy lake, including the exquisite Presque Isle, whose tannin-dark waters cut intricate patterns in the surrounding Nonesuch shale.

---

allowed along only a few roads that provide access to camping, and motorboats are permitted on only 2 of the national forest's 36 lakes.

In the wilderness, the only sounds are wildlife, wind, water lapping the shores, and the slap of a big fish breaking the surface. Because portages connect many of the lakes, one of the best ways to see the Sylvania Tract is by canoe, slicing quietly through still waters as the early morning mist lifts and bass, northern pike, and lake trout glide beneath. Outfitters in Watersmeet can provide canoes.

Needle-springy hiking trails are lined by red and white pines and an array of fungi: eggshell-colored shelf fungi, crimson amanitas, dark red cones of hygrophorous, and bright yellow bolete globes. Club mosses whorl over the ground, mimicking the needled look of the pines, and sunny tracks are splashed with daisies, goldenrod, buttercups, and orange jewelweed. In damper areas, maple, yellow birch, and hemlock soar in dim, primeval forests, as Indian pipes, bluebead lilies, bunchberry, Canada mayflowers, starflowers, and other wildflowers hug the ground of the open understory. Here and there, the trunks of old trees are riddled with the holes of yellow-bellied sapsuckers. And rivulets, dark with tannin, shine like strands of garnet in the patchy sunlight.

WISCONSIN

PART FOUR

W I S C O N S I N

T he last great ice age was named for Wisconsin because the deposits of that ice age were first understood in that state. The results of those mile-high glaciers are everywhere. In the far north, where thick forests blanket the land, thousands of lakes fill low spots left by the retreating ice. Of the 15,000 lakes beading Wisconsin, most are in the upper third of the state, the Northern Highlands, which boasts one of the highest concentrations of lakes in the world. The Northern Highlands is also etched by river upon wild river: the Pine, Popple, Peshtigo, Wolf, Brule, Bois Brule, Flambeau, Namekagon—some of the finest watercourses in the North Woods. The state's name, in fact, comes from the Winnebago word *ouisconsin,* which means "where waters meet."

Southeastern Wisconsin could be an ice-age textbook, so filled is it with glacial signatures: moraines resembling foothills stretch for miles; pyramidal kames rise like ziggurats in flat fields; skinny, snaking eskers loop through dairy farms; and potbellied kettle-hole lakes pock the terrain. Only about 12,000 years old, these relatively recent glacial features are so numerous and distinctive that the National Park Service's Ice Age National Scientific Reserve is located here.

Part of Wisconsin was not touched by the glaciers: a broad band at the western edge of the state paralleling the Mississippi River. Called the Driftless Area because no glacial drift (rock debris) covers its surface, it is full of deep valleys and bold bluffs and contains most of Wisconsin's remnant tallgrass prairie. At the center of the state, the glaciated and the driftless areas converge in a region full of glacially created wetlands, including the largest cattail marsh in the country. Here too are tracts of dry, sandy prairie more often associated with desertlike environments than with forested Wisconsin.

The state is bordered by big water on all but its southern edge,

---

PRECEDING PAGES: *Potato River Falls is one of many cascades in the lake-dotted vastness of Wisconsin's Chequamegon National Forest.*

where it meets Illinois. Lake Michigan washes its eastern shores, Lake Superior and Michigan's Upper Peninsula define its northern boundaries, and the great Saint Croix–Mississippi river system etches its western edge. One of Wisconsin's most distinctive geographic features is a thin needle of hard dolomite limestone—Door Peninsula—that thrusts into Lake Michigan, creating Green Bay.

Wisconsin is full of Native American and French place names: Chequamegon, Menominee, Peshtigo, Nicolet, Fond du Lac, Roche-a-Cri. Before the French fur traders and blackrobes—as the Jesuit missionaries were known—came, the Winnebago, Menominee, and people of other tribes fished the rivers and the lakes and gathered wild rice in the wetlands. In the early 1600s the French began building their presence in the New World. Because they were seeking a passage to the Far East, one of the first areas they explored was the western Great Lakes. Following Native American routes, the French journeyed through Lakes Huron, Michigan, and Superior, down into Wisconsin, and onto the Mississippi River. River highways, such as the Brule and Namekagon, then allowed voyageurs to reap riches exporting beaver pelts to Europe.

After statehood in 1848, people of German, Scandinavian, and other ancestries began populating the area. The southern part of the state was cleared for dairy farming, and the north became the domain of loggers. As in Michigan, Wisconsin's great white pine forests were leveled. From 1900 to 1905, Wisconsin led the nation in timber production.

By contrast, in this century Wisconsin has pioneered a progressive attitude toward conservation. Although much has disappeared, Wisconsin remains rich in rivers, lakes, forests, and other natural resources, which are as prized as the pelts and timber once were. America's conservation ethic was born here. Aldo Leopold and John Muir, two of the nation's first and finest protectors of the wild, lived in Wisconsin, and the state was one of the first to establish a park system. In 1951, Wisconsin had the vision to inaugurate the nation's first natural areas program, which preserves 200 pristine natural regions.

Most important, the state's natural splendors—copper-colored waterfalls thundering through granite canyons shaded by towering evergreens, wolves and moose roaming boreal forests, bald eagles circling wetlands and fish-filled lakes—remain for future generations in Wisconsin's broad spectrum of protected places.

NORTHWESTERN WISCONSIN

Q uintessential North Woods country, the northern tier of Wisconsin shelters vast forests, wild, rushing rivers, sylvan lakes, and a fine roster of wildlife including eagles, beavers, loons, and even wolves. Boreal forests like those that lay at the feet of ice-age glaciers cap the state's far northwestern corner and line Lake Superior. Emptying into the Great Lake, classic voyageurs' rivers create great clouds of mist as cold, tumbling waters meet the still-colder waters of Superior. Just before their confluence with Lake Superior, these rivers plunge over ledges in spectacularly scenic waterfalls: Copper and Amnicon falls, the Brule Cascades, and others.

In the Northern Highlands, which form the top third of the state, glaciers left a bumpy landscape of hummocks and meltwater-filled depressions. Kettle-hole lakes formed where huge chunks of glacial ice, embedded in glacial debris, melted, leaving deep, circular indentations. The thousands of lakes riddling the Northern Highlands—home to walleye, northern pike, and the prized native muskellunge, the marlin of the Midwest—make it the densest lake area of the world.

When lakes are not replenished by springs and streams, they often develop into marshes and shrub swamps that in turn fill in to become

---

LEFT: *Icy fingers clutch shoreline cliffs in the Apostle Islands when Lake Superior freezes in winter. Even in summer, a swimmer without a wetsuit can die within about 20 minutes in the 40-degree-Fahrenheit water.*

forests. Most of the Northern Highlands is forested with yellow birch, maple, and other northern hardwoods mixed with stands of conifers. Distinguishing so many conifers can be difficult. Briefly, if the conifer rises straight and clean for the first 50 to 100 feet before branching out, and its bark is black and deeply furrowed, it is white pine. Even if the tree is smaller and its lineage unclear, five needles in a cluster make it a white pine. Red and jack pine each have two-needled bundles, and jack pine, a pioneer tree, is likely to grow in the scruffiest, most nutrient-deficient soil. Spruce needles are four-sided; needles less than a half-inch-long belong to black spruce, more than a half-inch to white spruce. More important, white spruce hugs higher, drier ground, while black spruce inhabits swamps. Like all true firs, each aromatic balsam needle has two white lines along its underside. The scalelike needles of white cedar grow in fan-shaped sprays. Deciduous tamarack needles form light gray-green tufts along the branches, and hemlocks are dark—almost black-green—with lacy foliage.

Drier than the Highlands, western Wisconsin harbors most of the state's remnant prairies. The western section is also known as the Driftless Area because it has never been covered by glacial drift or debris, and never crushed by deep seas of ice. Its ancient topography is full of bluffs, ridges, and eroded, incised valleys. At the western edge of the state, bluffs line the broad Mississippi River and its floodplain. Where soil has managed to cover rock outcrops, ferny forests and vertical prairies cling to the sides of the bluffs. Vistas are long and broad to match the river.

To explore northwestern Wisconsin, an area north of the rough diagonal formed by the Wisconsin River as it bisects the state, this chapter begins across from Michigan's Upper Peninsula, heads west along the Lake Superior shoreline, and turns south beside the Saint Croix and Mississippi rivers. Near Prairie du Chien, the confluence of the Mississippi and Wisconsin rivers, the route follows the Wisconsin east and north.

NICOLET NATIONAL FOREST AND ENVIRONS

Spread over nearly 700,000 acres in the northeastern corner of the state, **Nicolet National Forest❖** is named for one of the most famous French explorers. Setting out from Quebec in 1634, at the request of

NORTHWESTERN WISCONSIN

25   0   25 Miles

25   0   25 Kilometers

ABOVE: *Cathedral of the Pines, a stand of stately trees in Nicolet National Forest, is one of the few virgin pine forests in Wisconsin to have survived the logging era.*
LEFT: *Martens live in trees of northern forests. Highly prized for their fur, they were nearly extirpated in Wisconsin but have now been reintroduced to Nicolet.*

Governor Samuel de Champlain, Jean Nicolet made his way across Lake Superior in search of the Orient and its riches. At the head of Green Bay, thinking he had reached his destination, Nicolet donned a Chinese damask robe brought for the occasion and went to meet Winnebago chiefs.

Within the national forest are the headwaters of some of the state's wildest rivers. The Pine, Popple, Peshtigo, Brule, Oconto, and Wolf all begin in this "cradle of rivers." Nicolet's moist forests are even the birthplace of the Wisconsin River, which swells to impressive width as it travels southwest to meet the Mississippi.

Near the southern end of Nicolet is **Cathedral of the Pines,** off Route 32 just west of Lakewood via Archibald Lake Road (Forest Road 2121) and Cathedral Drive. (Forest roads are often unpaved, and a good map is advisable.) In this "cathedral," the soaring pines block sunlight except for dramatic, slanting rays that spotlight portions of a forest floor thickly carpeted with needles. Entering Cathedral of the Pines is more like entering a lost world than a house of worship be-

cause the area teems with seeming latter-day pterodactyls. In this great blue heron rookery, two or three huge nests sit high in each pine. Crawking raucously and clacking their bony bills, the adult herons flap between trees, their attenuated bodies and reptilian heads confirming their common lineage with dinosaurs. Toward the end of the summer, when heron babies become fledglings, the noise is astonishing. Despite the racket, visitors should remember that this is a nursery and should be respected.

North on Route 32 and east along Route 8, about two miles short of Route U, a decent but unimproved road leads a couple of miles north to **Dunbar Barrens State Natural Area❖.** Just east of Nicolet National Forest, this area offers a total contrast to Nicolet's damp green forests. At Dunbar Barrens, jack pine, oak, and aspen—plants that tolerate drier, well-drained soils—form an open forest on the rolling outwash plain. Pine barrens are just part of the picture: Much of Dunbar presents the broad vistas and low grasses and sedges of a dry prairie—an unusual ecosystem in this part of Wisconsin. Sandpipers, eastern bluebirds, and other species not found in a forest flit among wild blueberries and sweet fern—an intriguing mix in an unexpected spot.

Head northwest on Route 32 toward Three Lakes. Nearly 10 miles beyond Hiles, Scott Lake Road (Forest Road 2183) leads east 3.5 miles to a small parking area for **Scott Lake–Shelp Lake Natural Area❖.** A trail and boardwalk allow visitors to see a variety of communities, from northern mesic forests to sedge meadows and bogs. A bog mat rims

LEFT: *The strikingly colored eastern black swallowtail is distinguished by its large wings and a long tail; it avoids woodlands, preferring the streams, meadows, and open spaces in Nicolet National Forest.*

part of Shelp Lake, whose shallow, mucky bottom makes a good home for water lilies.

One-quarter mile north of Scott Lake Road along Route 32, Forest Road 2178 traces a 4,000-year-old route that prehistoric people followed from the northern shores of Lake Michigan to the tip of Michigan's Keweenaw Peninsula. This **Heritage Drive Scenic Byway** was favored by Native Americans, French fur traders, and later the U.S. Postal Service because it is one of the few relatively high and dry routes in this exceptionally wet land. The curving, leisurely road displays and interprets classic Nicolet forest features so strikingly that cars are frequently outpaced by big yellow-and-black swallowtail butterflies.

Heritage Drive also leads to a typical collection of North Woods trees along the **Sam Campbell Memorial Trail,** on Old Military Road (Forest Road 2207). The Sam Campbell Trail slopes downward, past red and jack pines, red oaks, red maples, and others to a quiet, mossy bog where land and water are difficult to distinguish. Black spruces rise from the soup surrounded by soft, thick mats of bright green sphagnum moss. The sphagnum mats ripple over the entire floor of the bog, their luminescent, plushy green brightening the dark spruces and subdued tamaracks. Bunchberry and ferns crowd the edges of the bog, a copper butterfly flits lazily above, and dragonflies add their hypnotic drone. Beyond lie a cedar swamp and Four Mile Lake.

Also in Nicolet National Forest—a few miles south of where Route 55 crosses Route 70 near the town of Alvin—is a put-in point for the **Pine River,** a designated wild river best run in the spring. (The Florence County Chamber of Commerce can provide information about canoe liveries.) The Pine runs through deep forest, plunges down rapids, and entails a couple of portages. Pine trees and aspens line the

RIGHT: *Orange hawkweed carpets Wisconsin meadows. Its other common name, devil's paintbrush, is more apt, however, because this European invader is pushing out less aggressive native plants.*

banks, wildlife frequent the river, and trout cruise beneath its surface. Occasionally the watercourse is bordered by marshy wetlands and beaver-dam ponds. Pushed out during the logging era, pine marten and fishers have been reintroduced and have successfully reestablished themselves in Nicolet.

From Eagle River, take Routes 70, 155 north, and N west to **Northern Highland–American Legion State Forest❖.** So many lakes line the roads that these routes seem more like dikes than terra firma. Because the state forest is a checkerboard of private and public lands, a variety of cabins, fishing camps, backwoods vacation homes, and even rustic resorts dot the banks of some of the area's lakes. Punctuating the glittering lakes are dense forests of northern hardwoods and conifers.

West of Sayner, Route N leads to the parking area for Fallison Lake Nature Trail, whose sights graphically display the evolution from water to land that has been taking place over millennia in the Northern Highlands. Surrounded by forest, Fallison Lake's clear, quiet waters shine, but sedges and shrubs are filling in nearby smaller ponds. In some areas, the trail becomes a boardwalk through a shrub swamp that once was open water like Fallison Lake. These shrub swamps are dense with bog rosemary and bog laurel, whose evergreen leaves and pretty pink-and-white blossoms create a natural flower garden. On higher ground, evergreen pines complement dramatic white-barked paper birch. Here young balsams, drenched by sun, grow so full and fat that they are called double balsams. Another Highlands area, **Plum Lake Hemlock Forest State Natural Area,** off Hook Road from Route N near Sayner, protects one of the largest remaining stands of old-growth trees in the state.

LEFT: *Female loons lay two eggs in their lakeside nests. Parents carry the chicks on their backs, which protects the young from predators and conserves heat.* RIGHT: *This marshy mix of cattails and tamarack in the Northern Highland forest was probably a glacial kettle-hole lake that slowly filled in.*

The best way to experience this land of lakes is to find one and settle next to it. In pools cloaked by water lilies and edged by blue-flowered pickerelweed, loons pierce the early morning darkness with their quavering, plaintive cries. During the day, one of a mated pair sits on eggs in a waterside nest while the other fishes. Later, babies ride on their parents' backs as they paddle these relatively shallow lakes. Loons appear only in pristine places because they do not tolerate development or polluted waters. These birds of the north are also the oldest bird species extant: Their six-foot-long ancestors lived during the age of dinosaurs.

Another bird—the bald eagle—rules the skies. Vilas County boasts one of the highest concentrations of eagles in the nation, and visitors often see one, two, even a trio soaring and wheeling across the sky. Submerged among aquatic plants, tiger muskies grow to 20-plus pounds. Beavers shape the water world with their dams, creating more shallows for herons to fish, as otters do the backstroke in the lakes and muskrat paddle near the banks. To see this world alive with wildlife requires nothing more than a canoe, a rowboat, or a secluded spot along the shore.

THE FLAMBEAU RIVER AND CHEQUAMEGON NATIONAL FOREST

Back on Route 70, continue west about 45 miles to **Flambeau River State Forest❖.** From a put-in point at Nine-Mile Landing on Route 70, a few miles west of Fifield, the North Fork of the Flambeau meanders southeast with just enough rapids to make the river lively and placid stretches to allow boaters to spot wildlife or simply soak in the quiet. Winding through the forest are more than 20 miles of hiking and cross-country ski trails.

ABOVE: *The setting sun burnishes a still Lake of the Falls in the Turtle-Flambeau Flowage. The French brought the appellation* flambeau *to the region because they saw Chippewa night fishing with the aid of torches.*

Farther west on Route 70 just beyond Loretta, take Route B northwest to Hayward and turn east onto Route 77 into **Chequamegon National Forest❖**. Chequamegon, Chippewa for "place of shallow water," is the name of the bay on Lake Superior stretching north from the town of Ashland. The national forest covers huge swaths of northern Wisconsin, its more than 850,000 acres generally hillier and drier than Nicolet, Wisconsin's other national forest. A good overview is provided by the Great Divide Scenic Byway: Route 77 between Hayward and Glidden, a drive especially colorful in autumn.

These woods are reminiscent of a Russian fairy tale. Bathed in distinctly northern light, the scenic byway is bordered by maple, aspen, and balsam fir, whose dark, layered skirts are trimmed with light new growth. Mukwanago Lake, just off the highway a few miles east of Route A, is a kettle-hole lake that is slowly filling in and becoming bog. On the east side of the lake, drier ridges support pine. Beavers gnaw lakeside aspens, their favorite trees, within sight of their dam. Seductive in its strangeness, bog flora fringes the lake.

Thick mats of sphagnum peat moss fill much of the bog, the living mat lying atop layers of dead peat. Sphagnum binds the bog's nutrients, creating an acid environment in the cold waters where little besides it can live. And because nothing rots in these sterile, nutrient-

204

ABOVE: *In autumn, Penokee Overlook provides a colorful view of Chequamegon's overarching forests. The rolling hills of the iron-rich Penokee-Gogebic Range were four miles high before glacial leveling.*

poor waters, sphagnum bogs, which lay at the margins of ice-age glaciers, contain embalmed mastodons and other animals from those times. Native Americans made the sterile peat moss into the first disposable diapers, and in World War II it was used as dressings for wounds. Forced to adapt ways of obtaining nutrients, the pitcher plants, sundews, and other carnivorous plants in Mukwanago's bogs lure and trap insects and then devour them with powerful chemicals.

Continue traveling east on 77 and take the next road going north, Forest Road 203. After 6.2 miles on this gravel road, turn south on Forest Road 622, which leads in a third of a mile to the **Lynch Creek Waterfowl Area❖.** Here a viewing platform and a short trail allow visitors to watch mallard and wood ducks, kingfishers and herons, and other of Chequamegon's more than 200 bird species. Otters and deer may also appear.

At the town of Clam Lake, about ten miles farther east on Route 77, veer onto Route GG north to pass the McCarthy Lake area, where one of the forest's four timber wolf packs makes its home. Maintaining one of the most tight-knit social systems of any mammal, wolves have suffered from an undeserved reputation. Until the mid-1900s wolves were slaughtered to near extirpation in the contiguous United States, partly to safeguard livestock. Now protected within the few northern states where

205

they are slowly making a comeback, these endangered canids are helping to control deer populations. Chequamegon also harbors marten,
beavers, fishers, gray and red squirrels, ruffed grouse, and numerous
black bears. Glidden, in fact, bills itself as the Bear Capital of the World.

Four miles short of Mellen on Route GG is a turnout for the Penokee
Overlook. From the viewing platform, visitors looking north can see the
Penokee-Gogebic Range, among the oldest on earth and still filled with
quantities of iron ore. This range is the Great Divide that separates the
waters flowing into the Great Lakes from those flowing into the Saint
Croix–Mississippi river system. The forests stretching beyond the Penokee Overlook are a continuation of the vast timbered lands visible from
the Upper Peninsula's Porcupine Mountains.

Although now low and wooded, these mountains would have ri-
valed the Alps 1.6 billion years ago. After the great Penokee-Gogebic
orogeny, wind and water immediately began scouring down the
range, which once reached as far east as New York. Later the mountains were covered by layers of sandstone and limestone, which were
totally eroded over time, allowing the gently rolling remains of the
once-mighty mountains to reappear.

Just behind the viewing platform, a series of looped trails offer fine
hiking in summer—with insect repellent—or skiing in winter. Penokee forest paths cross the nationally designated **North Country Trail,**
which stretches 3,200 miles from New York to North Dakota and includes 60 miles within Chequamegon National Forest.

LAKE SUPERIOR COUNTRY AND THE APOSTLE ISLANDS
Copper Falls State Park❖, two miles northeast of Mellen on Route
169, showcases the state's most spectacular waterfalls. Loop trails
allow visitors to view the Bad River and Tyler's Fork of the Bad River,
which meet within the park, as they tumble over rock in Copper Falls,
Brownstone Falls, Tyler's Fork Cascades, and Red Granite Falls.

Like other waterfalls around the Great Lake, these result from the
Lake Superior syncline, the great bowl that contains the lake. The syncline was formed in Precambrian times, when lava oozed out in
sheets roughly ten miles thick. Its extreme weight caused the lava bed
to sag in the middle and the edges to tilt upward. Over succeeding
millennia, rock overlaid the lava and was eroded away. Lava is not

ABOVE: *The Apostle Islands attract eastern bluebirds, now rare due to competition from aggressive nonnative starlings.*

LEFT: *The Apostles' wet meadows harbor delicate prairie white fringed orchids, natives of the Great Lakes region.*

ABOVE: *Ground-dwelling, low-flying eastern meadowlarks trill melodiously from Outer Island's meadows.*

RIGHT: *Round-leaved sundews in the Apostles' bogs feed on insects attracted to their sticky, red hairs.*

easily eroded, so when rivers hit the ancient ledges of the sloping syncline, waterfalls are born.

Because it follows a fault, making erosion easier, the Bad River has carved a deeper canyon than Tyler's Fork, which runs counter to the fault. Devil's Gate, which forms a narrow waist on the Bad River, is chunky with conglomerate rock. All this geology creates scenic splendor: Tints and textures of black lava, red lava, sandstone, and peanut-brittle conglomerate form a backdrop for rippling cascades and thundering falls—equally dramatic in winter—colored copper by minerals and organic material.

The dark, heavily forested slopes are cloaked with maples, spruces, big-tooth aspens, yellow birches, hop hornbeams (whose wood is hard enough to break an ax), and hazelnuts near the river. Myriad wildflowers include wintergreen, bunchberry, delicate whorls of cucumber root, and bluebead lilies, whose fat oval leaves are topped by a stalk of fringed yellow flowers in summer and large blue berries in fall. Chiding chickadees and drumming woodpeckers are only the most obvious birds.

Bayfield on Lake Superior, the appealing town that is the embarkation point for **Big Bay State Park❖,** lies some 40 miles north of Copper Falls on Route 13. Car ferries cross regularly between Bayfield and Madeline Island, once a flourishing fur-trading center. At 14 miles long and 3 miles wide, Madeline is the largest in the 22-island Apostle Islands archipelago and the only one not included in Apostle Islands National Lakeshore. From the island town of La Pointe, Big Bay State Park is about seven miles east.

The park's long, curving sand beach is a perfect spot to contemplate the deep-blue beauty and oceanlike power of Lake Superior, the world's largest freshwater lake. Beyond the picnic area, a trail loops out to rocky ledges where lashing waves have eroded sea caves in the sandstone. Also within the park, sphagnum-sedge quaking bogs make the 120-acre **Bog State Natural Area** one of the best in the region. The succession from beach grass to heath to juniper-covered barrens and shrub-bordered lagoon makes an interesting botanical journey.

In autumn, the lake helps moderate temperatures, reds and yellows color the forest, and the beaches are quiet. In winter, when Lake Superior freezes around most of the Apostle Islands, the two-mile section between Bayfield and La Pointe is the only municipally maintained ice route in the nation.

Bayfield is also the jumping-off point for **Apostle Islands National Lakeshore❖.** At the Apostle Islands Visitor Center in town, travelers can decide which islands to visit (no cars are permitted) and choose from a variety of boat trips, from excursions to water taxis. High spots that remained after ice-age glaciers retreated, the Apostles are scattered at this edge of the vast lake like low green loaves, each slightly different from the others.

Stockton, the largest of the lakeshore's islands, welcomes visitors with a broad, quiet bay near red sandstone ledges where water cascades in crystal veils. Six thousand years ago Stockton was two islands, but currents piled sand between the big and little islands, eventually connecting them by a sandbar called a tombolo. Pines with blueberries, pink lady's slippers, and wintergreen at their feet have colonized one side of the tombolo, and the middle of this sand bridge features a sunny bog full of wild cranberry and tadpoles, one of the Apostles' six frog species. The rest of the island is etched by tannin-dark streams and covered by northern hardwoods and hemlocks. Berries and fish in its small lake make Stockton a fine place for black bears, which are rarely spotted.

The sweeping beach on easternmost Outer Island attracts birds migrating south for the winter. Exhausted by their flight across Lake Superior from Canada, birds fall out here and become easy pickings for peregrine falcons and other raptors. Even between migrations, Outer Island is alive with birds: meadowlarks, brown thrashers, kingbirds, and sleek cedar waxwings flitting among the branches of tall, gnarled pines. The wetland area attracts green-winged teal, red-winged blackbirds, and others. On the island, the slight lap of waves, birdsong, and the deep, banjo-string plunk of a green frog are the only sounds.

Most of the Apostles have individual distinctions. Tiny Gull and Eagle islands support the area's largest herring gull breeding populations. Protected from loggers, Raspberry Island retains its stands of virgin forest, as well as a picturesque lighthouse. The northernmost point in Wiscon-

---

OVERLEAF: *With Rocky Island foremost, this aerial view looking toward the Wisconsin mainland includes a half dozen of Apostle Lakeshore's 21 islands, which range from 3-acre Gull to 10,000-acre Stockton.*

sin and the most exposed to Lake Superior's twin furies of wind and wave, Devils Island supports rare arctic plants and displays perhaps the state's best example of boreal vegetation: white cedar, white pine, black and white spruce, and spiky lines of balsam fir fronted by gray-green pillows of reindeer moss dotted with red-berried wintergreen.

Arctic plants—the squat buttery leaves of butterwort, the nodding purple flowers of bird's-eye primrose, and a variety of rare sedges— cling to Devils Island's north-facing cliffs. The island got its name because even on a merely brisk day, Lake Superior pounds furiously against the cliffs, and the noise during storms is so tremendous that early visitors claimed it was the devil's noise. (Others hold that Native Americans attributed the clamor to evil spirits.) Over thousands of years, the crashing waters have carved a series of incomparable sea caves in the cliffs. On calm days, sea kayakers paddle out to explore these exquisite recesses, some resembling arched flying buttresses, some smooth, open maws—all sculpted and polished by water.

Lake Superior is central to a sense of the Apostles. In shallows near the islands, the lake water is so clear that polished pebbles 13 feet down are visible. From afar, light refracting off lake mist can elongate an island or create ghost islands. Early maps reflect this trick, showing

of its tranquil winter moods. In the 1800s similar sandstone cliffs near the park were quarried for the Midwest's "brownstone" buildings.

many more islands than actually exist. Loons and otters roam the relatively protected cobalt-colored interisland waters, where cormorants, their heads held high in cocktail-party attitudes, are also common. Lake trout, herring, lake sturgeon, northern pike, salmon, whitefish, and perch swim below.

LAKE SUPERIOR TO THE SAINT CROIX

Follow Route 13 west along the Superior lakeshore, then head south on Routes H and 27 through the **Brule River State Forest.** (Boats can put in at Winneboujou or upstream at Stone's Bridge, and a canoe livery is in Brule.) For centuries, Native Americans used the Brule as a link between Lake Superior and the Mississippi River. In 1680, Daniel Greysolon, Sieur du Lhut, was the first Frenchman to make this journey (Duluth, Minnesota, preserves his name).

A historic marker on Route A at the north end of Saint Croix Lake marks the beginning of the short but historic trail that served as a portage between the Brule and Saint Croix rivers. Although the Saint Croix runs southwest to the Mississippi and the Brule runs north to Lake Superior, both begin in a coniferous bog north of Saint Croix Lake.

Neither big nor boisterous, the Brule is an absolutely classy water-

213

ABOVE: *Small and shy, the red fox was imported from England in the 1700s as a better quarry for sportsmen; it is believed to have interbred with native species.*

RIGHT: *Bald eagles and ospreys nest and fish along the Brule River; its dark waters were plied by voyageurs traveling from Lake Superior to the Mississippi River.*

way from beginning to end and one of the best fishing rivers east of the Mississippi. Five presidents—Ulysses S. Grant, Grover Cleveland, Calvin Coolidge, Herbert Hoover, and Dwight Eisenhower—came here to fish for trout and absorb the North Woods calm.

At Stone's Bridge, the river flows through an outstanding conifer bog, parts of which are preserved as a state natural area. White cedar, spruce, and shrubs attract golden-crowned kinglets, saw-whet owls, black-backed woodpeckers, and a host of more common birds, and strewn through the woods bordering the Brule are red baneberry, Canada mayflower, and the bright violet blossoms of fringed polygala.

Most of the way, the Brule flows smoothly, parting boreal forest banked with blue forget-me-nots and passing alder thickets, cattail beds, and a few rustic cabins. The eagles and ospreys that nest along the river glide overhead in search of a fish dinner. Caribou disappeared and moose declined with widespread logging, but deer now abound in the second-growth forests. Campers may also hear the cries of bobcat or the drumming of grouse.

Just above Route FF, the river begins dropping in rapids: 328 feet over the next 19 miles through tree-rimmed chasms to the mouth of Lake Superior. At the Ledges, the river slides over tilted rock like a ride at an amusement park. Where it pours into Lake Superior, the Brule slows and widens, rippling over sandbars to a soft conclusion where Route 13 becomes Brule River Road.

From Route 13, Route P south and 2 west lead to **Amnicon Falls State Park❖,** southeast of Duluth, Minnesota. Here a sparkling display of linked cascades and three waterfalls curves around rocky points and foams over ledges, making the Amnicon River one of the loveliest

ABOVE: *Plants and wildlife of the prairie and bog abound at Crex Meadows. Settlers tried to drain this fertile area but the wetlands endure.*

watercourses in the Midwest. The watershed is also an important spawning ground for steelhead and coho and harbors northwest Wisconsin's only native muskellunge.

Big Manitou Falls, the highest in the state, plunges 165 feet at **Pattison State Park❖,** about 10 miles southwest on Route 35. Having cut its way through basalt, the Black River cascades over a lip of harder basalt in a thundering rush. Tall evergreen white cedars frame the falls in a lush tableau. Pattison is popular in summer because the river has been dammed above the falls, creating a lake and beach at one end and marshes farther south. Visitors can avoid the crowds and see wilder areas by following the interesting signs marking the nature or hiking trails in the southeastern part of the park. Hazelnut, musclewood, and other substory trees grow beneath a canopy of yellow birch, basswood, maple, and white spruce, and the forest floor is green with club mosses, tall ferns, bluebead lilies, and huge patches of large-leaved aster. One of 250 species of asters in North America, large-leaved asters almost always grow in large colonies because their roots exude a plant-inhibiting antibiotic that kills other vegetation. Asters even compete with themselves, consuming so much energy that they seldom flower. When they do, they produce lovely loose masses of purple daisies.

About 50 miles south of Pattison, Route 70 heads west to Route F, which turns north through Grantsburg to the intersection of Route D. At **Crex Meadows Wildlife Area❖,** far-reaching marshes and prairies attract huge numbers of waterfowl and a wide variety of prairie flow-

ABOVE RIGHT: *A vocal denizen of Crex Meadows, a yellow-headed black-bird straddles two cattails to get an overview of its marshy domain.*

ers: More than 200 prairie plant species live here, and nearly 250 bird species nest in or visit Crex Meadows. These wetlands were formed some 10,000 years ago when the lobe of a glacier blocked the Saint Croix River and created a large shallow glacial lake. Eventually the lake drained, leaving marshes and wet sedge meadows. The name Crex probably derives from the taxonomic name for sedge, *carex.*

An informative self-guided auto tour is a good way to see this interweaving of ponds, wet meadows, and upland prairies. Mid- to late summer is the best time to see blooming prairie plants. On their great wings, blue herons ascend from marshes filled with extravagant blue-flag irises. Terns, green-winged teal, a surprising number of wood ducks, and yellow-headed blackbirds are just a few of the species lighting on cattails, paddling the ponds, or skimming above the water. Mid-October brings thousands of migrating Canada geese, snow geese, sandhill cranes, and ducks. So many Canada geese and their fuzzy, gangly babies waddle around refuge roads that the who-goes-first dance between visitors and geese becomes comic.

Upland plover, goldfinches, meadowlarks, and others crisscross the prairies, where the colors of blue lupine, yellow goldenrod, pink wild bergamot, and even native coral bells are softened by undulating grasses. Each spring, certain prairie areas become drumming grounds for amorous sharp-tailed grouse. As brush prairies have declined throughout the nation, so have these grouse; Crex Meadows supports the largest sharp-tailed grouse population in Wisconsin. Deer, porcupines,

eagles, and endangered Karner blue butterflies are among the other inhabitants of this fecund area.

DRIFTLESS UPLANDS: ALONG THE SAINT CROIX AND MISSISSIPPI

The town of Saint Croix Falls, where the **Saint Croix National Scenic Riverway**❖ has its headquarters, is the approximate northern edge of Wisconsin's Driftless Area. This ancient topography is characterized by bluffs and deep valleys—untouched by glaciers—that form a suitably grand backdrop for the Saint Croix and Mississippi rivers.

The national riverway encompasses the Saint Croix River from its headwaters near the Brule River to its confluence with the Mississippi. In addition, the riverway protects the Saint Croix's major tributary, the renowned Namekagon River, which begins much farther north in Chequamegon National Forest. The best way to explore the riverway is by river (the National Park Service can provide a list of canoe liveries). Following a river from its source to its mouth is both philosophically and physically satisfying. Like getting to know a person well, seeing a river from beginning to end is learning its life and its personality.

Such a trip begins off Route 63 about 70 miles northeast, on the Namekagon north of Hayward, where the river is still the color of polished mahogany. Another of the many put-ins for this broad, smooth waterway is Trego, 15 miles southwest of Hayward. Low banks alternate with marshy edges, bottomlands, and high forested banks as the river gains volume and speed down the course of its 98 miles to the confluence with the Saint Croix.

Just south of the riverway's headquarters near Saint Croix Falls, **Interstate State Park** provides a good bird's-eye view of the Saint Croix's dramatic rocky outcrops. Equally dramatic is the National Park Service's

battle against invading zebra mussels moving north into the Saint Croix–Namekagon river system. These small aliens began their westward migration perhaps two centuries ago, when they slowly spread from their home waters in eastern Europe to western Europe via boats traveling on newly constructed canals. Researchers believe that the mussels reached the Great Lakes—as well as the Ohio, Illinois, and Mississippi rivers—by the mid-1980s. One Michigan city spent more than $300,000 in a year to keep the mussels from clogging its public water system. Because they outcompete native mussels, the aliens can affect entire food chains by consuming critical amounts of plankton.

Southeast of Eau Claire, eight miles east of the town of Black River Falls on Route 54, the entrance road to **Black River State Forest❖** headquarters approaches sandstone buttes rising high above forests of pine and oak. Castle Mound gives a good overview of the territory, which lies just between the driftless and glaciated areas. Although the forest is drier than those to the north, the river environs include some of the most extensive wetlands in the state forest system, attracting ducks, eagles, geese, ospreys, hawks, and a variety of turtles and other reptiles. The river gets its name from its iron content. (Canoe rentals are available in Black River Falls.)

High river bluffs are the centerpiece of **Perrot State Park❖,** which borders the Mississippi off Route 93 a mile north of Trempealeau and about 35 miles southwest of Black River Falls. The sandstones and dolomites layered in the bluffs were deposited 600 to 400 million years ago when inland seas repeatedly advanced and retreated over the middle of North America. Since then, the Mississippi River and its tributaries have been the master sculptors. At about 425 feet, one of the highest bluffs in the park is **Trempealeau Mountain,** or *La Montagne Qui Trempe à l'Eau*—"the mountain with its feet soaking in the water."

The trail to Brady's Bluff, a state natural area, winds through dark junipers, then into sloping woods of oak and hickory, and finally switchbacks up to exhilarating open prairies filled with wildflowers: goldenrod, sunflowers, black-eyed Susans, rosy blazing stars, purple spiderwort. This pristine prairie is known as a goat prairie because it is so steep and sunbaked that only goats—and park visitors—would venture into it. Yet the expansive views of the Mississippi River, its islands, its valley, and the Minnesota bluffs beyond are among the best in the state. Below, white pelicans fly in formation downriver while barges and heavily laden ships inch along in both directions. Bird chorales complement the collection of wildflowers. When the summer air is sweet and warm, Brady's Bluff is a fine place to be planted.

The Mississippi River has been breached by so many gates that some natural area officials consider it a series of managed ponds. The edges of the river, however, are rife with wildlife. The wooded islands, marshes, and sloughs lining the Mississippi here are part of the **Upper Mississippi River National Wildlife and Fish Refuge❖.** Although it averages only 3.5 miles wide, the refuge stretches 260 miles along the boundaries of Minnesota, Wisconsin, Iowa, and Illinois, making it the longest in the lower 48 states. For each mazelike section of the river, the U.S. Fish and Wildlife Service can provide detailed maps. Puzzle-piece islands and backwaters are habitat for all sorts of aquatic and wetland plants, hundreds of bird and fish species, and dozens of mammal, amphibian, and reptile species. The fall, for instance, brings huge numbers of canvasback ducks—some 70 percent of the known population—to feed in ponds near La Crosse.

Traveling Route 35, Wisconsin's Great River Road from Prescott to Prairie du Chien is another way to see the omnipresent river. Begin-

ABOVE: *A brilliant autumnal mosaic of deciduous hardwoods—scarlet, orange, and gold—is complemented by the darker greens of native conifers in the vast woodlands of Wisconsin's Black River State Forest.*

ning in Minnesota, the Mississippi travels 2,348 miles to the Gulf of Mexico. Like the broad claws of lions guarding the entrance to some unimaginably large civic building, bluffs frame the river valley. Above them, raptors ride the thermals of the valley's wide skies as the inexorable river, braided with islands, goes where it pleases.

WISCONSIN RIVER VALLEY

At 2,650-acre **Wyalusing State Park❖,** 500-foot bluffs mark the place where the Mississippi and Wisconsin rivers meet (take Route 18 south from Prairie du Chien, then Routes C and X west). A network of trails along bluff faces provide close-up looks at rocks from 500 to 400 million years old. Council Point and Point Lookout provide scenic panoramas of the river valleys below, but a plethora of sandbars,

---

OVERLEAF: *At Perrot State Park, a birch clings to the slopes of Brady's Bluff, a steep "goat" prairie with wildflowers, native grasses, and fine views of the great river—a good spot for Mississippi dreaming.*

222

sloughs, backwaters, islands, and patchwork pieces of forest make discerning the main river channels difficult.

Below the viewpoints, Bluff Trail leads to Treasure Cave, a huge slump-block enclosure. Clinging to the side of the bluff like a mountain-goat track, the trail traverses dense vegetation: A low canopy of trees shades tall ferns, pink hepatica, and jack-in-the-pulpit big enough to accommodate a squirrel. Rare Goldie's fern and walking fern border park trails, along with other unusual plants such as amethyst shooting star. Like faces cratered by pox, outcrops textured by time pierce the greenery.

The Sugar Maple Trail leads through deep deciduous forest past Pictured Rock Cave, another slump-block recess adorned by a waterfall. Other trails lead into **Wyalusing Walnut Forest State Natural Area❖,** along the Wisconsin River, and to meadows where visitors can spot deer and wild turkeys. Because Wyalusing is along one of the country's major migration flyways, dozens of bird species pass through. Mound Builders—the Hopewell and Effigy Mound cultures—lived here nearly 2,000 years ago, and dozens of ceremonial and burial mounds still dot the park.

East on Route 133 along the Wisconsin River, 1.5 miles past Avoca and north on Hay Lane Road, are parking areas for **Avoca Prairie–Savannah State Natural Area❖.** When the Wisconsin River is running high, however, these lowlands may be covered by water. Because the state retains so few of its prairies—less than one percent—Avoca's 2,000 acres constitute the most extensive prairie in Wisconsin and the largest tract of native tallgrass east of the Mississippi. Unlike the vast undulating grass oceans of big bluestem found farther west, Avoca is a prairie mosaic with bottomland forests, sandy oak stands, wet sedge meadows, classic bluestem terrain, and shrubs sprinkled everywhere. This diversity—more than 200 vascular plants live here—draws a wide variety of wildlife.

Farther upriver are two of many put-in points for the **Lower Wisconsin State Riverway** at **Tower Hill State Park** and the Route 23 bridge (canoe rentals are available in Spring Green). Beginning in the northeastern section, the upper Wisconsin flows 337 miles diagonally across the state to the Prairie du Sac dam. On its journey it is girded by 26 dams, making it the nation's hardest-working river. In contrast,

ABOVE: *The precipitous cliffs of Wyalusing State Park overlook the Wisconsin River where it joins the Mississippi. Wyalusing means "home of the warrior," and lowlands here were once common to 14 tribes.*

the lower Wisconsin's 92 miles are the longest stretch of free-flowing river in the state—and on warm summer weekends it lures a good portion of the nearby population. Canoeing the river at other times, however, can be luxuriantly peaceful.

The river valley is 150 to 200 feet thick with sand carried downstream from glacial deposits, yet the water averages only 10 to 12 feet deep. In late summer, when the river is low, huge sandbars appear. Lining its banks are sand barrens, wet prairies, sedge meadows, and bottomland forests where orange-and-black orioles flutter among silver maples. Although the great herds of bison and elk that Marquette and Joliet saw in the late 1600s are gone, wildlife is everywhere. Turtles bask on logs, swallows dive and soar over the water, and in a giant tree a bald eagle guards its nest.

Just upriver are Devils Lake State Park, the Baraboo Hills, and the beginning of a journey to Wisconsin's heartland and Lake Michigan's shores.

SOUTHEASTERN WISCONSIN

L ike most of the other Great Lakes states, Wisconsin can be roughly divided into areas affected by ice ages and those that were not. The Central Sands region forms the transition between the rolling glaciated lands to the east and the rough Driftless Area of unglaciated western Wisconsin. Smack in the middle of the state, the Central Sands are checkered by an odd juxtaposition of marshes—Wisconsin's largest—with dry prairies and savannas. When the glaciers retreated, their meltwaters formed huge glacial Lake Wisconsin over a thick bed of sand. Where Lake Wisconsin dried up, sand remained; other areas were merely reduced to marsh, now home to myriad waterfowl and other birds.

In southeastern Wisconsin, the glaciers pressed heavily upon the land, leaving behind strange shapes and terrain softened by their great weight. Kame cones, snaking eskers, and lakes deeper than they are wide are all part of the glacial legacy. More than any other state, Wisconsin is the center of ice-age studies because glaciers left so many clues on the land.

After the glaciers had their way, much of this area was covered by trees. Although second-growth forests are making a comeback in regions such as the Kettle Moraine State Forest, the southeastern section is the state's urban-industrial hub. In addition, its many farms are

LEFT: *In Door County's Peninsula State Park, Eagle Tower provides a broad view of the Lake Michigan shoreline. Nicolet Bay and Welcker's Point are in the foreground, Green Bay and Chambers Island beyond.*

the reason Wisconsin is called America's Dairyland. Driving through the gently rolling green hills of southeastern Wisconsin, dotted with flower-trimmed farmhouses and neat barns, is a bit like entering a bucolic landscape painting.

On the eastern side of the state, Lake Michigan country, the lake and its shores reveal habitats and moods ranging from rockbound, water-dashed coastlines rimmed by dark forests to gentle beaches and sunny dunes. Branching from the mainland, the long spine of the Door Peninsula divides Green Bay from Lake Michigan and offers some of the best scenery in Wisconsin, as well as nine state natural areas and five state parks.

Door County's limestone outcrops are evidence of the Niagara Escarpment, an enormous shelf of hard dolomite formed from the accretion of shells and marine skeletons in ancient, warm inland seas. The escarpment extends east (although not continuously) to Niagara Falls, where the Niagara River thunders over its edge. Door County and Canada's Bruce Peninsula, between Lake Huron and Georgian Bay, are practically mirror-image ridges on this vast dolomite reef.

This chapter begins its trip through southeastern Wisconsin near the lower Wisconsin River valley, hopscotches north along the river, and turns east toward the Wolf River. From there it proceeds to Door County and then south along the Lake Michigan shoreline.

CENTRAL WISCONSIN

In terms of size alone, **Devil's Lake State Park❖** (off Route 123 just south of Baraboo) must be counted Wisconsin's premier park. Its roughly 8,500 acres include more than 900 types of vascular plants, 239 species of birds, and a hundred other animal species, including badgers, deer, mink, and a half-dozen species of bats. Because the glaciers were busy here, Devil's Lake is one of nine units of the Ice Age National Scientific Reserve. Some of the most prominent features of the park, however, are far older than the last ice age.

The still blue waters of the lake—the heart of the park—are flanked by eroded bluffs exposing rocks more than a billion years old. The bluffs lined the valley of the Wisconsin River until the last ice age about 12,000 years ago, when glaciers carrying earth and rocks plugged Devil's Lake Gap with a terminal moraine and rerouted the

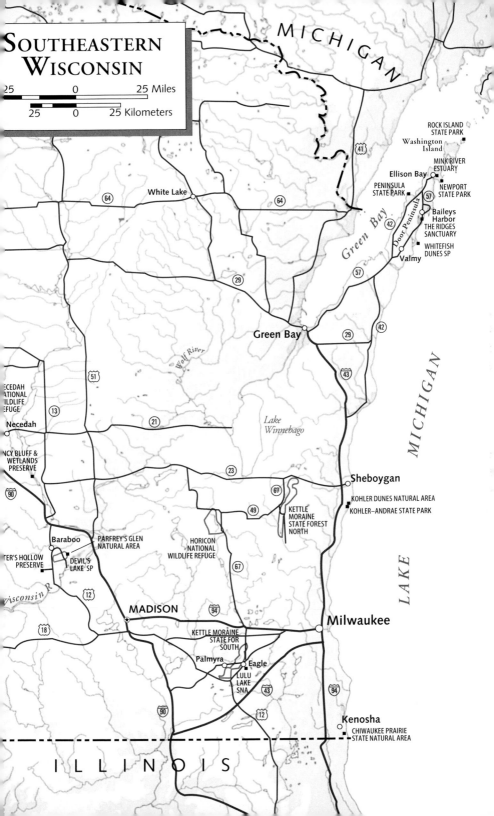

SOUTHEASTERN WISCONSIN

25   0   25 Miles

25   0   25 Kilometers

MICHIGAN

ROCK ISLAND
STATE PARK

Washington
Island

MINK RIVER
ESTUARY

Ellison Bay

PENINSULA
STATE PARK

NEWPORT
STATE PARK

41

64

White Lake

64

Baileys
Harbor
THE RIDGES
SANCTUARY

WHITEFISH
DUNES SP

Green Bay

Door Peninsula

42

57

57

Valmy

29

57

Green Bay

29

42

Wolf River

43

ECEDAH
ATIONAL
ILDLIFE
EFUGE

51

MICHIGAN

13

Necedah

21

Lake
Winnebago

NCY BLUFF &
WETLANDS
PRESERVE

23

Sheboygan

90

67

KOHLER DUNES NATURAL AREA

KOHLER–ANDRAE STATE PARK

49

KETTLE
MORAINE
STATE FOREST
NORTH

LAKE

Baraboo

PARFREY'S GLEN
NATURAL AREA

HORICON
NATIONAL
WILDLIFE REFUGE

TER'S HOLLOW
PRESERVE

DEVIL'S
LAKE SP

67

sconsin R

12

MADISON

94

Milwaukee

18

KETTLE MORAINE
STATE FOR
SOUTH

Palmyra

Eagle

LULU
LAKE
SNA

43

94

90

12

Kenosha

CHIWAUKEE PRAIRIE
STATE NATURAL AREA

I L L I N O I S

river, creating spring-fed Devil's Lake.

Serene and spectacular views from the bluffs await hikers on the Balanced Rock Trail up the East Bluff, which winds through a boulder field of gray and dark purple quartzite, formed when sandstone was radically compressed and partially recrystallized. In niches between lichen-covered boulders, the lacy leaves and nodding pink-and-yellow flowers of meadow rue have taken hold. Yellow birch, white pine, and oak appear near the top of the bluff, and where they shade the trail, stone blocks cut for stairs provide startling evidence of the inland sea that covered the Midwest long ago. Visible in some of the stair blocks are ripples of sand from the floor of that prehistoric sea, frozen in time.

Where it overlooks the lake, the East Bluff supports a pygmy forest. Although almost a hundred years old, the trees are only 10 to 15 feet high because the soil is thin and baked by the sun. Seemingly crafted in miniature, the ashes, oaks, hickories, and sinuously twisted redcedars are reminiscent of bonsai.

Below, turkey vultures glide the thermals and rowboats sprouting fishing poles dot the lake. Farther along the bluffs, rosy blossoms of shooting stars and the smell of warm, clean meadows fill a pocket prairie. The descent to the **Red Oak State Natural Area,** a full-size forest, passes potholes where water has scoured smooth bowls in the rock.

LEFT: *Near Baraboo, glacial moraines plug the end of Devil's Lake, once the valley of the Wisconsin River. The East Bluff (foreground) is now topped by a pygmy forest.*
RIGHT: *Balanced Rock, high on the East Bluff of Devil's Lake, is a five-ton chunk of quartzite: sandstone compacted and hardened by ancient mountain-building forces.*

Take the North Shore Road to Route 113, turn south for two miles to County Highway DL, then head east to the small parking lot for **Parfrey's Glen Natural Area❖,** the state's first natural area. Although it is within park boundaries, Parfrey's Glen feels like a secret spot. It is also fragile. After passing through an old field, the path enters moist woods bisected by a stream bubbling along in the dappled light of maples. Pink cranesbill geraniums and the creamy flowers of false Solomon's seal brighten the forest floor.

Imperceptibly, the gorge closes in. Becoming cooler and dimmer, the trail is lined with high walls of moss-covered rock. Ostrich and maidenhair ferns frame boulders of puddingstone—pebbles of quartzite embedded in sandstone. The glen is a place of seeps, small hanging gardens, and big trees.

The Baraboo Hills surround Devil's Lake, and the two complement rather than duplicate each other as natural areas. Because much of this green rolling countryside is not under government protection, conservation organizations arc working to preserve it in parcels. **Baxter's Hollow Preserve❖,** the largest remnant of deciduous upland forest in Wisconsin, is central to the Baraboo Hills, named for a French voyageur named Baribeau. From Route 12 south of Devil's Lake, take Kings Corner Road or Route C two miles west and Stones Pocket Road two miles north to several small Nature Conservancy parking lots and tranquil, lovely Otter Creek. A trail leads back into the forest for about a mile, passing old stands of oak, hickory, maple, and ash. One of the most important nesting areas for forest birds in southern Wisconsin, Baxter's Hollow is home to ovenbirds, veeries, Cooper's hawks, and pileated

LEFT: *Solitary, silent, and strongly territorial, a male mountain lion may cover 25 miles in one night hunting large mammals. The sleek native cats are occasionally spotted in highlands near Devil's Lake.*

RIGHT: *Bewhiskered river otters, known for their playfulness and agility in water, inhabit spring-fed Devil's Lake. Close relatives, mink and two species of weasel flourish within the state park as well.*

woodpeckers, which are rarely found beyond old-growth woods.

The banks of Otter Creek are perhaps the most inviting place in Baxter's Hollow. Part of the most undisturbed watershed in southern Wisconsin, the creek is rife with trout, which feed on more than 78 species of caddis flies and numerous other aquatic insects. Luminescent buttery yellow marsh marigolds crowd the damp banks, and skunk cabbage, ferns, and foam-flower and yellow Canada mayflowers flourish beneath a peeling, furrowed river birch arching over the tree-shaded creek. As they pour over small rocks, the creek waters sound like a calm heartbeat.

Although it is not a natural area, the **International Crane Foundation,** which protects the most complete collection of crane species in the world, is just north of Baraboo off Route 12 on Shady Lane Road and worth a visit. To the west is the **Elroy-Sparta State Trail,** the nation's first rail-to-trail (abandoned railroad beds converted to biking/hiking trails); the state's system of such trails provides a fine way to see natural Wisconsin.

Nearby are the Wisconsin Dells. (*Dells* comes from *dalles,* French for layers of rock resembling flagstones.) Along this section of the Wisconsin River glaciers carved and polished the 100-foot Cambrian sandstone cliffs into shapes prefiguring rounded modern sculpture. Unfortunately, almost as soon as the area's beauty was recognized, it was exploited: water shows, museums, every sort of entertainment. The Dells are still a major tourist mecca. In 1994 the state acquired ten miles of river, estab-

lishing the **Dells of the Wisconsin River State Natural Area,** to protect the molded gorge, shadowed side canyons, cliff tops, and rare species.

From the Dells, continue north on Routes 12 and 13 about 20 miles, then take Route H west, 16th Avenue north, Evergreen Avenue west, and 16th Drive north 2.2 miles to the Nature Conservancy parking lot for **Quincy's Bluff and Wetlands Preserve❖.** Because classic Wisconsin Central Sands habitats such as Quincy's Bluff are increasingly rare, some of the resident wildlife is too. Oak and pine forests have colonized a sandstone mesa, which provides a visible anchor to the wetlands on the east; below are sedge meadows and shrub wetlands, which attract sandhill cranes, raptors, and rare butterflies.

Routes 13 north and 21 west lead to the entrance of **Necedah National Wildlife Refuge❖.** Once part of glacial Lake Wisconsin, which covered much of the Central Sands region just after the glaciers retreated, this area became a vast peat bog as the glacial lake shrank. Because old sand ridges were claimed by woodlands, Necedah is a

43,000-acre mix of woodlands and wetlands interspersed with prairies. Thousands of geese, ducks, sandhill cranes, and other birds—about 220 species altogether—visit the wetlands, especially during spring and fall migrations. Muskrat, mink, beavers, grouse, deer, and coyotes are among the other Necedah residents.

Canoe liveries for the **Wolf River,** one of Wisconsin's first national wild and scenic rivers, can be found in White Lake (from Necedah, take Route 21 west, Route 51 north, and Route 64 east). Renowned as a premier Midwest white-water and trout-fishing river, the Wolf is far more than just a waterway dedicated to sport. The river, which flows 200 miles south to Oshkosh and the Fox River, begins unobtrusively in the wetlands of Nicolet National Forest, where a quiet current winds through open marshes framed by pines and northern hardwoods. When an eagle beats the air overhead and marsh grasses rustle hypnotically, the Wolf looks like a scene from the beginning of time. Growing at the edges of the marshy current is wild rice, a staple of the Menominee and other Algonquin peoples who lived here. When it is heavy with grain, wild rice fills the air with its nutty aroma.

The river then traverses the deep forests of the Menominee, among the few tribes to retain Wisconsin lands they once occupied. During the late 1800s, they were not allowed to cut and market their timber because they would have competed with the logging barons. Ironically, those laws gave the Menominee the richest mix of trees in Wisconsin, and their forests have long been intelligently managed for diversity and sustainability.

The Wolf gains volume from tributaries as it travels south. Lazy meanderings through wetlands become concentrated white-capped tumult. The rushing river and overhanging forest create morning mists that paint the scene with a soft, impressionistic haze, concealing black bears, deer, and otters. Occasionally, moose and wolves wander this far south. And the sound like a chain saw, explains one resident, is "a ruffed grouse looking for love."

Placid sections alternate with roaring rapids such as Wolf Dells, which runs through a narrow, high-walled rock slot. Below, on Menominee lands, the Wolf breaks around small islands and tumbles in waterfalls. Although its character changes along the way, the Wolf's constancy is its wildness. Whitewater Specialty in White Lake provides

ABOVE: *Henry Vianden (1814–99) was Wisconsin's first landscape painter. In his 1880's* View of the Fox River, Wisconsin, *the sunlit central oak epitomizes Vianden's belief that trees are "God's noblest creatures."*

not only guided canoe trips, but also a wealth of information about the natural history of the Wolf River and its watershed.

DOOR COUNTY AND THE LAKE MICHIGAN SHORELINE

Door County's chief resource—its natural beauty—has made it one of the top vacation destinations in the Great Lakes region, famous for fish boils, tangy cherries, Green Bay and Lake Michigan fishing, beaches, and picturesque towns. The best of the peninsula's bay side is on display at **Peninsula State Park❖** just north of Fish Creek (from the city of Green Bay, take Routes 57 and 42 northeast).

Peninsula is one of the state's oldest, largest, and most popular parks, containing historical buildings, a golf course, and hundreds of

OVERLEAF: *Door Peninsula extends a long, rocky finger into Lake Michigan, creating Green Bay. The 20 miles of scenic shoreline in Peninsula State Park feature dolomite cobbles and dense lakeshore forests.*

campsites. Although the park is developed, Peninsula is not without natural areas. Eagle Tower, which rises atop bluffs overlooking Green Bay some 250 feet below, presents a great perspective of land and water. Horseshoe and other islands are visible, as are sportfishing boats scattered across the bay. Lake trout, whitefish, sturgeon, and yellow perch were once abundant, but overfishing and pollution caused declines as early as the 1890s. Now perch have made a comeback, and trout, bass, walleye, and salmon are frequently caught here.

Steep, fern-edged Eagle Trail showcases the bluffs that line the bay side of the peninsula. From a bench of land at the bottom, the bluffs rise above the trees like stacked pancakes, layer upon layer of gray limestone—the legacy of billions of fish, shellfish, and corals composing this part of the vast Niagara Escarpment. Because subsidence has caused the peninsula's rock layers to slope toward the Lake Michigan–Huron geologic bowl, cliffs are sharp on the bay side of Door Peninsula while the Lake Michigan shore is bound only by low, rocky ledges and sand beaches.

In direct contrast to the bluffs, the land in **Peninsula Park White Cedar Forest State Natural Area** is moist to boggy, a transition to outright marsh. At the feet of water-loving white cedar and black spruce, the extravagant yellow slipper-shaped blossoms of lady's slippers are always a surprise. Mergansers, herons, mallard, and a chorus of chirruping frogs are the most obvious inhabitants of the marsh.

Continue north on Route 42 to land's end at Gill's Rock or Northport, then take a ferry to Washington Island and another to **Rock Island State Park❖.** French explorers named the straits between the peninsula and Washington Island Porte des Morts—Death's Door—because so many shipwrecks occurred there, and Door County also takes its name from this description. On tranquil Rock Island, where no cars are allowed, a six-mile trail roughly parallels the shoreline around the entire island, passing a sandy beach on the southern shores. After a few hours of perfect peace, visitors realize that the island's chief charm is its isolation from motors and busyness.

From Ellison Bay, take Route 42 a few miles east, then follow

---

RIGHT: *A fragrant yellow lady's slipper orchid brightens the forest floor in Peninsula Park White Cedar Forest State Natural Area, a biological crossroads of marsh, relict dune, and cedar-spruce swamp.*

Route NP to Newport Lane and the entrance to **Newport State Park❖.** At 2,000-plus acres, Newport is two-thirds the size of Peninsula, and administered as semiwilderness. Trails are less managed, amenities less evident. Fronting on Lake Michigan, the park possesses a rugged shoreline, and the lake exposure creates a boreal effect, producing forests more like those in northern Wisconsin.

The three-mile Fern Trail–Lynd Point Trail loop affords a good picture of the park. Whorls of club moss carpet the thick deciduous forest, which gives way to a grove of dark, lacy hemlocks followed by airy aspens. Beyond, deep-green white cedars are underlain with bunchberries whose attractive white dogwood flowers are followed by red berries in the fall. An opening of chest-high ferns hiding jack-in-the-pulpits strikes a jungle note. Eventually, outcrops of chalky white dolomite and the rhythmic slap of breakers announce the shoreline, where scented balsam, endangered dwarf lake irises, and yellow-flowered bluebead lilies crowd the rocky limestone shelves. Where cobbles end and a long stretch of sandy beach begins, spawning carp thrash in the shallows while a pair of mergansers float placidly by.

Newport's two-mile Ridge Trail presents another aspect of the park. Following the back of a low ridge that was once the shoreline of Lake Nipissing (a larger precursor of Lake Michigan), the trail feels like a deer path—nature with little human intervention. Clumps of white paper birch mix with maple, beech, and hemlock, and white-flowered trillium brightens the gloom of the forest floor. Rising where Ridge Trail passes

ABOVE: *Rowleys Bay laps at Newport State Park, where marsh grasses give way to white-cedar woods filled with songbirds.*
RIGHT: *In Newport's boreal forests, bunchberry's red fruits brighten the ground in fall.*

near Sand Cove are the largest trees in the park, white and red pines. Elsewhere, the floor is covered with starflowers, columbine, ferns, and hopeful saplings. Somewhere in a tree a veery sings its eloquent if melancholy song. Eventually, the trail intersects one that traces Rowleys Bay.

Mink River Estuary❖, also off Rowleys Bay, is best seen by boat, which means traveling south on Route 42 and east on Route Z to the Rowleys Bay Wagon Trail Resort, where canoe rentals and fishing charters are available. Mink River Estuary is a particularly pristine example of these fecund wildlife nurseries—all the more valuable because most Great Lakes estuaries have been destroyed by pollution and development.

At its swampy edges, the estuary is populated by white cedar, and a step farther into the marshes reveals shrub swamps of willow, dogwood, and alder. Sedges, reed grass, and wild rice clump where water is shallow. The abundant vegetative life provides protection and food for teeming fish and other aquatic species. Moving up the food chain,

ABOVE: *The Mink River Estuary, one of the nation's most pristine, attracts thousands of birds, one of which provides dinner for a threatened Cooper's hawk, a wily raptor and secretive woodland predator.*

Mink River Estuary's aquatic nurseries attract thousands of birds, including teal, wood ducks, black ducks, black-crowned night herons, cormorants, and threatened Cooper's hawks.

Just before the town of Baileys Harbor is the entrance to **Ridges Sanctuary**❖ (south on Route 57, then east on Route Q). One naturalist calls this state natural area owned and managed by a nonprofit foundation "a botanist's paradise." Forested with a vast array of boreal species, the more than a dozen parallel ridges that give the sanctuary its name are former shorelines of a larger predecessor of Lake Michigan. Between these ridges, long swales run like gutters—some filled with water, some with shrubs and sunshine. More than 500 plant species grow within the sanctuary's more than 1,000 acres, including 13 endangered or threatened species and 25 species of native orchids.

Many of the trails are shadowed and close with conifers, their needles and mosses carpeting the forest floor. Weaving in and out among the trees are the pink-white flowers of trailing arbutus. Labrador tea, blueberry, and huckleberry fill niches of the understory, and in open, sandy clearings, spreading juniper stretches its dark, needled fingers

ABOVE: *Threatened dwarf lake iris, a one- to three-inch-tall lavender wildflower native only to graveled or forested shores of the northern Great Lakes, grows among boreal conifers at Ridges Sanctuary.*

across white sand indented by deer tracks. The juniper anchors the sand, providing toeholds for orange paintbrush and shiny, leathery kinnikinnick (also known as bearberry because bears are fond of its red berries). Silvery gray reindeer moss—actually a lichen—twines around the kinnikinnick.

Lining one of the sanctuary's open areas are four conifers so perfect in form and so different from one another that they look like specimens in a botanical garden—the pinkish puzzle bark of red pine; black spruce displaying neat, clipped needles; tamarack trembling with light-colored bundled needles; and white cedar layered with deep green fans. To complete the picture, a red squirrel barks querulously from a branch.

Marsh marigolds and water-loving shrubs such as bog rosemary and potentilla bloom at the edges of the swales. Where water fills these long strips ducks and mosquitoes abound. Along the path leading to the beach are jewel-like scenes of lichen-covered fallen branches surrounded by the frilly blue flowers of dwarf lake iris and extravagantly purple polygala.

Continue south on Route 57 and turn east on County Road WD,

about three miles south of Jacksonport, to **Whitefish Dunes State Park❖** on the Lake Michigan side of Door Peninsula. Here the shoreline and lake are the focus, and the dunes, Wisconsin's largest, are especially significant because they are rare on the west shore of Lake Michigan.

Clark Lake, less than a mile inland, was part of Whitefish Bay until currents formed a sandbar across its mouth. During the last 3,000 years, the wind has blown the sand into dunes, some nearly 100 feet tall. In the northern part of the park past the dunes, Niagara Escarpment limestone forms low cliffs that overlook the Great Lake. At **Cave Point County Park,** where the shoreline reaches farthest into the lake, waves carve sea caves.

At the southern end of the cliffs, rock shelves are replaced by cobbles, then by long strands of white sand backed by dunes. On a warm day, the dunes are the perfect spot to contemplate wave patterns and whitecaps on Lake Michigan while terns and gulls wheel overhead. On warm summer weekends, when the dunes are crowded, visitors in need of solitude can head for the forest. Yellow and blue violets decorate the entrances to wooded trails behind the dunes. Whitefish Dunes is a transition area between boreal and beech-maple forests. Although beech-maple generally dominates, conditions are clearly right for some boreal types, and the ratio could change depending on temperature and precipitation. Cutting through the forest silence, the voice of the white-throated sparrow, that herald of northern forests, reiterates, "Oh, Canada, Canada, Canada," or as some people hear it, "Get-a-job, get-a-job, get-a-job."

A marshland trail wends through rushes and past downed trees sporting blue flag nurseries. The full succession of frog life—from tadpoles to old croakers—is apparent, and deer skirt the marsh edges. In winter, Whitefish Dunes is a fine place to roam on cross-country skis.

THE SOUTHEAST CORNER

Dunes, sandy beaches, swimming, and trails through forest and along the Black River all invite visitors to 1,000-acre **Kohler-Andrae State Park❖,** along Lake Michigan (a few miles south of Sheboygan, turn east

---

RIGHT: *Lake Michigan laps the shore of Whitefish Dunes State Park, where the dunes are among the highest in Wisconsin. Because prevailing winds blow eastward, sand dunes are generally bigger in Michigan.*

ABOVE: *Kettle Moraine State Forest, where two lobes of a glacier met about 20,000 years ago, provides an unparalleled lesson in ice age topography; a hazy sunset silhouettes a cone-shaped kame at right.*

on Route V, south on Route KK, then east again on Old Park Road). Along the lake in the northern part of the park, **Kohler Dunes Natural Area❖** offers a separate parking area and a good nature center. A dunes boardwalk allows visitors to enjoy views of Lake Michigan from atop the dunes without disturbing the fragile successional flora, and another part of the trail traverses woodlands and white pine forest. Kohler-Andrae encompasses interdunal wetlands, more than 400 plant species (many rare or threatened), and numerous birds.

Take I-43 north and Route 23 west to **Kettle Moraine State Forest❖** (Northern Unit), which lies almost directly west of Kohler-Andrae. The Ice Age Visitor Center (south on Route G) is a good place to start in this multifaceted area because its displays explain the workings of glacial activity particularly well.

The reasons why Kettle Moraine is part of the National Park System's Ice Age National Scientific Reserve are abundantly apparent: Every type of glacially created landform is represented here. Cone-shaped kames—the most striking in the world—rise from flat fields like props in an enormous Candyland game, and eskers slither along the land like Brobdingnagian snakes. Kettle Moraine itself, the largest glacial signature, is about 300 feet high and 1 to 30 miles wide. The

ABOVE: *Now surrounded by farm fields and other kettle lakes, Moraine Lake was formed when giant chunks of ice buried in glacial debris finally melted; the resulting cavities in the earth then filled with water.*

moraine stretches about a hundred miles from Green Bay to Whitewater Lake, north of the Wisconsin-Illinois border.

Long Lake and the nearby small towns look as carefully groomed as Norman Rockwell illustrations, and rolling green farms are checkered between broad-leaved forests and groves of pine and spruce. Within **Spruce Lake Bog,** where woolly mammoths once grazed, grass-pinks, moccasin-flower orchids, and other rare plants now flourish.

Of the number of hiking-skiing trails showcasing the 30,000-acre forest, the Zillmer and Greenbush are among the best. Along Zillmer Trail, mayapples and large-flowered trilliums nod in the dappled forest shadows of maple and oak. Sumac, elderberry, and poison ivy populate the understory, and a swampy section sometimes affords views of increasingly rare leopard frogs. As the trail climbs the crest of an esker so narrow that it's like treading the back of a stegosaurus, a deer springs for cover below.

The lakes and streams in Kettle Moraine's Northern Unit—which

OVERLEAF: *A great egret silently stalks the shallow waters of the nation's largest freshwater cattail marsh, Horicon National Wildlife Refuge. Created by glacial meltwater, Horicon is now fed by streams.*

contain walleye, northern pike, trout, and largemouth bass—are good places to spot waterfowl. Because the state forest is near Milwaukee, visitors may also spot a lot of other people during the summer months. Aglow with color in the fall, Kettle Moraine Scenic Drive connects the northern and southern forest units.

A premier place for birding is **Horicon National Wildlife Refuge❖,** which is west of Kettle Moraine/North via Routes 67 and 49. Route Z runs south from 49 to refuge headquarters, where pheasants roam through swaths of grass. The drive also suggests the refuge's size: Its 21,000 acres contain the largest freshwater cattail marsh in the nation—cattails to the horizon and beyond. Like other marshes in Wisconsin's Central Sands region, Horicon was once part of a postglacial lake that silted in over time. Human habitation at Horicon began more than 12,000 years ago, roughly when the glaciers retreated. Although recently attempts were made to drain the marsh for agriculture, this "land of clean water" in Algonquian has been returned to its wildlife.

Passing marshes, open water, woods, and fields, the six miles of trails in the northwest section of the refuge, just off Route 49, afford the best place to see Horicon's more than 220 bird species. Terns, black-crowned night herons, egrets, and Canada geese are all residents, and where the cattails are thick, yellow-headed blackbirds sit atop the stalks to rule their small domains. Buffleheads, mergansers, shovelers, and other ducks dive and dabble in open waters while blue-winged teal rise into the air from hidden places. Dark coots lead strings of fuzzy babies, meadowlarks trill in the fields, and yellow warblers sing in the trees. Among the mammals inhabiting Horicon, muskrat help keep the waters open by eating vegetation and using it to build lodges.

From Horicon, take Route 67 about 50 miles south, then Route 59 west to headquarters for **Kettle Moraine State Forest❖** (Southern Unit), between Eagle and Palmyra. Like the northern unit, Kettle Moraine/South displays a variety of glacial features via a 75-mile trail system. The Scuppernong and John Muir trails, for example, pass dry kettles, kames, moraines, and some of the forest's dozen lakes, including one 80 feet deep.

Asters, goldenrod, monarda, and pasqueflowers are a few of the prairie species that thrive in **Blue Spring Oak Opening,** a state natural area within Kettle/South and the largest oak savanna complex in the

The male hooded merganser (above) sports a flamboyant crest during mating season; the common merganser (right) is a strong flier and among the first birds to migrate in the spring.

upper Midwest. Although the wildfires that regularly consumed the underbrush once left little but thick-barked oaks and perennial prairie species, the oak openings are now maintained by safer prescribed burns.

Even along such forest trails as the Wood Duck, pockets of prairie filled with sun and pink-and-white shooting stars appear like secret gardens, and bluebirds swoop across golden rolling meadows dotted with flowers. In the woods, viburnums nod their lacy white flower heads, red columbine tints the forest floor, and the anise fragrance of sweet cicely floats past. Only occasionally do unwelcome aliens, such as invasive honeysuckle, intrude.

Southwest of Kettle Moraine/South is **Lulu Lake State Natural Area❖,** jointly owned by the state and the Nature Conservancy (for tours of the area, contact the Conservancy's state office in Madison). One of the best examples of a kettle lake in southeastern Wisconsin, Lulu Lake contains relict ice-age fish species such as blackchin shiners and Iowa darters.

The area's oak opening is perhaps the finest in Wisconsin. Characterized by large well-spaced oaks surrounded by grasses and wildflowers, these fire-caused openings formerly covered five million acres of the Midwest, which once encompassed the best and largest oak openings in the world. Now only 300 acres remain.

Lulu Lake's fen, whose calcium-rich groundwaters nourish rare plants such as lesser-fringed gentian and grass-of-parnassus, offers another natural delight. Frogs, cranes, ospreys, and other rare and common animals populate the preserve, which is said to enjoy the widest biotic diversity in Wisconsin—outside Chiwaukee Prairie.

Set in an unlikely spot—near Lake Michigan halfway between Chicago and Milwaukee—**Chiwaukee Prairie State Natural Area❖** is just far enough off megalopolis highways to remain the finest prairie in Wisconsin and one of the most diversified in the nation. To get there, head south past Kenosha to 116th Street, then east across the railroad tracks. Turn south on Marina Road and then follow 121st Street one block west to Second Avenue. Go north to 119th and the parking lot for the Al Crampert Trail.

Just after the last ice age, when the lake basin was much higher, Chiwaukee Prairie was part of the ridge-and-swale lakeside. Sands and clays gathered in different areas, creating sandy ridges and clay-bottomed marshes. As the lake retreated, plants advanced, finding niches in a wide array of habitats. Within Chiwaukee's 350 acres grow an astonishing 400-plus native prairie species.

On the ridges that surround the prairie, oaks and willows form permeable green walls separating the prairie from the road beyond. Within, only the buzz of dragonflies punctuates the quiet. As great drifts of colors sway in the Lake Michigan breezes, Chiwaukee beckons softly, like the field of poppies in the *Wizard of Oz*. In early summer, the clouds of pink and white shooting stars covering large parts of the prairie are punctuated with yellow spikes of lousewort and clumps of violets. Later, the prairie glows with deep yellow goldenrod accompanied by fuzzy spikes of rose-purple liatris, the statuesque flowered crowns of joe-pye weed, and omnipresent undulating grasses.

Foxes, deer, and many smaller mammals live in Chiwaukee Prairie, along with a host of birds: meadowlarks, kingbirds, and clutches of burbling bobolinks, their yellow stripes and white patches matching patterns in the meadow. Here, less than an hour from Chicago, lies an authentic prairie landscape, once one of America's defining features and now one of its most endangered.

RIGHT: *In spring, pink and white shooting stars, with their delicate nodding heads, cover huge swaths of Chiwaukee Prairie, a rare mosaic of virgin grasslands, wetlands, shrub patches, and oak openings.*

FURTHER READING ABOUT THE GREAT LAKES

DANIEL, GLENDA, AND JERRY SULLIVAN. *A Sierra Club Naturalist's Guide to the North Woods of Michigan, Wisconsin, and Minnesota.* San Francisco: Sierra Club Books, 1981. This book delves into the specifics about North Woods natural history, from bog plants to ducks. Details about such things as the formation of particular mountain ranges and lake systems answer most questions about the northern Great Lakes.

EIFERT, VIRGINIA LOUISE SNIDER. *Journeys in Green Places: The Shores and Woods of Wisconsin's Door Peninsula.* New York: Dodd, Mead, 1963. The author accompanies her prose journeys through this midwestern Eden with her own photos and illustrations.

ELLIS, WILLIAM DONOHUE. *Land of the Inland Seas.* Palo Alto, California: American West, 1974. This illustrated book provides a fine overview of the region, from the geological intricacies of how the Great Lakes were formed to distinctions among the Native American peoples of the Great Lakes region.

GERBER, DAN. *Grass Fires.* Winn Books: Seattle, 1987. A collection of clean, fine stories set among the landscapes—both exterior and interior—of the lands around the Great Lakes.

HAVIGHURST, WALTER, ED. *Great Lakes Reader.* New York: Macmillan, 1969. Havighurst has assembled a revealing cultural history of the Great Lakes region, from the earliest French explorers to the modern era of thousand-foot freighters. Journal excerpts allow historical figures tell the Great Lakes stories in their own words.

HEMINGWAY, ERNEST. *The Nick Adams Stories.* New York: Charles Scribner's Sons, 1972. Hemingway may have perfected plain speak, but he probably heard plenty of it in the forests and along the dark, fast rivers of Michigan, where a number of these luminous stories are set.

HOLLING, CLANCY. *Paddle-to-the-Sea.* Boston: Houghton Mifflin, 1969. This superbly drawn, classic children's book follows a Native American boy's carved toy through the Great Lakes to the sea, telling the tale of the surrounding region in the process.

LAFFERTY, MICHAEL B. *Ohio's Natural Heritage.* Columbus: Ohio Academy of Science, 1979. From geology to ecotones, early settlement to flora and fauna, this lucid book presents a wealth of information about Ohio's natural heritage.

LEOPOLD, ALDO. *A Sand County Almanac.* New York: Ballantine Books, 1966. In this preeminent work by one of America's first conservationists, Leopold eloquently delights in the Wisconsin nature surrounding him, from dreamlike rivers to the autumn gold of a tamarack.

MUIR, JOHN. *The Story of My Boyhood and Youth.* Sierra Club Books: San Francisco, 1988. From Scotland to a farm in Wisconsin, Muir tells how experience and the land shaped him as one of the country's preeminent environmentalists and mountaineers.

SANDERS, SCOTT R. *Wilderness Plots.* Morrow: New York, 1983. These terse tales tell of taming the wilderness when the wilderness was the Ohio Valley. Using an economy of language, each poignant story reveals a facet of the then unspoiled land, illuminating the lives of the people who came and the people who had been there for centuries.

SUTTON, ANN, AND MYRON SUTTON. *Eastern Forests: The Audubon Society Nature Guides.* Knopf, New York, 1985. Part of an excellent series on American ecosystems, this well-illustrated guide clarifies forest types—plus flora and fauna—found in the Great Lakes region.

TEALE, EDWIN WAY. *Dune Boy.* Indiana University Press: Bloomington, 1957. This award-winning nature writer remembers childhood summers spent with his grandparents along the Indiana Dunes. His evocative stories re-create both the land and the people of pre–World War I Indiana.

ABOVE: *In the 1800s, a burgeoning timber industry claimed most of the region's old-growth forests. Here loggers maneuver massive lumber rafts along the Chippewa River near Eau Claire, Wisconsin, in the 1870s.*

Glossary

archipelago group of closely scattered islands in a large body of water
bog wetland, formed in glacial kettle holes, common to cool climates of the Northern Hemisphere; called a *muskeg* in Canada and northern U.S.
boreal relating to the northern biotic area characterized especially by dominance of coniferous trees
coniferous describing the cone-bearing trees of the pine family, usually evergreen
conglomerate rock composed of rounded waterworn fragments of older rock, usually combined with sand
deciduous describing trees that shed leaves seasonally and remain leafless for part of the year
delta flat, low-lying plain that forms at the mouth of a river as the river slows and deposits sediment gathered upstream
drumlin hill of glacial debris smoothed by overriding ice into the shape of an overturned spoon
escarpment cliff or steep rock face, formed by faulting or fracturing of the earth's crust, that separates two comparatively level land surfaces
esker long, winding rise of gravel and sand that marks the trail where a river once flowed beneath a glacier
fen any low land covered wholly or partly with water, often with an outlet
floodplain flat area along a watercourse, subject to periodic flooding
igneous referring to rock formed by cooled and hardened lava or magma
kame cone-shaped hill of rock debris deposited by glacial meltwater
karst area of land lying over limestone dotted with sinkholes, underground streams, and caves formed by erosion of the limestone by rainwater
kettle hole glacial depression that may evolve into a bog, pond, or lake
moraine debris (rock, sand, gravel, silt, and clay) carried by a glacier and left along its sides or terminus wherever it pauses or retreats
orogeny mountain-building process
outwash plain area of gravel and sand carried from glaciers by meltwater and deposited below the glaciated area
oxbow lake that forms where a meandering river overflows and forms a crescent-shaped body of standing water; looks like a U-shaped ox harness frame
sandstone sedimentary rock composed of sand grains
sedimentary referring to rocks formed from deposits of such debris as gravel, sand, mud, silt, or peat
sinkhole funnel-shaped hole formed where water has collected in the cracks of limestone, dissolved the rock, and carried it away; also formed when roofs of caves collapse
stalactite icicle-shaped piece of dripstone formed when water containing dissolved limestone drips from the roof of a cave and evaporates, leaving the mineral formation
stalagmite spire formed when water drips onto a cave floor and deposits of dissolved minerals build up
swale moist, low area in a tract of land
tombolo sandbar connecting an island to the mainland or to another island
wetland area of land covered or saturated with groundwater; includes swamps, marshes, and bogs

LAND MANAGEMENT RESOURCES

The following public and private organizations are among the important administrators of the preserved and protected areas described in this volume. Brief explanations of the various legal and legislative designations of these areas follow.

MANAGING AGENCIES

Indiana Division of Fish and Wildlife

Intensively manages 17 fish and wildlife areas for multiple uses, and administers wetland conservation areas, game bird habitat areas, and natural resource areas. Also regulates hunting and fishing and administers the sale of licenses. Part of the Department of Natural Resources.

Indiana Division of Forestry

Manages nine state forests and two tree nurseries for public recreation as well as timber production. Regulates and licenses state timber buyers. Part of the Department of Natural Resources.

Indiana Division of Nature Preserves

Manages 149 nature preserves for recreation and protection of the areas' natural features. Part of the Department of Natural Resources.

Indiana Division of State Parks

Manages and maintains 23 state parks for public recreation. Part of the Department of Natural Resources.

Michigan Forest Management Division

Manages six state forests for multiple uses including recreation, timber production, and wildlife protection. Provides statewide forest-fire protection and assists private forest landowners and industry in planning and forestry services. Part of the Department of Natural Resources.

Michigan Parks and Recreation Division

Manages 260,000 acres within 96 state parks and recreation areas. Also manages approximately 600 boating access sites both inland and on the Great Lakes. Part of the Department of Natural Resources.

Michigan Wildlife Division

Manages 300,000 acres in 85 state game and wildlife areas and comanages all 3.8 million acres of state forest land with the Forest Management Division. Also regulates hunting and fishing and administers licensing. Part of the Department of Natural Resources.

National Park Service (NPS) Department of the Interior

Regulates the use of national parks, monuments, and preserves. Resources are managed to preserve and protect the landscape, natural and historic artifacts, and wildlife. Administers historic and national landmarks, national seashores and lakeshores, wild and scenic rivers, and the national trail system.

The Nature Conservancy (TNC) Private organization

International nonprofit organization that owns the largest private system of nature sanctuaries in the world, some 1,300 preserves. Aims to preserve significant and diverse plants, animals, and natural communities. Some areas are managed by other private or public conservation groups, some by the Conservancy itself.

Ohio Division of Forestry

Manages 19 state forests totaling more than 175,000 acres. Forests are managed for multiple uses including recreation, timber production, and wildlife management. Part of the Department of Natural Resources.

Ohio Division of Natural Areas and Preserves

Manages 87 state nature preserves and approximately 20 natural areas for the purpose of protecting tracts of the state's rare and diverse ecological communities. Also administers the state's Scenic River Program and the ten rivers included. Part of the Department of Natural Resources.

Ohio Division of Parks and Recreation

Manages and maintains the state's 72 state parks. Part of the Department of Natural Resources.

Ohio Division of Wildlife

Manages 130,000 acres within 86 wildlife areas. Land is managed for public hunting, fishing, trapping, and conservation. Part of the Department of Natural Resources.

U.S. Fish and Wildlife Service (USFWS) Department of the Interior

Principal federal agency responsible for conserving, protecting, and enhancing the country's fish and wildlife and their habitats. Manages national wildlife refuges and fish hatcheries as well as programs for migratory birds and endangered and threatened species.

U.S. Forest Service (USFS) Department of Agriculture

Administers more than 190 million acres in the national forests and national grasslands and is responsible for the management of their resources. Determines how best to combine commercial uses such as grazing, mining, and logging with conservation needs.

Wisconsin Department of Natural Resources

Office which oversees the Bureaus of Fisheries Management, Wildlife Management, Forestry, and Parks and Recreation, among many others. Responsibilities include management of all state parks, wildlife areas, fisheries, and forests.

LAND DESIGNATIONS

Fish and Wildlife Area

Natural area owned, protected, and maintained by a state for conservation and recreation. Aside from seasonal restrictions, hunting, fishing, and public access are allowed. Managed by state wildlife divisions.

National Forest

Large acreage managed for the use of forests, watersheds, wildlife, and recreation by the public or private sectors. Managed by the USFS.

National Lakeshore
Area of pristine, natural freshwater lakeshore designated to protect its natural form and appearance and provide public recreation. All four national lakeshores are on the Great Lakes. Managed by the NPS.

National Park
Spacious primitive or wilderness area with scenery and natural wonders so outstanding it has been preserved by the federal government for public recreation. Managed by the NPS.

National Recreation Area
Site established to conserve and develop for recreational purposes an area of national scenic, natural, or historic interest. Powerboats, dirt and mountain bikes, and ORVs allowed with restrictions. Managed by the NPS.

National Wildlife Refuge
Public land set aside for wild animals; protects migratory waterfowl, endangered and threatened species, and native plants. Managed by the USFWS.

Nature Preserve
Tract of land formally dedicated to protect specific natural resources and remnants of high-quality ecosystems such as old-growth forests and prairies. Managed by individual state's Department of Natural Resources.

Wild and Scenic River System
National program set up to preserve selected rivers in their natural free-flowing condition; stretches are classified as wild, scenic, or recreational, depending on the degree of development on the river, shoreline, or adjacent lands. Management shared by the BLM, NPS, and USFWS.

Wilderness Area
Area with particular ecological, geological, scientific, scenic, or historic value that has been set aside in its natural condition to be preserved as wild land; limited recreational use is permitted. Managed by the BLM and NPS.

Wildlife Area
State land managed to protect wildlife. Aside from seasonal restrictions, hunting, fishing, and public access are allowed. Managed by individual states.

NATURE TRAVEL

The following is a selection of national and local organizations that sponsor nature-related travel activities or can provide specialized regional travel information.

NATIONAL

National Audubon Society
700 Broadway
New York, NY 10003
(212) 979-3000
Offers a wide range of ecological field studies, tours, and cruises throughout the United States

National Wildlife Federation
1400 16th St. NW
Washington, D.C. 20036
(703) 790-4363
Offers training in environmental education for all ages, wildlife camp and teen adventures, conservation summits involving nature walks, field trips, and classes

The Nature Conservancy
1815 North Lynn St.
Arlington, VA 22209
(703) 841-5300
Offers a variety of excursions based out of regional and state offices. May include hiking, backpacking, canoeing, horseback riding. Contact above number to locate state offices

Sierra Club Outings
730 Polk St.
San Francisco, CA 94109
(415) 923-5630
Offers tours of different lengths for all ages throughout the United States. Outings may include backpacking, hiking, biking, skiing, and water excursions

Smithsonian Study Tours and Seminars
1100 Jefferson Dr. SW
MRC 702
Washington, D.C. 20560
(202) 357-4700
Offers extended tours, cruises, research expeditions, and seminars throughout the United States

REGIONAL

Indiana Department of Tourism
One North Capitol, Ste. 700
Indianapolis, IN 46204
(800) 289-6646
Publishes free travel guides and maps and can answer specific questions regarding travel, transportation, and recreation

Michigan Travel Bureau
PO Box 30226
Lansing, MI 48909
(800) 543-2937
(517) 373-0670
Answers specific travel and recreation queries. Call to request travel publications and maps

Ohio Travel and Tourism
Vern Riffe Ctr.
77 South High St.
Columbus, OH 43215
(800) BUCKEYE (282-5393)
Publishes Getaway packet including maps, event calendar, and travel coupons. Can also answer specific questions regarding travel and accommodations.

Wisconsin Division of Tourism
123 W. Washington Ave.
P.O. Box 7607
Madison, WI 53707
(608) 266-2161
(800) 432-8746
Answers specific questions regarding travel and accommodations. Publishes and distributes seasonal guidebooks and auto tour brochures.

How to Use This Site Guide

The following site information guide will assist you in planning your tour of the natural areas of Indiana, Ohio, Michigan, and Wisconsin. Sites set in boldface and followed by the symbol ❖ in the text are here organized alphabetically by state. Each entry is followed by the mailing address (sometimes different from the street address) and phone number of the immediate managing office, plus brief notes and a list of facilities and activities available. (A key appears on each page.)

Information on hours of operation, seasonal closings, and fees is often not listed, as these vary from season to season and year to year. Please bear in mind that responsibility for the management of some sites may change. Call well in advance to obtain maps, brochures, and pertinent, up-to-date information that will help you plan your adventures in the Great Lakes region.

Each site entry in the guide includes the address and phone number of its immediate managing agency. Many of these sites are under the stewardship of a forest or park ranger or supervised from a small nearby office. Hence, in many cases, those sites will be difficult to contact directly, and it is preferable to call the managing agency.

The following umbrella organizations can provide general information for individual natural sites, as well as the area as a whole:

REGIONAL

National Park Service
Great Lakes Systems Office
1709 Jackson St.
Omaha, NE 68102
(402) 221-3477

INDIANA

Indiana Division of Fish and Wildlife
402 W. Washington St.
Rm. W273
Indianapolis, IN 46204
(317) 232-4080

Indiana Division of Forestry
402 W. Washington St.
Rm. W296
Indianapolis, IN 46204
(317) 232-4105

Indiana Division of Nature Preserves
402 W. Washington St.
Rm. W267
Indianapolis, IN 46204
(317) 232-4052

Indiana Division of State Parks
402 W. Washington St.
Rm. W298
Indianapolis, IN 46204
(317) 232-4124

MICHIGAN

Michigan Forest Management Division
PO Box 30452
Lansing, MI 48909
(517) 373-1275

Michigan Parks and Recreation Division
PO Box 30257
Lansing, MI 48909
(517) 373-9900

Michigan Wildlife Division
PO Box 30444
Lansing, MI 48909
(517) 373-1263

OHIO

Ohio Division of Forestry
1855 Fountain Sq.

Bldg. H1
Columbus, OH 43224
(614) 265-6694

Ohio Division of Natural Areas and Preserves
1889 Fountain Sq.
Bldg. F1
Columbus, OH 43224
(614) 265-6453

Ohio Division of Parks and Recreation
1952 Belcher Dr.
Columbus, OH 43224
(614) 265-6561

Ohio Division of Wildlife
1840 Belcher Dr.
Columbus, OH 43224
(614) 265-6300

WISCONSIN

Wisconsin Department of Natural Resources
PO Box 7921
Madison, WI 53707
(608) 266-2621

261

INDIANA

ACRES LAND TRUST
2000 N. Wells St., Fort Wayne, IN 46808
(219) 422-1004
Protects 31 nature preserves

BW, H, MT, TG

BROWN COUNTY STATE PARK
Indiana Div. of State Parks
PO Box 608, Nashville, IN 47448
(812) 988-6406
Includes a nature center

**BW, C, F, GS, H, HR, I,
L, MT, PA, RA, S, T, XC**

CHAIN O' LAKES STATE PARK
Indiana Div. of State Parks
402 W. Washington St., Rm. 298
Indianapolis, IN 46204
(219) 636-2654
Cabins available **BW, C, CK, F, GS,
H, L, MT, PA, RA, S, T**

CHARLES DEAM WILDERNESS
Hoosier National Forest
811 Constitution Ave.
Bedford, IN 47421
(812) 275-5987
Groups limited to 10 or less; horses must
stay on marked trails; maps sold at information center at edge of wilderness

BW, C, CK, F, H, HR, I, MT

CLARK STATE FOREST
Indiana Div. of Forestry
PO Box 119, Henryville, IN 47126
(812) 294-4306
Permit requires for horseback riding;
self-registration required for primitive
camping **BW, C, F, H, HR, MT, PA, T**

CLIFTY FALLS STATE PARK
Indiana Div. of State Parks
1501 Green Rd., Madison, IN 47250
(812) 265-1331 (office)
(812) 265-1324 (nature center)
(812) 265-4135 (inn)

BW, C, GS, H, L, MT, PA, RA, S, T

CROOKED LAKE NATURE PRESERVE
Acres Land Trust
2000 N. Wells St.
Fort Wayne, IN 46808
(219) 422-1004 **BW, H, MT, TG**

DUNES NATURE PRESERVE
Indiana Div. of Nature Preserves
c/o Indiana Dunes State Park
1600 North 25 East
Chesterton, IN 46304
(219) 926-1952 (park office)
(219) 926-1390 (nature center)
Nature center located in state park

BW, H, I, MT, RA, XC

FALLEN TIMBER NATURE PRESERVE
Indiana Div. of Nature Preserves
PO Box 205
Versailles, IN 47042
(812) 689-6424 **BW, H, MT**

FALLS OF THE OHIO STATE PARK
Indiana Div. of State Parks
PO Box 1327
Jeffersonville, IN 47131-1327
(812) 280-9970
Admission fee; day use only; suitable
footgear needed for exploring rock beds

**BW, F, GS, H, I,
MT, PA, RA, T, TG**

FOX ISLAND NATURE PRESERVE
Allen County Parks and Recreation Board
7324 Yohne Rd.
Fort Wayne, IN 46809
(219) 747-7846
Closed Mondays; dogs allowed in cer-
tain areas only **BW, F, GS, H, I, MT,
PA, RA, S, T, TG, XC**

GIBSON WOODS NATURE PRESERVE
Lake County Parks and Recreation Dept.
2293 North Main
Crown Point, IN 46307
(219) 844-3188; (219) 755-3685

BW, GS, H, I, MT, RA, T

HARRISON-CRAWFORD
WYANDOTTE COMPLEX
Indiana Div. of Forestry
7240 Old Forest Rd.
Corydon, IN 47112
(812) 738-8232 **BW, C, CK, F, H, HR,
I, MT, PA, S, T, TG**

HEMLOCK CLIFFS RECREATION AREA
Hoosier National Forest
811 Constitution Ave.
Bedford, IN 47421
(812) 547-7051; (812) 547-5144 (TTY)
Primitive development **BW, H**

BT Bike Trails	**CK** Canoeing, Kayaking	**F** Fishing	**HR** Horseback Riding
BW Bird-watching		**GS** Gift Shop	
C Camping	**DS** Downhill Skiing	**H** Hiking	**I** Information Center

HEMMER WOODS NATURE PRESERVE
Indiana Div. of Nature Preserves
402 W. Washington St., Rm. W-267
Indianapolis, IN 46204
(317) 232-4052   **BW, H, MT**

HOOSIER PRAIRIE NATURE PRESERVE
Indiana Div. of Nature Preserves
402 W. Washington St., Rm. W-267
Indianapolis, IN 46204
(317) 232-4052   **BW, H, MT**

HOVEY LAKE FISH AND WILDLIFE AREA
Indiana Div. of Fish and Wildlife
1298 W. Graddy Rd.
Mount Vernon, IN 47620
(812) 838-2927
    Primitive camping, pit toilets
                BW, C, CK, F, H, I, PA, T

INDIANA DUNES NATIONAL LAKESHORE
National Park Service
1100 North Mineral Springs Rd.
Porter, IN 46304
(219) 926-7561, ext. 225
    Access to Pinhook Bog by ranger escort
    only, reservation required
                BW, C, F, GS, H, I, MT,
                PA, RA, S, T, TG, XC

INDIANA DUNES STATE PARK
Indiana Div. of State Parks
1600 North 25 East
Chesterton, IN 46304
(219) 926-1952 (park office)
(219) 926-1390 (nature center)
    BW, C, GS, H, I, MT, PA, PA, RA, S, T, XC

JACKSON-WASHINGTON STATE FOREST
Indiana Div. of Forestry
1278 East State Rd. 250
Brownstown, IN 47220
(812) 358-2160
    Includes Starve Hollow Lake and Skyline
    Drive; horses must stay on trails; no hors-
    es in campground; pets on leashes only
                BT, BW, C, CK, F, H,
                HR, I, MT, PA, RA, T

**JASPER-PULASKI FISH
AND WILDLIFE AREA**
Indiana Div. of Fish and Wildlife
Rte. 1, Box 216
Medaryville, IN 47957
(219) 843-4841
Primitive camping   **C, PA**

McCORMICK'S CREEK STATE PARK
Indiana Div. of State Parks
Rte. 5, Box 282
Spencer, IN 47460-9456
(812) 829-2235 (park office)
(812) 829-4344 (nature center)
(812) 829-4881 (inn)
                BW, C, GS, H, HR, I,
                L, MT, PA, RA, S, T, TG

MORGAN-MONROE STATE FOREST
Indiana Div. of Forestry
6220 Forest Rd.
Martinsville, IN 46151
(317) 342-4026   **BW, C, F, H, MT, PA, T**

**MUSCATATUCK NATIONAL
WILDLIFE REFUGE**
U.S. Fish and Wildlife Service
12985 East Rte. 50
Seymour, IN 47274
(812) 522-4352
    Self-guided auto tour
                BW, F, GS, H, I, MT

PIGEON RIVER FISH AND WILDLIFE AREA
Indiana Div. of Fish and Wildlife
PO Box 71, Mongo, IN 46771
(219) 367-2164
                BW, C, CK, F, H, I, PA, T, XC

PINE HILLS NATURE PRESERVE
c/o Shades State Park
RR 1, Box 72
Waveland, IN 47989
(317) 435-2810   **BW, H, MT**

PIONEER MOTHERS MEMORIAL FOREST
Hoosier National Forest
811 Constitution Ave.
Bedford, IN 47421
(812) 547-705
(812) 547-6144 (TTY)   **BW, H**

POKAGON STATE PARK
Indiana Div. of State Parks
450 Lane 100, Lake James
Angola, IN 46703
(219) 833-2012   **BW, C, CK, F, GS, H, HR,**
                I, L, MT, PA, RA, S, T, XC

PORTLAND ARCH NATURE PRESERVE
Indiana Div. of Nature Preserves
402 W. Washington St., Rm. 298
Indianapolis, IN 46204
(317) 232-4052   **BW, MT**

L	Lodging	**PA**	Picnic Areas	**RC**	Rock Climbing	**TG**	Tours, Guides
MB	Mountain Biking	**RA**	Ranger-led Activities	**S**	Swimming	**XC**	Cross-country Skiing
MT	Marked Trails			**T**	Toilets		

POTATO CREEK STATE PARK
Indiana Div. of State Parks
25601 State Rd. 4
North Liberty, IN 46554
(219) 656-8186
Cabins available   **BT, BW, C, F, GS, H, I,**
L, MT, PA, RA, S, T, TG, XC

POTAWATOMI NATURE PRESERVE
c/o Pokagon State Park
450 Lane 100, Lake James
Angola, IN 46703
(219) 833-2012   **BW, F, H, MT**

ROCKY HOLLOW NATURE PRESERVE
c/o Turkey Run State Park
Rte. 1, Box 164, Marshall, IN 47859
(317) 597-2654 (nature center)
(317) 597-2635 (park office)
                    BW, CK, H, HR,
                    I, MT, T, TG

SALAMONIE RIVER STATE FOREST
Indiana Div. of Forestry
4934 East Rte. 524, Lagro, IN 46941
(219) 782-2349
Pit toilets   **BW, C, F, H, HR,**
                    MT, PA, T, XC

SHADES STATE PARK
Indiana Div. of State parks
RR 1, Box 72, Waveland, IN 47989
(317) 435-2810
Entrance fee; ranger activities
summer only   **BW, C, F, H, MT, PA, RA**

SPRING MILL STATE PARK
Indiana Div. of State Parks
402 W. Washington St., Rm. 298
Indianapolis, IN 46204
(812) 849-4129
Entrance fee   **BW, C, CK, F, GS, H,**
                    HR, I, L, MT, PA, RA, S, T

TAMARACK BOG NATURE PRESERVE
c/o Pigeon River Fish and Wildlife Area
PO Box 71, Mongo, IN 46771
(219) 367-2164   **BW, CK**

TEFFT SAVANNA NATURE PRESERVE
The Nature Conservancy
1330 West 38th St.
Indianapolis, IN 46208
(317) 923-7547
(219) 843-4841 (Jasper-Pulaski Fish and
Wildlife Area)   **BW,H**

TIPPECANOE RIVER STATE PARK
Indiana Div. of State Parks
RR 4, Box 95 A
Winemac, IN 46996
(219) 946-3213   **BW, C, CK, F, GS,**
                    H, HR, I, MT, PA, S, T, XC

TRI-COUNTY STATE FISH AND
WILDLIFE AREA
Indiana Div. of Fish and Wildlife
8432 North 850 East
Syracuse, IN 46567-8378
(219) 834-4461   **BW, F, H, XC**

TURKEY RUN STATE PARK
Indiana Div. of State Parks
Rte. 1, Box 164
Marshall, IN 47859
(317) 597-2635 (park office)
(317) 597-2654 (nature center)
(317) 597-2211 (inn)
                    BW, C, CK, F, GS, H, HR,
                    I, L, MT, PA, RA, S, T, TG

TWIN SWAMPS NATURE PRESERVE
Indiana Div. of Nature Preserves
402 W. Washington St., Rm. W-267
Indianapolis, IN 46204
(317) 232-4052   **BW, H, MT**

VERSAILLES STATE PARK
Indiana Div. of State Parks
PO Box 205
Versailles, IN 47042
(812) 689-6424   **BW, C, CK, F, H, HR,**
                    I, MT, PA, RA, S, T

WESSELMAN WOODS NATURE PRESERVE
Wesselman Woods Nature Preserve Society
551 N. Boeke Rd.
Evansville, IN 47711
(812) 479-0771   **BW, GS, H, I,**
                    MT, RA, T, TG

WHITE OAK NATURE PRESERVE
c/o Clark State Forest
PO Box 119
Henryville, IN 47126
(812) 2947-4306   **BW, H**

WILLOW SLOUGH STATE FISH AND
WILDLIFE AREA
Indiana Div. of Fish and Wildlife
2042 South 500 West
Morocco, IN 47963
(219) 285-2704   **BW, C, CK, F, I, PA, T**

BT	Bike Trails	**CK**	Canoeing, Kayaking	**F**	Fishing
BW	Bird-watching			**GS**	Gift Shop
C	Camping	**DS**	Downhill	**H**	Hiking
				HR	Horseback Riding
				I	Information Center

YELLOWWOOD STATE FOREST
Indiana Div. of Forestry
772 South Yellowwood Rd.
Nashville, IN 47448
(812) 988-7945
No hookups for camping
BW, C, CK, F, H,
HR, I, MT, PA, T

MICHIGAN

ALGONAC STATE PARK
Michigan Parks and Recreation Div.
8732 River Rd.
Marine City, MI 48039
(810) 765-5605
(800) 543-2937 (camping reservations)
BW, C, F, H, MT, PA, T

BETSY LAKE RESEARCH NATURAL AREA
c/o Tahquamenon Falls State Park
Box 225, Star Route 48
Paradise, MI 49768
(906) 492-3415
No motors   BW, CK, F, H, MT

COLONIAL POINT MEMORIAL FOREST
University of Michigan
Biological Station
Pellston, MI 49769
(616) 539-8406; (616) 539-8408 (seasonal)
Tours offered occasionally
during summer   BW, H, TG, XC

CRAIG LAKE STATE PARK
Michigan Parks and Recreation Div.
PO Box 66, Champion, MI 49814
(906) 339-4461   BW, CK, F, H, MT

ERIE STATE GAME AREA
Michigan Wildlife Div.
PO Box 30028, Lansing, MI 48909
(517) 373-1263
Caution during hunting season, October
and November   BW, F, II, MT

ESCANABA RIVER STATE FOREST
Michigan Forest Management Div.
6833 Rtes. 2 and 41
Gladstone, MI 49837
(906) 786-2351   BW, C, CK, F, H, HR,
MB, MT, PA, RC, S, T, XC

ESTIVANT PINES SANCTUARY
Michigan Nature Association
PO Box 102, Avoca, MI 48006
(810) 324-2626   BW, H, MT

FAYETTE STATE PARK
Michigan Parks and Recreation Div.
13700 13.25 Lane, Garden, MI 49835
(906) 644-2603
(800) 543-2937 (camping reservations)
BW, C, F, H, I, MT,
PA, RA, S, T, TG, XC

GRAND MERE STATE PARK
Michigan Parks and Recreation Div.
12032 Red Arrow Hwy.
Sawyer, MI 49125
(616) 426-4013   BW, H, MT, PA, T

GRASS RIVER NATURAL AREA
PO Box 231, Bellaire, MI 49615
(616) 533-8314   BW, CK, F, GS, H,
I, MT, RA, T, TG, XC

HARBOR ISLAND NATURE PRESERVE
U.S. Fish and Wildlife Service
c/o Seney National Wildlife Refuge
HCR 2, Box 1, Seney, MI 49883
(517) 777-5930   BW, CK, F, H

HARTWICK PINES STATE PARK
Michigan Parks and Recreation Div.
Rte. 3, Box 3840, Grayling, MI 49738
(517) 348-7068; (800) 543-2937 (camping
reservations)   BT, BW, C, F, GS, H,
I, MB, MT, PA, RA, T, TG, XC

HIAWATHA NATIONAL FOREST
U.S. Forest Service
2727 N. Lincoln Rd., Escanaba, MI 49829
(906) 786-4062
ATV use restricted to certain areas
BT, BW, C, CK, F, H, HR, I, L,
MB, MT, PA, RA, S, T, TG, XC

HIGHLAND RECREATION AREA
Michigan Parks and Recreation Div.
Proud Lake Management Unit
3500 Wixom Rd., Milford, MI 48382
(810) 685-2433
Canoeing by reservation; no biking in
natural area; rustic camping
BT, BW, C, CK, F, H,
HR, MB, MT, PA, S, T, XC

HURON NATIONAL FOREST
U.S. Forest Service
1755 S. Mitchell St., Cadillac, MI 49601
(616) 775-2421; (616) 775-3183 (TTY)
BT, BW, C, CK, F, H,
HR, I, MB, MT, PA, S, T, XC

L	Lodging	**PA**	Picnic Areas	**RC**	Rock Climbing	**TG**	Tours, Guides
MB	Mountain Biking	**RA**	Ranger-led Activities	**S**	Swimming	**XC**	Cross-country Skiing
MT	Marked Trails			**T**	Toilets		

ISLE ROYALE NATIONAL PARK
National Park Service
800 East Lakeshore Dr.
Houghton, MI 49931-1895
(906) 482-0984
(906) 337-4993 (lodge)
Cabins available; no vehicles or
pets on island   **BW, C, CK, F, GS, H, I, L, MT, RA, T, TG**

LAKE SUPERIOR STATE FOREST
Michigan Forest Management Div.
PO Box 77, Newberry, MI 49868
(906) 293-5131   **BW, C, F, H, S, T, XC**

LAUGHING WHITEFISH FALLS STATE SCENIC SITE
c/o J. W. Wells State Park
N. 7670 Hwy. M-35
Cedar River, MI 49813
(906) 863-9747   **BW, H, MT, T**

LITTLE PRESQUE ISLE TRACT
Escanaba River State Forest
Ishpeming Area
1985 Rte. 41 West, Ishpeming, MI 49849
(906) 485-1031; (906) 249-1497
BW, C, CK, F, H, HR, MB, MT, PA, RC, S, XC

LUDINGTON STATE PARK
Michigan Parks and Recreation Div.
PO Box 709, Ludington, MI 49431
(616) 843-8671; (800) 543-2937 (camping reservations)   **BT, BW, C, CK, F, GS, H, I, MT, PA, RA, S, T, XC**

MANISTEE NATIONAL FOREST
U.S. Forest Service
1755 S. Mitchell St., Cadillac, MI 49601
(616) 775-2421; (616) 775-3183 (TTY)
BT, BW, C, CK, F, H, I, MB, MT, PA, S, T, XC

NORDHOUSE DUNES WILDERNESS AREA
Manistee National Forest
1755 S. Mitchell St.
Cadillac, MI 49601
(616) 775-2421; (616) 723-2211
BW, C, H, S

OTTAWA NATIONAL FOREST
U.S. Forest Service
2100 East Cloverland Dr.
Ironwood, MI 49938
(906) 932-1330
BT, BW, C, CK, DS, F, GS, H, I, L, MB, MT, PA, RA, S, T, XC

PALMS BOOK STATE PARK
Michigan Parks and Recreation Div.
Rte. 2, Box 2500
Manistique, MI 49854
(906) 341-2355   **BW, GS, T**

PICTURED ROCKS NATIONAL LAKESHORE
National Park Service
PO Box 40
Munising, MI 49862
(906) 387-3700
Permit required for back-country camping   **BT, BW, C, CK, F, GS, H, I, MT, PA, RA, S, T, TG**

PIGEON RIVER COUNTRY STATE FOREST
Michigan Forest Management Div.
9966 Twin Lakes Rd.
Vanderbilt, MI 49795
(517) 983-4101
Wild area; no paved roads; primitive camping; pit toilets
C, CK, F, H, HR, MB, MT, PA, T, XC

P. J. HOFFMASTER STATE PARK
Michigan Parks and Recreation Div.
6585 Lake Harbor Rd.
Muskegon, MI 49441
(616) 798-3711
(800) 543-2937 (camping reservations)
BW, C, GS, H, I, MT, PA, RA, S, T, TG, XC

PORCUPINE MOUNTAINS WILDERNESS STATE PARK
Michigan Parks and Recreation Div.
412 South Boundary Rd.
Ontonagon, MI 49953
(906) 885-5275; (800) 543-2937 (camping reservations)   **BW, C, DS, F, GS, H, I, MT, PA, RA, S, T, XC**

SENEY NATIONAL WILDLIFE REFUGE
U.S. Fish and Wildlife Service
HCR 2, Box 1, Seney, MI 49883
(906) 586-9851   **BT, BW, CK, F, GS, H, I, MT, RA, T, TG, XC**

SHIAWASSEE NATIONAL WILDLIFE REFUGE
U.S. Fish and Wildlife Service
6975 Mower Rd. Saginaw, MI 48601
(517) 777-5930
Includes the Green Point Environmental Learning Center; day use only; no pets
BT, BW, CK, F, H, I, MB, MT, RA, T, TG, XC

BT	Bike Trails	**CK**	Canoeing, Kayaking	**F**	Fishing
BW	Bird-watching			**GS**	Gift Shop
C	Camping	**DS**	Downhill	**H**	Hiking

HR	Horseback Riding
I	Information Center

SKEGEMOG SWAMP WILDLIFE AREA
Michigan Forest Management Div.
PO Box 30028, Lansing, MI 48909
(517) 373-1275; (517) 373-1263
Tours by prearrangement; no motors
BW, CK, F, H, MT, TG

SLEEPING BEAR DUNES NATIONAL LAKESHORE
National Park Service
9922 Front St.
Empire, MI 49630
(616) 326-5134
BW, C, CK, F, H, I, MT, PA, RA, S, T, XC

STERLING STATE PARK
Michigan Parks and Recreation Div.
2800 State Park Rd.
Monroe, MI 48161
(313) 289-2715
(800) 543-2937 (camping reservations)
BT, BW, C, F, H, MT, PA, S, T

SYLVANIA WILDERNESS
Ottawa National Forest
Watersmeet Ranger District
PO Box 276
Watersmeet, MI 49969
(906) 358-4551   **BW, C, CK, F, H, I, XC**

TAHQUAMENON FALLS STATE PARK
Michigan Parks and Recreation Div.
Box 225, Star Rte. 48
Paradise, MI 49768
(906) 492-3415
(800) 543-2937 (camping reservations)
BW, C, CK, F, GS, H, MT, PA, RA, T, TG, XC

TAWAS POINT STATE PARK
Michigan Parks and Recreation Div.
686 Tawas Beach Rd.
East Tawas, MI 48730
(517) 362-5041; (800) 543-2937 (camping reservations)   **BW, C, F, H, MT, PA, S, T**

THOMPSONS HARBOR STATE PARK
Michigan Parks and Recreation Div.
Rte. 23 North, Rogers City, MI 49779
(517) 734-2543   **BW, H, MT, T**

TOBICO MARSH
Bay City State Recreation Area
3582 State Park Dr., Bay City, MI 48706
(517) 667-0717
Vehicle permit fee
BT, BW, H, I, MB, MT, RA, T, TG

VAN RIPER STATE PARK
Michigan Parks and Recreation Div.
PO Box 66, Champion, MI 49814
(906) 339-4461
(800) 543-2937 (camping reservations)
BW, C, F, H, MT, PA, S, T, XC

WARREN DUNES STATE PARK
Michigan Parks and Recreation Div.
12032 Red Arrow Hwy.
Sawyer, MI 49125
(616) 426-4013;
(800) 543-2937 (camping reservations)
BW, C, H, MT, PA, RA, S, T

WARREN WOODS NATURAL AREA
Michigan Parks and Recreation Div.
12032 Red Arrow Hwy.
Sawyer, MI 49125
(616) 426-4013
Day use only   **BW, H, MT**

WATERLOO STATE RECREATION AREA
Michigan Parks and Recreation Div.
16345 McClure Rd., Rte. 1
Chelsea, MI 48118
(313) 475-8307
(800) 543-2937 (camping reservations)
BW, C, CK, F, GS, H, HR, I, MB, MT, PA, RA, S, T, TG, XC

WHITEFISH POINT BIRD OBSERVATORY
Whitefish Point Rd., Box 115
Paradise, MI 49768
(906) 492-3596
Ranger-led activities in spring only
BW, GS, H, I, MT, RA, T

WILDERNESS STATE PARK
Michigan Parks and Recreation Div.
PO Box 380
Carp Lake, MI 49718
(616) 436-5381;
(800) 543-2937 (camping reservations)
BW, C, F, H, MT, PA, S, T, XC

OHIO

BATELLE-DARBY METROPARK
Columbus and Franklin Counties
Metropolitan Park District
PO Box 29169
Columbus, OH 43229
(614) 891-0700
Stay on trail; no collecting
BW, CK, F, H, I, MT, PA, RA, T, TG, XC

L Lodging	**PA** Picnic Areas	**RC** Rock Climbing	**TG** Tours, Guides
MB Mountain Biking	**RA** Ranger-led Activities	**S** Swimming	**XC** Cross-country Skiing
MT Marked Trails		**T** Toilets	

BEAVER CREEK STATE PARK
Ohio Div. of Parks and Recreation
12021 Echo Dell Rd.
East Liverpool, OH 43920
(216) 385-3091 **BW, C, CK, F, H, HR, I, MB, MT, PA, RA, T**

BEDFORD RESERVATION
Cleveland Metroparks
4101 Fulton Pkwy.
Cleveland, OH 44144
(216) 351-6300
BW, F, H, HR, MT, PA, RA, T, TG, XC

BLACKHAND GORGE STATE NATURE PRESERVE
Ohio Div. of Natural Areas and Preserves
1889 Fountain Square, F-1
Columbus, OH 43224-1331
(614) 763-4411 **BT, BW, CK, F, H, MT, PA, RA, T, TG, XC**

CAESAR CREEK GORGE STATE NATURE PRESERVE
Ohio Div. of Natural Areas and Preserves
1889 Fountain Square, F-1
Columbus, OH 43224
(614) 265-6453; (513) 932-2347
Special programs available to groups
upon request **BW, H**

CEDAR BOG STATE MEMORIAL
Ohio Historical Society
980 Woodburn Rd.
Urbana, OH 43078
(513) 484-3744
Admission fee; guided tours by appointment; open April–October, Wednesday–Sunday; winter visits by appointment
BW, I, MT, RA, T, TG

CLIFTON GORGE STATE NATURE PRESERVE
Ohio Div. of Natural Areas and Preserves
3790 Rte. 370, Yellow Springs, OH 45387
(513) 767-1274 **BW, H, MT, T**

CONKLES HOLLOW STATE NATURE PRESERVE
Ohio Div. of Natural Areas and Preserves
1889 Fountain Square, F-1
Columbus, OH 43224
(614) 265-6456 (main office)
(614) 653-2541 (field office)
Hiking strenuous in places
BW, H, MT, PA, RA, T, TG

CRANE CREEK STATE PARK
c/o Maumee Bay State Park
1400 Park Rd. #1
Oregon, OH 43618
(419) 836-7758 **BW, F, PA, S, T**

CUYAHOGA VALLEY NATIONAL RECREATION AREA
National Park Service
15610 Vaughn Rd.
Brecksville, OH 44141
(216) 526-5256;
(800) 445-9667 (Canal Vs. Ctr.)
(800) 257-9477 (Happy Days Vs. Ctr.)
Includes Ohio and Erie Canal Towpath; camping and swimming in privately owned facilities within park
BT, BW, C, DS, F, GS, H, I, MB, MT, PA, RA, S, T, TG

DYSART WOODS
Ohio University, Athens, OH 45701
(614) 593-1126 **BW, H, MT**

EDGE OF APPALACHIA PRESERVE
Cincinnati Museum of Natural History
19 Abner Hollow Rd., Lynx, OH 45650
(513) 544-2880 (Museum)
(614) 486-4194 (The Nature Conservancy)
Groups of more than 10 contact the museum in advance
BW, H, MT, TG

FORT ANCIENT STATE MEMORIAL
Ohio Historical Society
6123 Rte. 350, Oregonia, OH 45054
(513) 932-4421
Admission fee; open April–October, Wednesday–Sunday; tours by appointment **BT, BW, CK, F, GS, H, I, MT, PA, RA, T, TG**

FOWLER WOODS STATE NATURE PRESERVE
Ohio Div. of Natural Areas and Preserves
1435 TR 38 W
Tiffin, OH 44883
(419) 981-6319
Day use only; no pets; no collecting;
stay on trails **BW, H, I, MT, RA, TG**

GOLL WOODS STATE NATURE PRESERVE
Ohio Div. of Natural Areas and Preserves
26093 County Rd. F
Archbold, OH 43502
(419) 445-1775 **BW, H, MT, RA, T, XC**

BT	Bike Trails	**CK**	Canoeing, Kayaking	**F**	Fishing
BW	Bird-watching			**GS**	Gift Shop
C	Camping	**DS**	Downhill Skiing	**H**	Hiking

HR	Horseback Riding
I	Information Center

GRAND WILD AND SCENIC RIVER
Ohio Div. of Natural Areas and Preserves
1889 Fountain Square, F-1
Columbus, OH 43224
(614) 265-6460   **BW, CK, F, H, I, PA, T**

**HEADLANDS DUNES STATE
NATURE PRESERVE**
Ohio Div. of Natural Areas and Preserves
1889 Fountain Square, F-1
Columbus, OH 43224
(216) 563-9344; (614) 265-6453
    Day use only; foot traffic only; no col-
    lecting   **BW, H, RA, TG**

HOCKING HILLS STATE PARK
Ohio Div. of Parks and Recreation
20160 Rte. 6645
Logan, OH 43138
(614) 385-6841   **BW, C, F, GS, H, I, L,
MT, PA, RA, S, T, TG**

**HUESTON WOODS STATE
NATURE PRESERVE**
Ohio Div. of Natural Areas and Preserves
1889 Fountain Square, F-1
Columbus, OH 43224
(614) 265-6453
    Day use only; stay on trails; information
    center at park office   **BW, H, I, MT,
RA, TG**

IRWIN PRAIRIE STATE NATURE PRESERVE
Ohio Div. of Natural Areas and Preserves
26093 County Rd. F, Archbold, OH 43502
(419) 445-1775   **BW, H, MT, RA, T**

JOHN BRYAN STATE PARK
Ohio Div. of Parks and Recreation
3790 Rte. 370, Yellow Springs, OH 45387
(513) 767-1274
    Preregistration required for
    rock climbing   **BW, C, F, H, I, MT,
PA, RC, T, XC**

KELLEYS ISLAND STATE PARK
c/o Lake Erie Islands State Park
4049 E. Moores Dock Rd.
Port Clinton, OH 43452
(419) 746-2546 (Kelleys Island seasonally)
(419) 797-4530 (Lake Erie year-round)
    BT, BW, C, F, H, MT, PA, RA, S, T

LAKE HOPE STATE PARK
Ohio Div. of Parks and Recreation
Rte. 2, Box 3000

McArthur, OH 45651
(614) 596-5253
    Ranger-led activities May–November
    BW, C, CK, F, H, I, MT, PA, RA, S, T

**LAKE KATHERINE STATE
NATURE PRESERVE**
Ohio Div. of Natural Areas
and Preserves
784 Rock Run
Jackson, OH 45640
(614) 286-2487
    Special free permits required for any use
    of the lake   **BW, CK, F, H, MT, RA, TG**

LAKE VESUVIUS RECREATION AREA
Wayne National Forest
Ironton Ranger District
6518 Rte. 93
Pedro, OH 45659
(614) 532-3225
    Parking fee   **BW, C, CK, F, H,
HR, I, MT, PA, S, T**

**LITTLE MIAMI STATE AND NATIONAL
SCENIC RIVER**
Ohio Div. of Natural Areas and Preserves
4675 North Diamond Mill Rd.
Trotwood, OH 45426-4254
(513) 854-0350
    Camping in designated areas only;
    information at state parks
    **BT, BW, C, CK, F, H,
HR, I, MB, MT, PA, S, T**

MAGEE MARSH WILDLIFE AREA
Ohio Div. of Wildlife
13229 West St., Rte. 2
Oak Harbor, OH 43449
(419) 898-0960
    Visitation restricted in some areas
    BW, F, H, I, MT, PA, RA, S, T, TG

MAUMEE BAY STATE PARK
Ohio Div. of Parks and Recreation
1400 Park Rd. #1
Oregon, OH 43618
(419) 836-7758   **BT, BW, C, CK, F, GS,
H, I, L, MT, PA, RA, S, T, XC**

MOHICAN MEMORIAL STATE FOREST
Ohio Div. of Forestry
3060 County Rd. 939
Perrysville, OH 44864
(419) 938-6222   **BW, C, CK, F,
H, HR, MT, T, XC**

L	Lodging	**PA**	Picnic Areas	**RC**	Rock Climbing	**TG**	Tours, Guides
MB	Mountain Biking	**RA**	Ranger-led Activities	**S**	Swimming	**XC**	Cross-country Skiing
MT	Marked Trails			**T**	Toilets		

MOHICAN STATE PARK
Ohio Div. of Parks and Recreation
3116 Rte. 3, Loudonville, OH 44842
(419) 994-5125; (419) 994-4290
Includes Clearfork Gorge State Nature
Preserve **BW, C, CK, F, H,
L, MT, PA, RA, S, T**

NORTH CHAGRIN RESERVATION
Cleveland Metroparks
4101 Fulton Pkwy., Cleveland, OH 44144
(216) 351-6300
(216) 473-3370 (nature center)
**BW, CK, F, GS, H, HR,
I, MT, PA, RA, T, XC**

OAK OPENINGS METROPARK
Metropolitan Park District of the
Toledo Area
5100 West Central Ave.
Toledo, OH 43615-2100
(419) 535-3058 **BT, BW, F, H, HR, I, L,
MB, MT, PA, RA, T, TG, XC**

OTTAWA NATIONAL WILDLIFE REFUGE
U.S. Fish and Wildlife Service
14000 West Rte. 2
Oak Harbor, OH 43449
(419) 898-0014
Day use only
BT, BW, H, I, MT, RA, T, TG, XC

SCIOTO TRAIL STATE PARK AND FOREST
Ohio Div. of Parks and Recreation
1952 Belcher Dr., Bldg. C-3
Columbus, OH 43224-1388
(614) 663-2125; (800) 282-5393
**BT, BW, C, CK, DS, F, GS,
H, HR, I, MB, MT, PA, T, XC**

**SHALLENBERGER STATE
NATURE PRESERVE**
Ohio Div. of Natural Areas and Preserves
1889 Fountain Square, F-1
Columbus, OH 43224
(614) 265-6546 (main office); (614) 653-
2541 (field office) **BW, H, MT, RA, TG**

SHAWNEE STATE FOREST
Ohio Div. of Forestry
13291 Rte. 52
West Portsmouth, OH 45663-8906
(614) 858-6685 (forest); (614) 858- 6652
(park); (614) 858-6621 (lodge)
**BW, C, CK, F, GS, H,
HR, L, MT, PA, RA, S, T**

**SHELDON MARSH STATE
NATURE PRESERVE**
Ohio Div. of Natural Areas and Preserves
2514 Cleveland Rd. East
Huron, OH 44839
(419) 433-4601; (614) 265-6453
No pets, bikes, or picnics **BW, MT, XC**

**SPRINGVILLE MARSH STATE
NATURE PRESERVE**
Ohio Div. of Natural Areas and Preserves
1435 TR 38 W, Tiffin, OH 44883
(419) 981-6319
Day use only; no pets; no collecting;
stay on trails **BW, H, I, MT, RA, TG**

**TAR HOLLOW STATE
PARK AND FOREST**
Ohio Div. of Parks and Recreation
16396 Tar Hollow Rd.
Laurelville, OH 43135
(614) 887-4818
Ranger activities and gift shop
summers only **BW, C, CK, F, GS, H,
HR, I, MT, PA, RA, S, T**

WAYNE NATIONAL FOREST
U.S. Forest Service
219 Columbus Rd., Athens, OH 45701
(614) 592-6644
Write for hiking maps; first-come first-
served camping **BT, BW, C, CK, F, GS,
H, HR, I, MT, PA, S, T, XC**

WILDCAT HOLLOW
Wayne National Forest
Athens Ranger District
219 Columbus Rd.
Athens, OH 45701
(614) 592-6644
Primitive camping **BW, C, H, MT**

ZALESKI STATE FOREST
Ohio Div. of Forestry
PO Box 330
Zaleski, OH 45698
(614) 596-5781; (614) 596-5476
BW, C, CK, F, H, HR, MT, T

WISCONSIN

AMNICON FALLS STATE PARK
Wisconsin Dept. of Natural Resources
5294 S Rte. 35
Superior, WI 54880
(715) 398-3000 (summer); (715) 399-8073,
(rest of year) **BW, C, F, H, I, MT, PA, RA, T**

BT Bike Trails	**CK** Canoeing,	**F** Fishing	**HR** Horseback
BW Bird-watching	Kayaking	**GS** Gift Shop	Riding
C Camping	**DS** Downhill	**H** Hiking	**I** Information
	Skiing		Center

APOSTLE ISLANDS NATIONAL LAKESHORE
National Park Service
Rte. 1, Box 4, Bayfield, WI 54814
(715) 779-3397   **BW, C, CK, F, H, I, MT,**
PA, RA, S, T, TG, XC

AVOCA PRAIRIE–SAVANNAH STATE
NATURAL AREA
c/o Tower Hill State Park
5808 County Hwy. C
Spring Green, WI 53588
(608) 588-2591   **BW, H**

BAXTER'S HOLLOW PRESERVE
The Nature Conservancy of Wisconsin
PO Box 1642, Madison, WI 53701
(608) 251-8140   **BW, H**

BIG BAY STATE PARK
Wisconsin Dept. of Natural Resources
PO Box 589, Bayfield, WI 54814
(715) 779-3346; (715) 747-6425
BW, C, CK, F, H, I, MT,
PA, RA, S, T, TG, XC

BLACK RIVER STATE FOREST
Wisconsin Dept. of Natural Resources
910 Rte. 54 E, Black River Falls, WI 54615
(715) 284-1400; (715) 284-4103
BT, BW, C, CK, F, H,
HR, MB, MT, PA, S, T, XC

CHEQUAMEGON NATIONAL FOREST
U.S. Forest Service
1170 4th Ave. S., Park Falls, WI 54552
(715) 762-2461
BT, BW, C, CK, F, H, HR, I, MB,
MT, PA, RA, S, T, TG, XC

CHIWAUKEE PRAIRIE STATE
NATURAL AREA
c/o Bong State Recreation Area
26313 Burlington Rd.
Kansasville, WI 53139
(414) 878-5605   **BW**

COPPER FALLS STATE PARK
Wisconsin Dept. of Natural Resources
RR 1, Box 17AA, Mellen, WI 54546
(715) 274-5123
BW, C, F, GS, H, MB, MT, PA, S, T

CREX MEADOWS WILDLIFE AREA
Wisconsin Dept. of Natural Resources
PO Box 367, Grantsburg, WI 54840
(715) 463-2899; (715) 463-2896

Camping in fall only; group tours by appointment   **BW, C, CK, H, I, MT,**
PA, RA, T, TG, XC

DEVIL'S LAKE STATE PARK
Wisconsin Dept. of Natural Resources
S 5975 Park Rd., Baraboo, WI 53913
(608) 356-8301   **BT, BW, C, CK, F, GS, H,**
I, MB, MT, PA, RA, RC, S, T, XC

DUNBAR BARRENS STATE NATURAL AREA
Wisconsin Dept. of Natural Resources
PO Box 16, Marinette, WI 54143
(715) 732-5511   **BW**

FLAMBEAU RIVER STATE FOREST
Wisconsin Dept. of Natural Resources
W 1613 County W. South
Winter, WI 54896
(715) 332-5271
Fees charged for some recreational activities   **BT, BW, C, CK, F,**
H, MB, PA, S, T, XC

HORICON NATIONAL WILDLIFE REFUGE
U.S. Fish and Wildlife Service
W 4279 Headquarters Rd.
Mayville, WI 53050
(414) 387-2658
BT, BW, F, H, I, MT, T, XC

KETTLE MORAINE STATE FOREST-
NORTHERN UNIT
Wisconsin Dept. of Natural Resources
N 1765 Rte. G, Campbellsport, WI 53010
(414) 626-2116
Includes the Ice Age Visitor Center; vehicle admission sticker required in fee areas
BT, BW, C, CK, DS, F, GS, H, HR,
I, MB, MT, PA, RA, S, T, TG, XC

KETTLE MORAINE STATE
FOREST-SOUTHERN UNIT
Wisconsin Dept. of Natural Resources
S 91 W 39091 Rte. 59
Eagle, WI 53119-0070
(414) 594-6200
Pit toilets   **BT, BW, C, CK, F, H, HR,**
MB, MT, PA, RA, S, T, XC

KOHLER-ANDRAE STATE PARK
Wisconsin Dept. of Natural Resources
1520 Old Park Rd., Sheboygan, WI 53081
(414) 451-4080
BT, BW, C, GS, H, HR, I, MB,
MT, PA, RA, S, T, TG, XC

L	Lodging	**PA**	Picnic Areas	**RC**	Rock Climbing	**TG** Tours, Guides
MB	Mountain Biking	**RA**	Ranger-led Activities	**S**	Swimming	**XC** Cross-country Skiing
MT	Marked Trails			**T**	Toilets	

KOHLER DUNES NATURAL AREA
c/o Kohler-Andrae State Park
1520 Old Park Rd.
Sheboygan, WI 53081
(414) 451-4080   **BW, H, I, MT, RA, TG**

LULU LAKE STATE NATURAL AREA
c/o Kettle Moraine State Forest-
Southern Unit
S 91 W 39091 Rte. 59
Eagle, WI 53119-0070
(414) 594-6215   **BW, CK, F, H**

LYNCH CREEK WATERFOWL AREA
Chequamegon National Forest
Glidden/Hayward Ranger Districts
Rte. 10, Box 508
Hayward, WI 54843
(715) 762-2461   **BW, MT, TG**

MINK RIVER ESTUARY
The Nature Conservancy of Wisconsin
633 W. Main St.
Madison, WI 53703
(608) 251-8140   **BW, CK, H, I**

NECEDAH NATIONAL WILDLIFE REFUGE
U.S. Fish and Wildlife Service
W 7996 20th St. W
Necedah, WI 54646-7531
(608) 565-2551   **BW, F, H, XC**

NEWPORT STATE PARK
Wisconsin Dept. of Natural Resources
475 County Rd. NP
Ellisin Bay, WI 54210
(414) 854-2500
Vehicle admission fee; backpack
camping   **BT, BW, C, CK, F, H,
I, MB, MT, PA, RA, S, T, TG, XC**

NICOLET NATIONAL FOREST
U.S. Forest Service
68 South Stevens St.
Rhinelander, WI 54501
(715) 362-1300
**BT, BW, C, CK, F, GS, H, HR, I,
MB, MT, PA, RA, S, T, XC**

**NORTHERN HIGHLAND-
AMERICAN LEGION STATE FOREST**
Wisconsin Dept. of Natural Resources
8770 Rte. J, Woodruff, WI 54568
(715) 356-5211; (715) 385-2727
**BT, BW, C, CK, F, GS, H,
HR, I, MT, PA, RA, S, T, TG, XC**

PARFREY'S GLEN NATURAL AREA
Wisconsin Dept. of Natural Resources
S 5975 Park Rd., Baraboo, WI 53913
(608) 356-8301; (608) 356-6618
BW, H, MT, PA, T

PATTISON STATE PARK
Wisconsin Dept. of Natural Resources
6294 S Rte. 35, Superior, WI 54880
(715) 399-8073   **BW, C, CK, F, H, I, MT,
PA, RA, S, T, TG, XC**

PENINSULA STATE PARK
Wisconsin Dept. of Natural Resources
PO Box 218, Fish Creek, WI 54212
(414) 868-3258
**BT, BW, C, CK, F, H, I, MB,
MT, PA, RA, S, T, TG, XC**

PERROT STATE PARK
Wisconsin Dept. of Natural Resources
Rte. 1, Box 407, Trempealeau, WI 54661
(608) 534-6409
Vehicle admission sticker required
**BT, BW, C, CK, F, H, I,
MB, MT, PA, RA, T, XC**

**QUINCY'S BLUFF AND
WETLANDS PRESERVE**
The Nature Conservancy of Wisconsin
PO Box 1642
Madison, WI 53701
(608) 251-8140   **BW, H, I**

RIDGES SANCTUARY
PO Box 152
Baileys Harbor, WI 54202
(414) 839-2802
BW, GS, H, I, MT, T, TG, XC

ROCK ISLAND STATE PARK
Wisconsin Dept. of Natural Resources
Washington Island, WI 54246
(414) 847-2235
Primitive camping; dogs on leashes; un-
guarded swimming
BW, C, CK, F, H, I, MT, PA, RA, S, T

**SAINT CROIX NATIONAL
SCENIC RIVERWAY**
National Park Service
PO Box 708
Saint Croix Falls, WI 54024
(715) 483-3284
BW, C, CK, F, H, I, MT, PA, RA, T, TG, XC

BT	Bike Trails	**CK**	Canoeing, Kayaking	**F**	Fishing	**HR** Horseback Riding
BW	Bird-watching			**GS**	Gift Shop	
C	Camping	**DS**	Downhill Skiing	**H**	Hiking	**I** Information Center

SCOTT LAKE–SHELP LAKE NATURAL AREA
Nicolet National Forest
68 South Stevens St.
Rhinelander, WI 54501
(715) 362-1300
Primitive camping; no motors in
wilderness   **BW, C, CK, F, H, HR, MT**

**UPPER MISSISSIPPI RIVER NATIONAL
WILDLIFE AND FISH REFUGE**
U.S. Fish and Wildlife Service
51 East 4th St., Winona, MN 55987
(507) 454-7351
Includes the Great River State Trail;
primitive camping on islands accessible
only by boat   **BT, BW, C, CK, F**

WHITEFISH DUNES STATE PARK
Wisconsin Dept. of
Natural Resources

3701 Clark Lake Rd.
Sturgeon Bay, WI 54235
(414) 823-2400
Day use only; beach and one trail acces-
sible to wheelchairs   **T, BW, F, GS, H, I,
MT, PA, RA, S, T, TG, XC**

WYALUSING STATE PARK
Wisconsin Dept. of Natural Resources
13342 County Hwy. C
Bagley, WI 53801
(608) 996-2261   **BT, BW, C, CK, F, H, I,
MB, MT, PA, RA, T, XC**

**WYALUSING WALNUT FOREST
STATE NATURAL AREA**
c/o Wyalusing State Park
13342 County Hwy. C
Bagley, WI 53801
(608) 996-2261   **BW, H, MT**

ABOVE: *Eschewing standard portraits, H. H. Bennett carted his unwieldy
camera into a rugged Wisconsin River gorge in the late 1800s. His on-
site photographs helped make the Dells a thriving tourist attraction.*

L	Lodging	**PA**	Picnic Areas	**RC**	Rock Climbing	**TG**	Tours, Guides
MB	Mountain Biking	**RA**	Ranger-led Activities	**S**	Swimming	**XC**	Cross-country Skiing
MT	Marked Trails			**T**	Toilets		

INDEX

Numbers in **bold** indicate illustrations; numbers in *bold italics* indicate maps.

PHOTOGRAPHY CREDITS

All photography by Gary Irving except for the following:

i: Skip Moody/Dembinsky Photo Associates, Owosso, MI
iv: John and Ann Mahan, Gaylord, MI
viii, right: Skip Moody/Dembinsky Photo Associates, Owosso, MI
ix, right: Sharon Cummings/Dembinsky Photo Associates, Owosso, MI
xvi, 3: Tom Bean, Flagstaff, AZ
10: Gary Meszaros/Dembinsky Photo Associates, Owosso, MI
11: John and Ann Mahan, Gaylord, MI
20–21: Dominique Braud/Dembinsky Photo Associates, Owosso, MI
23, left: Skip Moody/Dembinsky Photo Associates, Owosso, MI
23, right: Dick Scott/Dembinsky Photo Associates, Owosso, MI
26, 29: Sharon Cummings/Dembinsky Photo Associates, Owosso, MI
30, left: Skip Moody/Dembinsky Photo Associates, Owosso, MI
37: Gary Meszaros/Dembinsky Photo Associates, Owosso, MI
51, top: Dusty Perin/Dembinsky Photo Associates, Owosso, MI
51, bottom: Stan Osolinski/Dembinsky Photo Asociates, Owosso, MI
54: Dominique Braud/Dembinsky Photo Associates, Owosso, MI
55: Skip Moody/Dembinsky Photo Associates, Owosso, MI
57: A.B. Sheldon/Dembinsky Photo Associates, Owosso, MI
63: Cincinnati Art Museum, Gift of Norbert Heerman and Arthur Helbig (1926.18)
73: Alan and Sandy Carey, Bozeman, MT
75: Skip Moody/Dembinsky Photo Associates, Owosso, MI
80: Alan and Sandy Carey, Bozeman, MT
81: Yale Collection of Western Americana, Beinecke Rare Book and Manuscript Library, Yale University, New Haven, CT
85: Library of Congress, Washington, D.C.
86: Carl R. Sams II/Dembinsky Photo Associates, Owosso, MI

89: Doug Locke/Dembinsky Photo Associates, Owosso, MI
91: Skip Moody/Dembinsky Photo Associates, Owosso, MI
92: Jean and Ted Reuther/Dembinsky Photo Associates, Owosso, MI
100: Carl R. Sams II/Dembinsky Photo Associates, Owosso, MI
101: Carl R. Sams II, Milford, MI
103: John Gerlach/Dembinsky Photo Associates, Owosso, MI
104, 107: Carl R. Sams II, Milford, MI
110, left: Mark J. Thomas/Dembinsky Photo Associates, Owosso, MI
110, center, right: Barbara Gerlach, Chatham, MI
113, left: John Gerlach/Dembinsky Photo Associates, Owosso, MI
113, right: Bates Littlehales, Arlington, VA
116–117: Dan Dempster/Dembinsky Photo Associates, Owosso, MI
119, top left: Skip Moody/Dembinsky Photo Associates, Owosso, MI
119, bottom left: Randall B. Henne/Dembinsky Photo Associates, Owosso, MI
119, right: John Gerlach, Chatham, MI
120–121: Rod Planck/Dembinsky Photo Associates, Owosso, MI
124–125: The Detroit Institute of Arts, Gift of James L. Edison (#05.411)
132: Doug Locke/Dembinsky Photo Associates, Owosso, MI
133: Skip Moody/Dembinsky Photo Associates, Owosso, MI
134: A.B. Sheldon/Dembinsky Photo Associates, Owosso, MI
146: John Gerlach/Dembinsky Photo Associates, Owosso, MI
149: Skip Moody/Dembinsky Photo Associates, Owosso, MI
151: Arthur Morris/Birds As Art, Deltona, FL
154, 163: George E. Stewart/Dembinsky Photo Associates, Owosso, MI
165: Alan and Sandy Carey, Bozeman, MT
168: Barbara Gerlach/Dembinsky Photo Associates, Owosso, MI
175, top left: George E. Stewart/Dembin-

sky Photo Associates, Owosso, MI
175, top right: John Hendrickson, Clipper Mills, CA
175, bottom left: Gary Meszaros/Dembinsky Photo Associates, Owosso, MI
175, bottom right: Alan G. Nelson/Dembinsky Photo Associates, Owosso, MI
176: Skip Moody/Dembinsky Photo Associates, Owosso, MI
177, left: John Gerlach/Dembinsky Photo Associates, Owosso, MI
177, top right: George E. Stewart/Dembinsky Photo Associates, Owosso, MI
177, bottom right: John and Ann Mahan, Gaylord, MI
178–179: Tom Bean, Flagstaff, AZ
180: John Gerlach/Dembinsky Photo Associates, Owosso, MI
181: Skip Moody/Dembinsky Photo Associates, Owosso, MI
182, 183: John and Ann Mahan, Gaylord, MI
185, top: Carl R. Sams II/Dembinsky Photo Associates, Owosso, MI
185, bottom: Sharon Cummings/Dembinsky Photo Associates, Owosso, MI
198, bottom: Leonard Lee Rue III, Blairstown, NJ
200: Tom Bean, Flagstaff, AZ
201: Skip Moody/Dembinsky Photo Associates, Owosso, MI
202: Carl R. Sams II/Dembinsky Photo Associates, Owosso, MI
207, top left: Marv L. Dembinsky, Jr./Dembinsky Photo Associates, Owosso, MI

207, top right: John Mielcarek/Dembinsky Photo Associates, Owosso, MI
207, bottom left: Mark J. Thomas/Dembinsky Photo Associates, Owosso, MI
207, bottom right: Skip Moody/Dembinsky Photo Associates, Owosso, MI
210–211: John and Ann Mahan, Gaylord, MI
214: Tom Bean, Flagstaff, AZ
217: John Gerlach/Dembinsky Photo Associates, Owosso, MI
218: Anthony Mercieca/Dembinsky Photo Associates, Owosso, MI
219, 226, 230: Tom Bean, Flagsatff, AZ
232, 233: Dominique Braud/Dembinsky Photo Associates, Owosso, MI
235: Milwaukee Art Museum, Layton Art Collection, Gift of Friends of the Artist
239, 241, bottom: Rod Planck/Dembinsky Photo Associates, Owosso, MI
242: Anthony Mercieca/Dembinsky Photo Associates, Owosso, MI
243: Skip Moody/Dembinsky Photo Associates, Owosso, MI
247: Tom Bean, Flagstaff, AZ
251, left: Dr. Scott Nielsen, Superior, WI
251, right: Rod Planck/Dembinsky Photo Associates, Owosso, MI
255: State Historical Society of Wisconsin, Madison, WI
273: H. H. Bennett Studio Foundation, Wisconsin Dells, WI
Back Cover: Skip Moody/Dembinsky Photo Associates (trillium); Dominique Braud/Dembinsky Photo Associates (mink); Tom Bean (butterfly)

ACKNOWLEDGMENTS

The editors gratefully acknowledge the professional assistance of Susan Kirby and Patricia Woodruff. We wish to thank those site managers and naturalists whose time and commitment contributed to this volume. The following consultants also helped in the preparation of this volume: Guy L. Denny, Chief, Ohio Department of Natural Resources, Division of Natural Areas and Preserves; Roger Hedge, Michael A. Homoya, and Hank Huffman, Indiana Department of Natural Resources, Division of Nature Preserves; Paul Matthiae, Chief, Natural Areas Section, Wisconsin Department of Natural Resources; Ron Nagel,Visitor Services, Michigan Department of Natural Resources; Dallas Rhodes, Professor and Chair of Geology, Whittier College; and Keith P. Tomlinson, Principal Naturalist, Biogeographic, Inc.